Frommer's®

Las Vegas
day BY day®

3rd Edition

by Rick Garman

WILEY

John Wiley & Sons, Inc.

Contents

Published by:

John Wiley & Sons, Inc.

111 River St.
Hoboken, NJ 07030-5774

ISBN 978-1-118-28753-8
Editor: Naomi P. Kraus
Production Editor: Lindsay Beineke
Photo Editor: Alden Gewirtz
Cartographer: Liz Puhl
Production by Wiley Indianapolis Composition Services

For information on our other products and services or to obtain technical
support, please contact our Customer Care Department within the U.S.
at 800/762-2974, outside the U.S. at 317/572-3993 or fax 317/572-4002.

Wiley also publishes its books in a variety of electronic formats. Some
content that appears in print may not be available in electronic formats.

Manufactured in China

5   4   3   2   1

A Note from the Editorial Director

Organizing your time. That's what this guide is all about.

Other guides give you long lists of things to see and do and then expect you to fit the pieces together. The Day by Day guides are different. These guides tell you the best of everything, and then they show you how to see it *in the smartest, most time-efficient way*. Our authors have designed detailed itineraries organized by time, neighborhood, or special interest. And each tour comes with a bulleted map that takes you from stop to stop.

Hoping to hit it big at the blackjack tables, visit the dolphins at The Mirage, take in a Cirque du Soleil show, or just stroll The Strip? Planning a walk through Downtown, or dinner and drinks where you can rub shoulders with rich and infamous? Whatever your interest or schedule, the Day by Days give you the smartest routes to follow. Not only do we take you to the top attractions, hotels, and restaurants, but we also help you access those special moments that locals get to experience—those "finds" that turn tourists into travelers.

The Day by Days are also your top choice if you're looking for one complete guide for all your travel needs. The best hotels and restaurants for every budget, the greatest shopping values, the wildest nightlife—it's all here.

Why should you trust our judgment? Because our authors personally visit each place they write about. They're an independent lot who say what they think and would never include places they wouldn't recommend to their best friends. They're also open to suggestions from readers. If you'd like to contact them, please send your comments our way at feedback@frommers.com, and we'll pass them on.

Enjoy your Day by Day guide—the most helpful travel companion you can buy. And have the trip of a lifetime.

Warm regards,

Kelly Regan

Kelly Regan, Editorial Director
Frommer's Travel Guides

About the Author

Rick Garman began visiting Las Vegas as soon as he was not barred from doing so by pesky things like laws. He started writing about the city in 1997 and went on to create *Vegas4Visitors.com*, one of the most respected Las Vegas travel resources on the Web. He's appeared in various outlets as a self-proclaimed Vegas expert, although most of that expertise has been gained sitting at a slot machine with a glazed look in his eye while mumbling incoherently to himself. When not gambling away his life savings, Rick lives in Los Angeles and works in the travel industry.

Advisory & Disclaimer

Travel information can change quickly and unexpectedly, and we strongly advise you to confirm important details locally before traveling, including information on visas, health and safety, traffic and transport, accommodations, shopping, and eating out. We also encourage you to stay alert while traveling and to remain aware of your surroundings. Avoid civil disturbances, and keep a close eye on cameras, purses, wallets, and other valuables.

While we have endeavored to ensure that the information contained within this guide is accurate and up-to-date at the time of publication, we make no representations or warranties with respect to the accuracy or completeness of the contents of this work and specifically disclaim all warranties, including without limitation warranties of fitness for a particular purpose. We accept no responsibility or liability for any inaccuracy or errors or omissions, or for any inconvenience, loss, damage, costs, or expenses of any nature whatsoever incurred or suffered by anyone as a result of any advice or information contained in this guide.

The inclusion of a company, organization, or website in this guide as a service provider and/or potential source of further information does not mean that we endorse them or the information they provide. Be aware that information provided through some websites may be unreliable and can change without notice. Neither the publisher nor author shall be liable for any damages arising herefrom.

Star Ratings, Icons & Abbreviations

Every hotel, restaurant, and attraction listing in this guide has been ranked for quality, value, service, amenities, and special features using a **star-rating system.** Hotels, restaurants, attractions, shopping, and nightlife are rated on a scale of zero stars (recommended) to three stars (exceptional). In addition to the star-rating system, we also use a **kids icon** to point out the best bets for families. Within each tour, we recommend cafes, bars, or restaurants where you can take a break. Each of these stops appears in a shaded box marked with a coffee-cup-shaped bullet ☕ .

The following **abbreviations** are used for credit cards:

AE	American Express	DISC	Discover	V	Visa
DC	Diners Club	MC	MasterCard		

Travel Resources at Frommers.com

Frommer's travel resources don't end with this guide. Frommer's website, **www.frommers.com**, has travel information on more than 4,000 destinations. We update features regularly, giving you access to the most current trip-planning information and the best airfare, lodging, and car-rental bargains. You can also listen to podcasts, connect with other Frommers.com members through our active-reader forums, share your travel photos, read blogs from guidebook editors and fellow travelers, and much more.

A Note on Prices

In the "Take a Break" and "Best Bets" sections of this book, we have used a system of dollar signs to show a range of costs for 1 night in a hotel (the price of a midseason standard double-occupancy room) or the cost of a midpriced *a la carte* entree at a restaurant. Use the following table to decipher the dollar signs:

Cost	Hotels	Restaurants
$	under $100	under $20
$$	$100–$150	$40–$75
$$$	$150–$200	$20–$40
$$$$	over $200	over $75

How to Contact Us

In researching this book, we discovered many wonderful places—hotels, restaurants, shops, and more. We're sure you'll find others. Please tell us about them, so we can share the information with your fellow travelers in upcoming editions. If you were disappointed with a recommendation, we'd love to know that, too. Please write to:

Frommer's Las Vegas Day by Day, 3rd Edition
John Wiley & Sons, Inc. • 111 River St. • Hoboken, NJ 07030-5774

15 Favorite **Moments**

15 Favorite **Moments**

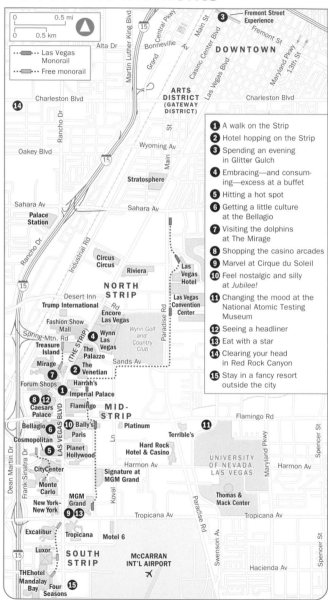

1. A walk on the Strip
2. Hotel hopping on the Strip
3. Spending an evening in Glitter Gulch
4. Embracing—and consuming—excess at a buffet
5. Hitting a hot spot
6. Getting a little culture at the Bellagio
7. Visiting the dolphins at The Mirage
8. Shopping the casino arcades
9. Marvel at Cirque du Soleil
10. Feel nostalgic and silly at *Jubilee!*
11. Changing the mood at the National Atomic Testing Museum
12. Seeing a headliner
13. Eat with a star
14. Clearing your head in Red Rock Canyon
15. Stay in a fancy resort outside the city

Previous page: The Las Vegas Strip at night.

Elvis sang "Viva, Las Vegas," wishing there were more than 24 hours in the day to spend in the city that set his soul on fire. But some respond by saying, "Yeah, it's not my kind of thing." For me, that's like saying the Grand Canyon isn't your kind of thing. Sure, the latter is one of the great natural wonders of the world, but Las Vegas is *the* great unnatural wonder of the world. It's a life experience like no other. It has to be seen to be believed, and to see it is to experience it. And once you have, you may be singing along with the King, because even in a 24/7 kind of town, there aren't enough hours to handle it all. My favorite picks should help you manage this sprawling mass of fun.

❶ **Walking on the Strip.** The heart of the city, a 13-block stretch of Las Vegas Boulevard South, is lined left and right with behemoth hotel casino resorts, all wonders of excess and each with its own particular absurd delight, from gaudy outside decor to attention-grabbing free attractions to a theme run amok. It's less spectacular during the day, but the lights at night are so head spinning you might be too distracted to take it all in. Truth be told, it's too far to walk in one go, so plan to do it in stretches. See p 42.

❷ **Hotel hopping on the Strip.** It's Vegas, after all, and even if you don't want to drop a dime (though isn't that partly what you came here for?), you'll want to see what's inside those flashy facades. The trend has been toward resort spas on steroids—what would be quiet good taste were it on a smaller scale—but there is still plenty, from ancient Egypt and Rome to medieval Venice to a scaled-down New York City to keep you agog. Remember, in other cities, hotels are built *near* the attractions. In Vegas, they *are* the attractions. See p 42.

❸ **Spending an evening in Glitter Gulch.** The original heart of the city, the pedestrian-only section of Fremont Street comes as a relief after the overwhelming Strip. Sure, there's still sensory overload, but the scale is such that by comparison, it's practically small-town Main Street. Each casino is an easy

The Venetian is one of the Strip's best re-created locales.

Sassy Sally is among Glitter Gulch's most famous icons.

distance from the next, the crowds seem less daunting, and you don't have to jostle for position to view the overhead Fremont Street Experience light show. *See p 58,* **14**.

4 **Embracing—and consuming— excess at a buffet.** All-you-can-eat, low-cost buffets have long been a symbol of the city's bargain vacation status. Vegas is no longer a bargain, but the buffets remain, though similarly increased in price. Still, the sight of rows of prep stations, offering varieties of international and American cuisine, not to mention mounds of shrimp and prime rib, remains a sybaritic treat. And though prices have gone up, so has quality—and it's still cheaper than multicourses at a costly restaurant. The Wynn Las Vegas Buffet is tops in appeal, though also in price. *See p 98.*

5 **Hitting a hot spot.** Vegas rivals LA and NYC in its nightlife scene, with every hotel offering multiple nightclubs, lounges, and bars that draw hordes of partiers vying for attention behind the velvet ropes. You have to endure long lines and high prices, but the wild abandon inside is why they came up with that "What happens in Vegas . . ."

catchphrase. The hottest of the hot right now is Marquee, a massive, multiroom club with a little something for every taste. *See p 106.*

6 **Getting a little culture at the Bellagio.** Vegas still remains too busy with the bang and the bustle to really dedicate itself to the quieter arts, but the Bellagio Gallery of Fine Art continues to defy the odds and offers excellent retrospective shows on everything from photography (Ansel Adams) to fine art (Monet). Ducking into a gallery from a casino is nearly an exercise in cognitive dissonance, but a little intellectual nutrition helps keep your balance in a city designed to throw you off same. *See p 15,* **3**.

7 **Visiting the dolphins at The Mirage.** An unexpected oasis in the midst of the Strip's pleasurable madness. Visitors can watch these playful mammals swim and frolic in a meticulously designed environment; they'll even interact a bit thanks to cute and lively trainers, glorying in the best job in Vegas. Take as long as you like to enjoy the

Stuff yourself silly at one of the city's many buffets; it's a quintessential Vegas experience.

An exhibit inside the Smithsonian-affiliated National Atomic Testing Museum, one of the best museums in the city.

dolphins' company; if you are really lucky, they might even play ball with you. *See p 16,* **5**.

8 Shopping the casino arcades. Vegas is a shopper's paradise only if you don't demand cute, quirky, and original stores. In other words, chains and other recognizable names rule the day, but rule they do, in shopping centers largely attached to the casino hotels and every bit as extravagantly designed. From Versace to Old Navy, there is something for every budget, and in the case of The Forum Shops, it's all set in an overblown Roman streetscape that adds fanciful (if not tasteful) glamour. Buy some shoes in between rounds of blackjack—maybe your winnings will pay for them! *See p 68.*

9 Marveling at Cirque du Soleil. The tacky postvaudevillian variety shows that were once the standard for Strip entertainment have almost entirely vanished in favor of the great many offerings from the idiosyncratic human circus, Cirque du Soleil. Truth be told, there can be too much of a good thing, and at six different shows and counting (another was ramping up at press time), not every one is worth the high ticket price. But the good ones certainly are, so much so that it's hard to choose. Right now, my favorite is *KÀ* at the MGM Grand, a near-perfect blend of Cirque artistry, athleticism, visuals, and storytelling. *See p 45,* **12**.

10 Feeling nostalgic and silly at Jubilee! Classic, over-the-top (not to mention topless) Vegas revues are a dying breed, hedged out by special-effects-laden modern productions and just a modicum of good taste. But if you are nostalgic for some old-fashioned glamour and barely naughty fun, come see the pinnacle of what was once the dominant theatrical art form in town, the shameless and delightful *Jubilee! See p 115.*

11 Changing the mood at the National Atomic Testing Museum. With the National Atomic Testing Museum, the city delivers something unexpected and unique. For 4 decades, Sin City's neighbor was the country's primary nuclear weapons testing ground. This admirable facility offers perspectives, technical and personal, on the science and implications of the work done there. *See p 15,* **2**.

12 Seeing a headliner. Time was, all the big names in show business did stands of varying lengths in Vegas. And though the decline of the Rat Pack left a longtime hole in the name-brand entertainment market, big deals such as Celine Dion, Garth Brooks, and Elton John have taken up residency at various showrooms. Ticket availability varies, as do the performance schedules. If you can splurge on only one, make it Garth. *See p 116.*

You haven't really done Las Vegas properly if you haven't seen one of the city's famous showgirls; Jubilee! is the best show in town to check them out.

⓭ **Eating with a star.** A Michelin-starred chef, that is. A number of celebrity chefs have set up outposts in town, but only at Joël Robuchon (in the MGM Grand) can you dine on the work of the youngest chef in history to win three consecutive Michelin stars. It'll cost you, make no mistake about it, but it's also been hailed by the country's most prominent food critics as some of the finest French food on the continent. You won't regret spending the big bucks. *See p 92.*

⓮ **Clearing your head in Red Rock Canyon.** Less than 20 miles (32km) from the overstimulated artifice of Vegas is one of the great wonders of the natural world, an impossible set of sandstone monoliths stretching across an unspoiled vista. Take a car through the 13-mile (21km) scenic drive, or hike around on your own and marvel at what is possible given a mere 300 million years or so. *See p 19,* ❶.

⓯ **Staying in a fancy resort off the Strip.** There are so many Vegas hotel possibilities, but for a truly relaxing experience, you have to get off the Strip. For pampering luxury, I like the M Resort, an actual boutique property where the rooms are fabulously appointed, the spa and pool are great, and the staff is friendly. And it's just a short drive away from all the major Vegas action. If only they'd lose the "resort fee"—the sort of money-grubbing best left to one-arm bandits. *See p 132.* ●

The M Resort Spa & Casino offers a true boutique experience away from the hubbub of the Strip

The Best **in One Day**

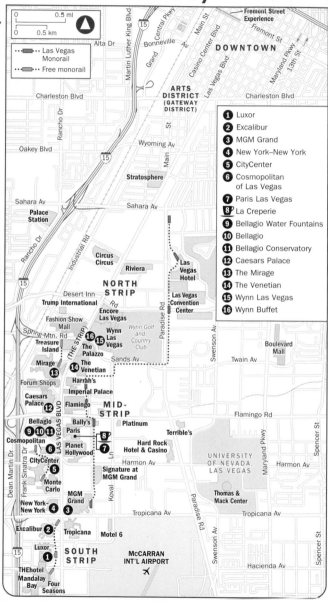

0 | 0.5 mi
0 | 0.5 km

···■··· Las Vegas Monorail
···■··· Free monorail

DOWNTOWN

Fremont Street Experience

ARTS DISTRICT (GATEWAY DISTRICT)

1 Luxor
2 Excalibur
3 MGM Grand
4 New York–New York
5 CityCenter
6 Cosmopolitan of Las Vegas
7 Paris Las Vegas
8 La Creperie
9 Bellagio Water Fountains
10 Bellagio
11 Bellagio Conservatory
12 Caesars Palace
13 The Mirage
14 The Venetian
15 Wynn Las Vegas
16 Wynn Buffet

Charleston Blvd
Oakey Blvd
Sahara Av
Palace Station
Stratosphere
Circus Circus
Riviera
Las Vegas Hotel
Las Vegas Convention Center
NORTH STRIP
Desert Inn Rd
Trump International
Encore Las Vegas
Fashion Show Mall
Wynn Las Vegas
Treasure Island
The Palazzo
Mirage
The Venetian
Forum Shops
Harrah's
Imperial Palace
Caesars Palace
Flamingo
MID-STRIP
Bellagio
Bally's
Platinum
Terrible's
Cosmopolitan
Paris
CityCenter
Planet Hollywood
Hard Rock Hotel & Casino
Monte Carlo
Signature at MGM Grand
UNIVERSITY OF NEVADA, LAS VEGAS
New York-New York
MGM Grand
Thomas & Mack Center
Excalibur
Tropicana
Motel 6
Luxor
SOUTH STRIP
McCARRAN INT'L AIRPORT
THEhotel
Mandalay Bay
Four Seasons
Boulevard Mall

Previous page: Caesars Palace, a prime example of the Las Vegas theme hotel.

If all you know of Las Vegas is the Strip, that's okay—that's really all you need to know. This stretch of Las Vegas Boulevard South is the heart of the city—sometimes it's mistaken for the city itself. That's an understandable error, because here is what Vegas is all about: mammoth hotel casinos, glittering with electricity both real and metaphorical. See nothing else and you will see Las Vegas. START: **The main entrance to the Luxor.**

① ★ **Luxor.** With its glass pyramid-shaped main building (designed by noted architect Veldon Simpson), complete with a 315,000-watt light beam emanating from its peak, this hotel is an appropriate introduction to all things Vegas. There's a touch of historical accuracy (say howdy to those replicas of the Sphinx and Cleopatra's Needle), there's more than a bit of braggadocio (that light beam is allegedly visible from space), and it's all a bit weirdly wrong (not least because Luxor execs have done their best to make the place more "chic" by obliterating the interior traces of Egypt in a 30-story pyramid). ⏱ *20 min. 3900 Las Vegas Blvd. S.* ☎ *888/777 0188 or 702/262-4000. www.luxor.com.*

② **Excalibur.** Though its interior's King Arthur mythology has been toned down over the years, this castle-shaped resort is still one of the largest in Vegas and continues to give a sense of what the city was like at its kitsch-and-cash height. Note the battlements, the drawbridge, and even a moat, though the spoilsports ditched the larger-than-life Merlin that used to overlook the realm. ⏱ *20 min. 3850 Las Vegas Blvd. S.* ☎ *800/937-7777 or 702/597-7700. www.excalibur.com.*

③ **MGM Grand.** The biggest of the big, the MGM Grand's emerald exterior (left over from its original incarnation as an homage to MGM's most beloved *Wizard of Oz*) is garish

A marvel of modern design, CityCenter cost over $9 billion.

in the daytime, glowing at night, and enormous at all times. The biggest hotel in the U.S., it certainly is the greenest. A stately 100,000-pound (45,359kg) bronze lion guards the entrance beneath high-tech video screens. Once upon a time, this was the pinnacle of the ill-conceived—and hastily discarded—"Vegas is for families" campaign, but today it caters to more adult-oriented tastes. ⏱ *25 min. 3799 Las Vegas Blvd. S.* ☎ *800/929-1111 or 702/891-7777. www.mgmgrand.com.*

④ ★★ **New York–New York.** Take the Big Apple's skyline, squash it down and turn it into a hotel exterior, and presto—you have this

It's less Egyptian than it used to be, but you can still lose yourself in the Luxor's impossibly large atrium.

pinnacle of over-the-top fantasy Vegas. The Empire State and Chrysler buildings, a half-scale Statue of Liberty, and more are represented in brightly colored, semicartoon detail—and a roller coaster (whose cars appropriately resemble NYC taxis) swooshes through it all. Ridiculous and fantastic all at once—even if the hotel execs deserve a Bronx cheer for toning down the

theme on the inside. ⏱ *20 min. 3970 Las Vegas Blvd. S.* ☎ *800/693-6763 or 702/740-6969. www.nyny hotelcasino.com.*

⑤ ★ CityCenter. The big question hanging over this futuristic "urban community" of resorts, retail, and entertainment options, which debuted to great fanfare in December 2009, is whether it will ever recoup the zillion-dollar investment it took to open it. Still, that money bought some pretty nifty modern architecture, a sustainable environment (it has the highest casino LEED certification in Vegas), and one of the largest public art installations in the U.S. Stroll past artworks by such notables as Maya Lin and Henry Moore and marvel at the sheer scale of this steel-and-glass wonder. ⏱ *25 min. Las Vegas Blvd. S. & Harmon Ave. www.city center.com. See p 137 for details on CityCenter's hotels & p 69 for details on shopping.*

⑥ ★★ Cosmopolitan of Las Vegas. If you want to know what the future Las Vegas will look like, this is where you need to pay attention. The audacious, deliriously over-the-top decor eschews traditional Vegas themes (no lions or tigers or roller coasters, oh my!) and

The Cosmopolitan Las Vegas embraces Sin City's love of over-the-top glitz.

The Eiffel Tower replica at Paris Las Vegas is half as tall as the original but still impressive.

goes for a bold luxury that emphasizes art and modern design. From the three-story chandelier in the casino to the LCD-TV covered support columns in the lobby, from the 6-foot-tall (1.8m) high-heel-pump art pieces on the second floor to the "hidden" pizzeria that has no signage, the Cosmopolitan creates an atmosphere that is both wholly original and completely true to what Sin City is all about. ⏲ *20 min. 3700 Las Vegas Blvd. S.* ☎ *877/551-7778 or 702/698-7000. www.cosmopolitan oflasvegas.com.*

❼ ★ Paris Las Vegas. More reproductions of famous landmarks (including a half-scale Eiffel Tower and a two-thirds replica of the Arc de Triomphe), though without much regard to actual geographical location, as the Hôtel de Ville is crammed on top of the Louvre. It is one of the few Strip resorts that still embraces its theme to the max and is no less chic for it. Vive la France! ⏲ *15 min. 3655 Las Vegas Blvd. S.* ☎ *888/BONJOUR (266-5687) or 702/946-7000. www.parislv.com.*

Sidewalk creperies are everywhere in Paris, so continue your ooo-la-la mood and grab a traditional snack, with either a sweet or savory filling, at ❽ **La Creperie.** *Inside Paris Las Vegas.* ☎ *702/946-7000. $. See* ❼.

❾ ★★★ Bellagio Water Fountains. The best free show in Vegas. Giant spouts send water shooting (as high as 500 ft./152m in the air), dancing, swaying, and even twirling to music ranging from Sinatra to symphonic. A sophisticated lighting array adds a dash of color to the proceedings. You may think it sounds a bit silly, but catch a show and see if you can stop with just one; for a cinematic preview, check out the action in the 2001 remake of *Ocean's Eleven.* ⏲ *30 min., to allow for 2 different shows. In front of the Bellagio, see* ❿. *Shows every half-hour starting early afternoon, every 15 min. 8pm–midnight, weather permitting.*

An immense bronze lion, the largest statue in the United States, guards the entrance to the equally mammoth MGM Grand hotel.

The dancing fountains that front the Bellagio are the best free attraction in Las Vegas.

⑩ **Bellagio.** The turning point for modern-day Vegas, this elegant cross between hotel as attraction and hotel on steroids set back original owner/visionary Steve Wynn about $1 billion. As you stroll by, admire the ever-so-slightly classy strip mall version of a charming Italian village strung along an 8-acre (3.2-hectare) invocation of Lake Como. ⏰ *20 min. 3600 Las Vegas Blvd. S.* ☎ *888/987-6667 or 702/693-7111. www.bellagio.com.*

⑪ ★★ **Bellagio Conservatory.** A staff of more than 140 horticulturists creates Rose Parade float–worthy seasonal displays of flowers and plants in this botanical garden on steroids. Spring, summer, and fall displays are quite lovely, but the holiday and Chinese New Year themes are especially noteworthy. Yes, that dragon is made entirely out of flowers, and yes, you will want to take pictures, so have a camera ready. ⏰ *20 min. Inside the Bellagio, see* ⑩. *Open 24 hrs.*

⑫ ★ **Caesars Palace.** Vegas's original, simultaneously goofy and romantic hotel—and one of the oldest venues (it opened in 1966) still extant on the Strip. It's expanded so much that the Rat Pack wouldn't recognize it, but you should still

The Mirage kicked off the modern hotel era in Las Vegas and still holds its own today.

enjoy the tacky and oversize replicas of Greco-Roman statuary that decorate the front. Watch for the four-sided Bhrama shrine, an 8,000-pound (3,629kg) replica of the venerated Thai Buddhist good-luck landmark, on the north lawn. ⏲ *25 min. 3570 Las Vegas Blvd. S.* ☎ *877/427-7243 or 702/731-7110. www.caesars.com.*

⓭ ★ **The Mirage.** The hotel that, in 1989, kicked off the "more is more" modern Vegas era. This gleaming gold structure cost $630 million (a record when it was built) and set the pattern for pretty much every hotel that followed, down to its mirrored facade and Y shape, to say nothing of the attention-getting outdoor free attractions. The volcano (revamped in 2008) out front doesn't spew lava, but it does set off an entertaining display of fire, lights, and smoke every 15 minutes after dark. ⏲ *15 min. 3400 Las Vegas Blvd. S.* ☎ *800/627-6667 or 702/791-7111. www.mirage.com.*

⓮ ★★ **The Venetian.** Arguably the best representative of the be-in-Vegas-but-pretend-you-are-elsewhere architecture craze (not least because it's still proudly embracing its theme heritage); in this case, a rather admirable (and $1.5-billion) simulation of Venice. There's part of the Doge's palace, there's the Campanile, there's St. Mark's Square, and there are even guys in gondolier outfits. All that is missing is the smell from the canals and those pesky attack pigeons (we forgive them this trespass). And unlike similar storybook lands at New York–New York and Paris, you can actually wander this Italian cityscape. ⏲ *25 min. 3355 Las Vegas Blvd. S.* ☎ *888/2-VENICE*

The jaw-dropping lobby of The Venetian is loaded with marble and exquisitely detailed frescoes.

(283-6423) or 702/414-1000. www. venetian.com.

⓯ ★ **Wynn Las Vegas.** A nearly $3-billion, 60-story effort from Steve Wynn, the man who transformed Las Vegas forever. Disappointingly, you can't see that much from the outside; unlike Wynn's previous efforts, the eye-catching accouterments—in this case, a 150-foot-tall (46m) man-made mountain—can be properly viewed only from inside. Spoilsport! ⏲ *20 min. 3400 Las Vegas Blvd. S.* ☎ *800/627-6667 or 702/791-7111. www.wynnlasvegas. com.*

⓰ **Wynn Buffet.** For the most part, buffets are no longer the bastion of budget Vegas (itself a thing of the past), but they're still cheaper than dining at one of the city's fabled high-end, celebrity-chef restaurants (and a Vegas tradition, to boot). The buffet at Wynn is a fancy affair, with options running from tandoori chicken to Southern specialties, as well as sublime desserts. *See p 98 for full details on the restaurant.*

The Best **in Two Days**

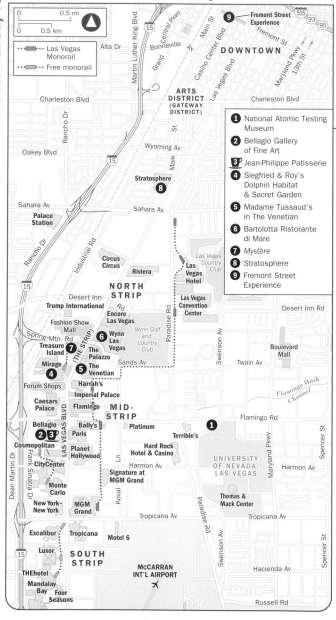

Las Vegas Monorail

Free monorail

1 National Atomic Testing Museum

2 Bellagio Gallery of Fine Art

3 Jean-Philippe Patisserie

4 Siegfried & Roy's Dolphin Habitat & Secret Garden

5 Madame Tussaud's in The Venetian

6 Bartolotta Ristorante di Mare

7 *Mystère*

8 Stratosphere

9 Fremont Street Experience

Vegas doesn't have a lot of cuhl-cha, but it does have four compelling and wildly different museums, each with its own charms—two are located on casino property! Today, I'll also give you a glimpse of life off the Strip, which might reinforce why most visitors rarely leave Las Vegas Boulevard South; except for a few architectural bright spots, design imagination seems to be exhausted and what remain are mostly strip malls. The treasures found inside, however, should more than make up for the bland exteriors. **START: National Atomic Testing Museum (755 E. Flamingo Rd.). It's best to drive here from your hotel; you can park in the free lot outside the museum.**

The Stratosphere offers pricey but breathtaking views of the city, especially at night.

1 ★★ **National Atomic Testing Museum.** Nevada, in addition to its other dubious contributions to the cultural history of the world, was the primary location for the testing of atomic weapons from 1951 to 1992. Indeed, aboveground blasts at the nearby Atomic Testing Site were once a tourist attraction in the way hotel implosions are today. This Smithsonian-affiliated museum soberly and carefully explores the development and implications of 40 years of nuclear weapons development.

Particularly affecting is a rather intense simulation of an explosion The docents (some of them former site employees) are chock-full of information, so quiz them at will. ⏱ *1 hr. 755 E. Flamingo Rd.* ☎ *702/ 794-5161. www.atomictesting museum.org. Admission $14 adults; $11 seniors, students & military; free for kids 6 & under. Mon–Sat 10am– 5pm; Sun noon–5pm. Closed Thanksgiving, Christmas, and New Year's Day.*

2 **Bellagio Gallery of Fine Art.** Originally opened as a showcase for former owner Steve Wynn's personal art collection, this small gallery now hosts often critically lauded temporary exhibits, ranging from fine art to Ansel Adams retrospectives. It's pricey, but it's good to rest your eyes on something of true value and quiet impact in a town that's renowned for Its

Las Vegas once promoted nuclear test explosions as a tourist attraction; check out this part of the city's history at the National Atomic Testing Museum.

Few things in the city are more fun than visiting the residents of the Dolphin Habitat at The Mirage.

loud and busy landscape. ⏱ *45 min. In Bellagio, 3600 Las Vegas Blvd. S.* ☎ *702/693-7871. www.bellagio.com. Reservations suggested; walk-ins taken every 15 min. Admission $15 adults, $12 seniors & Nevada residents, $10 teachers & students. Sun–Tues & Thurs 10am–6pm; Wed & Fri–Sat 10am–7pm. Last admission half-hour prior to closing.*

Have a sandwich or, best of all, a delectable dessert at the award-winning **3 Jean-Philippe Patis-serie,** whose signature attraction is a 27-foot-tall (8.2m) chocolate fountain that Willie Wonka would love. *In Bellagio, 3600 Las Vegas Blvd. S.* ☎ *702/693-8788. $.*

Drive to The Mirage, park your car, and walk until further notice.

4 ★★★ **kids Siegfried & Roy's Dolphin Habitat & Secret Garden.** You can get fairly close to some good-looking white tigers and lions at the **Secret Garden,** the day-time quarters for some of Siegfried & Roy's animals (they really live on the duo's ranch). But the best thing here is the **dolphin exhibit,** where a number of the delightful mammals (all born in captivity) live in a state-of-the-art habitat, designed to their specifications. There are no shows per se, but you can watch the dolphins happily cavort with their doting

trainers to your heart's content. ⏱ *1 hr. In The Mirage, 3400 Las Vegas Blvd. S.* ☎ *702/791-7188. www.miragehabitat.com. Admission $17 adults, $12 kids 4–12, free for kids 3 & under if accompanied by an adult. Mon–Fri 11am–6:30pm; Sat–Sun & holidays 10am–6:30pm.*

5 ★ **kids Madame Tussaud's in The Venetian.** A branch of London's legendary wax museum, here you will find lifelike—or creepy, sometimes it's a fine line—replicas of famous folks. Unlike in other museums, you can actually touch the free-standing exhibits. Go ahead, fondle J. Lo's butt or give Brad Pitt a little smooch. ⏱ *45 min. In The Venetian, 3355 Las Vegas Blvd. S.* ☎ *702/862-7800. www.mtvegas.com. Admission $25 adults, $18 seniors & students, $15 kids 7–12, free for kids 6 & under. Discounts for booking online. Sun–Thurs 10am–9:30pm; Fri–Sat 10am–10:30pm.*

6 Bartolotta Ristorante di Mare. To get the full Vegas experience, you need to dine with at least one celebrity chef, and better with James Beard–nominated Paul Bartolotta, who is actually likely to be in his kitchen. Plus, this beauty of a multilevel restaurant, featuring simple yet not simplistic classic Italian seafood cuisine, is a jewel box in its own right. Worth every dime. ⏱ *At least 2 hr. In Wynn Las Vegas, 3131 Las Vegas Blvd. S.* ☎ *888/352-3463* or 702/248-3463. www.wynnlasvegas.com. See p 88 for details on the restaurant.

7 ★★★ **kids** *Mystère.* The artistically superb productions of the world-famous Cirque du Soleil have largely replaced the old Vegas jiggle top revues. This is the first and most representative of classic Cirque, before it went nuts (happily) with the possibilities afforded by a big budget and elaborate staging. The result is a weird and wonderful mix of choreography, acrobatics, and music. ⏲ *1½ hr. In TI Las Vegas, 3300 Las Vegas Blvd. S.* ☎ *800/963-9634 or 702/796-9999. www.cirquedusoleil.com. Tickets $69–$109 (plus tax). Shows Sat–Wed 7 & 9:30pm. No shows Thurs–Fri.*

Take the TI shuttle back to The Mirage (or walk to the parking lot) and drive to the Stratosphere.

8 **Stratosphere.** The tallest building west of the Mississippi (1,149 ft./350m) offers eagle-eyed views of the desert, the mountains, and the Strip from its observation deck. It stays open until 1am, and though lines to get up here can be lengthy, you can stay as long as you like. The panorama up here can't be beat, as the lights of this ridiculous and marvelous city twinkle below

Mystère *launched the onslaught of Cirque du Soleil productions in Las Vegas.*

and around you. If you want, you can have a drink at the deck's Top of the World bar. Check out the adjacent restaurant (the desserts aren't bad); it revolves, which is a retro hoot. ⏲ *30 min. if you stay for a drink. 2000 Las Vegas Blvd. S.* ☎ *702/380-7777. Admission to observation deck $16 adults, $12 seniors & hotel guests, $10 kids 4–12, free for kids 3 & under. Sun–Thurs 10am–1am; Fri–Sat & holidays 10am–2am. Hours vary seasonally.*

Drive to Downtown Las Vegas and park in the Golden Nugget parking garage (validation available in the casino).

9 ★ **kids** **Fremont Street Experience.** In the heart of Downtown Vegas is a pedestrian-only zone that's covered with a video screen about five football fields in length known as Viva Vision. The screen's 12.5 million LED modules, and a 550,000-watt sound system, deliver a rotating light-and-sound show with themes like Area 51 (watch out for aliens!) and Retro Vegas, plus tributes to groups like the Rolling Stones, Queen, and the Doors. The shows don't necessarily make the best use of the technology, but they are still the best freebie in Vegas after the Bellagio fountains (p 11, **9**). ⏲ *20 min., longer if you see more than 1 show. Fremont St. (btw. Main St. & Las Vegas Blvd. S.). www.vegas experience.com. Shows nightly every hour, dusk–midnight.*

Even in a restaurant mecca such as Vegas, Bartolotta Ristorante di Mare stands out thanks to its superb Italian cuisine.

The Best **in Three Days**

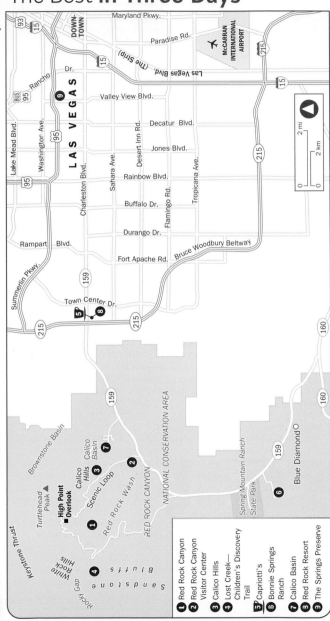

1 Red Rock Canyon
2 Red Rock Canyon Visitor Center
3 Calico Hills
4 Lost Creek— Children's Discovery Trail
5 Capriotti's
6 Bonnie Springs Ranch
7 Calico Basin
8 Red Rock Resort
9 The Springs Preserve

Even the most dedicated gambler needs to get outside for some real oxygen, so today I send you off to discover some of the natural wonders surrounding Vegas and how the city came to be. This tour has a lot of wholesome, child-appropriate activities, but adults need not fear—there's also a stop at a casino hotel, in case you need a fix. START: **Drive west from the Strip on Charleston Boulevard, which becomes NV 159, until you get to the Red Rock Canyon Visitor Center.**

❶ ★★★ kids Red Rock Canyon. In startling contrast to the sparkling madness of a city that sheds its skin about once every 10 years is this geological wonder, a mere 600 million years in the making. Sandstone monoliths—yes, some of them are quite red, though others are, frankly, sand colored—rugged canyons, cliffs, and other topographical thrills thrust up from the desert thanks to serious fault action. The **Red Rock Canyon National Conservation Area** consists of 197,000 acres (79,723 hectares), accessible to the public via a 13-mile (21km) scenic driving loop and 19 hiking trails. In addition to even better photo ops and encounters with local flora and fauna, the hikes provide opportunities to view petroglyphs and pictographs. Red Rock is also one of the most popular rock-climbing destinations in the world. ⏱ 30 min., longer if you stop to take photos or hike. On NV 159. ☎ 702/515-5350. www.nv.blm.gov/redrockcanyon. Admission $7 for 1-day vehicle pass. Daily dawn–dusk.

The magnificent natural scenery of Red Rock Canyon is only 30 minutes from the Strip.

❷ kids Red Rock Canyon Visitor Center. Stop here for brochures, suggestions for hikes, and other practical advice. The center has indoor and outdoor exhibits that helpfully illustrate the natural history of Red Rock. If you time it right—spring and summer—you can also visit with Mojave Max, a 65-plus-year-old desert tortoise, who is the charismatic star of the center. ⏱ 30 min. Just past the park entrance on the scenic loop. Daily 8am–4:30pm.

❸ Calico Hills. The parking lot at the start of the second trail along the scenic loop provides one of the two best views at the red rocks that give this area its name. ⏱ 20 min. for photographs; 3 hr. to hike, depending on level of fitness. Look for route marker just under a mile (1.6km) from the visitor center.

❹ kids Lost Creek—Children's Discovery Trail. The easiest of the park's trails, with no more than a 200-foot (61m) gentle elevation, lasts only about an hour round-trip (depending on how fast you go). It's perfect for kids and anyone who doesn't want to commit to a more demanding hike. Vegetation here is a bit more lush, due in part to the year-round stream, and there are some pictographs and an agave (a plant that was once a major source of food for local tribes) roasting pit. ⏱ 1 hr. to hike. Look for route marker, approximately 7 miles (11km) from Visitor Center.

Its glory days might be in the past, but Bonnie Springs Ranch still offers lots of old-style fun, especially for families.

Take advantage of the picnic tables at the start of the Lost Creek—Children's Discovery Trail by splitting a sandwich you picked up before entering the park, at **5** **Capriotti's,** the justly lauded local submarine sandwich place. Its outlet in the Red Rock Resort is on the drive in from the Strip to the park. *11011 W. Charleston Blvd.* ☎ *702/257-3337. $.*

6 kids **Bonnie Springs Ranch.** A deliberately hokey re-creation of an old Western town, where it's hard to tell if the weather-beaten look is authentic or the sign of a somewhat aging attraction. The regular satirical dramatic skits provide old-fashioned fun; not slick, but sweet and silly. Play cowboys with your kids as you wander past the saloon, the mill, and the old general store. Next door is a petting zoo, a maze of (scrupulously clean) wire pens with goats, rabbits, snooty llamas, elderly deer living in fat retirement, and a couple of wolves. The aviary provides glimpses of peacocks, while a riding stable offers trail rides into the mountains.

🕐 *1–2 hr. NV 159, 5 miles (8km) past Red Rock Canyon.* ☎ *702/875-4191. www.bonniesprings.com. Admission $20 per car. Daily Nov–Apr 10:30am–5pm, May–Oct 10:30am–6pm.*

7 **Calico Basin.** About 2 miles (3.2km) west of the turnoff into the Red Rock scenic loop is a half-mile-long (.8km) boardwalk trail, an alternative way for travelers with disabilities or for those with other mobility issues to get out of the car and into the scenery. Look for wildflowers and the foundations of an old cabin. 🕐 *1 hr. Look for signs 2 miles (3.2km) west of park entrance, on north side of Charleston Blvd.*

8 **Red Rock Resort.** This fancy resort is the getaway of choice for the famous of face to hide in Vegas. It's a good spot to ease yourself back into a Vegas frame of mind with a drink, and maybe even a little gambling. 🕐 *30 min., longer if you gamble. 11011 W. Charleston Blvd.* ☎ *866/767-7773 or 702/797-7777. See p 134 for more information on the resort.*

9 ★★ kids **The Springs Preserve.** Vegas was first settled around natural springs in the middle of an otherwise arid desert. Those springs have long since dried up, but they made the city possible and this 180-acre (73-hectare) facility celebrates that with a fun museum exploring the region's history, environmental displays, wetlands, gardens, and more. The interactive exhibits that put you in the center of a desert flash flood or atop Hoover Dam, keep this from being a "dry" experience. 🕐 *1 hr. 333 S. Valley View Blvd.* ☎ *702/822-7700. www. springspreserve.org. Admission $19 adults, $17 seniors & students, $11 kids 5–17, kids 4 & under free. Daily 10am–6pm.* ●

Las Vegas for **Sinners**

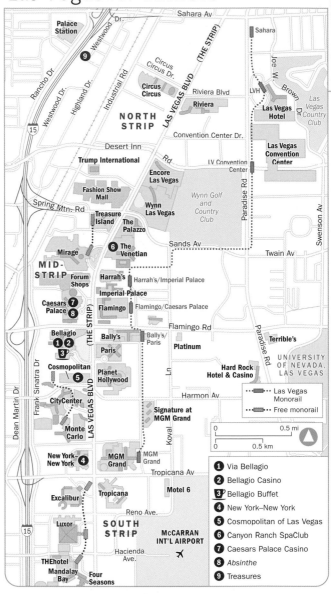

1. Via Bellagio
2. Bellagio Casino
3. Bellagio Buffet
4. New York–New York
5. Cosmopolitan of Las Vegas
6. Canyon Ranch SpaClub
7. Caesars Palace Casino
8. *Absinthe*
9. Treasures

Previous Page: Both the young and young at heart will enjoy the interactive Looney Tunes fun at the Chuck Jones Experience.

A dmit it . . . you didn't come here to have a good time. You came here to have a naughty time. More power to you. Vegas is ready to accommodate, having shifted over to a much more, let's say, adult perspective toward rest and relaxation. In fact, let's see if we can fit in all seven deadly sins, shall we? START: **Drive to Bellagio; there is a convenient parking lot by the far entrance to Via Bellagio, so you need not navigate the distance from Bellagio's main parking structure.**

1 ★★ Via Bellagio. Start your day off with a little envy, as you window-shop such high-priced boutiques as Tiffany, Chanel, Hermès, Dior, Prada, and more. There are plenty of shopping malls all over Vegas, and in just about every hotel, but there is something so classy, so high-end about this one that it gives off the impression that you can't even afford the oxygen. And yet, you are surrounded by people who can. ⏱ *45 min. In Bellagio, 3600 Las Vegas Blvd. S.* ☎ *702/693-7111. www.bellagio. com. Daily 10am–midnight.*

2 Bellagio Casino. Not jealous enough? Drop by the high rollers section of the Bellagio casino, where well-heeled types drop $500 on one pull of a slot. Notice how even the machines look fancier here, appearing to be encased in marble and wood. Now slink off and go find some penny slots. Bummer. ⏱ *20 min. See p 77.*

Nothing says gluttony like a meal at a Vegas buffet. The **3 ★★ Bellagio Buffet** is particularly large and especially indulgent, with elaborate pastas, duck and game hen, mounds of cold seafood, and more. *In Bellagio.* ☎ *877/234-6358. $$–$$$.*

4 New York–New York. Summon up the wrath felt by locals stuck in a NYC gridlock as you wander around this remarkable re-creation of Manhattan. Outside, the famous skyline is squashed down into a multicolored pastiche. Inside, all the famous neighborhoods are similarly crammed together, from Central Park to Times Square to the Village (though the decor inside has been tamed just enough to stir the anger of those who miss the themed architecture). Though the

If you have to ask how much it costs, you probably can't afford it at the mucho upscale Via Bellagio.

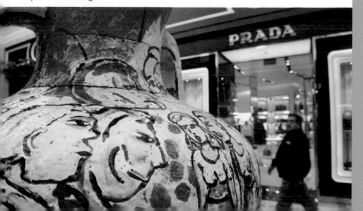

interior is now more sleek and modern, the hotel remains a bit of a nightmare to navigate. Toss in a few thousand (at minimum) other visitors, not to mention the inevitability of getting turned around and heading in the wrong direction, and you'll feel pretty steamed. It won't help if you just lost at blackjack, either. ⏲ 45 min. 3790 Las Vegas Blvd. S. ☎ 702/740-6969. www.newyork newyork.com.

⑤ Cosmopolitan of Las Vegas. The Cosmo's casino may not be the biggest in Las Vegas but it certainly is the boldest visually, and it almost seems to preen like a peacock, full of pride in its audacious, over-the-top design. The public spaces are done up as a Sin City version of a modern art museum with bold colors, patterns, and materials drawing almost as much attention as the slot machines they surround. Your eyes will be drawn to the big stuff like the massive three-story chandelier in the front, but take some time to explore and

Take a breather from the buzz of the Strip at the ultrarelaxing Canyon Ranch SpaClub.

note the smaller details like the midcentury cigarette machines that now dispense little packs of art or the French boudoir–style telephones positioned carefully in the lobby seating areas. ⏲ 30 min. 3708 Las Vegas Blvd. S. ☎ 702/698-7000. www.cosmopolitanlasvegas.com.

⑥ ★★ Canyon Ranch Spa-Club. Get your sloth on with some pampering in the largest spa in Las Vegas. Measuring in at more than 140,000 square feet (13,006 sq. m), it is a wonderland of indulgences from traditional massages and facials to ayurvedic treatments derived from ancient India customs and beyond. A full fitness center and rock climbing wall help tame your sinful indulgences. ⏲ 1½ hr. In The Venetian, 3355 Las Vegas Blvd. S. ☎ 702/414-3600. www.canyon ranch.com. Open to the public. No kids 17 or under. Massages $150–$305. Open daily 6am–8pm.

⑦ Caesars Palace Casino. Go ahead, play those slots or try a hand or two at the tables. And when you win, play some more . . . you greedy thing. ⏲ At least 30 min. See p 77.

New York–New York is loaded with re-created Big Apple landmarks, including this one of the Brooklyn Bridge.

Stripping 101

Want to learn to work a pole like a pro, get in touch with your inner vixen, or strut sexily in those stilettos you love? Stripping, when done right (think more tease than strip), is actually hard work, and **Stripper 101,** in the Miracle Mile Mall, 3663 Las Vegas Blvd. S. (☎ 702/260-7200; www.stripper101.com), teaches this very Vegas art form to women (sorry guys, you're strictly *verboten!*), ranging from 50-year-old housewives to 20-something celebrities. The hour-long classes are actually pretty nifty and confidence boosting, showing you the proper way to strut, slide down that pole, and give a lap dance. The shy shouldn't worry; you keep your clothes on for the entire experience. And you'll also burn a couple of hundred calories, so you can go sin without guilt at a buffet afterward. Classes cost $40 (they throw in a drink), and you must be at least 18 years of age.

A Deadly Bet

Some thrill seekers, when faced with a seriously long walk to that next crosswalk on the Strip, might be tempted to try the pedestrian version of Russian roulette in Vegas: darting across Las Vegas Boulevard without benefit of a traffic signal. Don't! That bet is a guaranteed loser.

❽ ★★★ Absinthe. Lust is a Las Vegas staple crop, but there are few places where it is as flagrantly, giddily displayed than in *Absinthe* at Caesars Palace. Mixing gasp-inducing acrobatics with topless performers, fever-dream theatrics, and outrageous, X-rated comedy, the show is what Cirque du Soleil would look like if Howard Stern was producing it. Definitely not for the faint of heart. 🕐 1½ hr. See p 114 for full details on the show.

❾ ★★★ Treasures. You can never have too much of a good thing, so continue your lustfest at this fancy strip joint, whose interior looks like it's straight out of a Victorian sporting house. The stage is strictly modern, as gals twirl in

some actual routines on light-up poles, action often complete with fog machines and other effects. Be careful about prices and hidden fees, lest you fall victim to someone else's greed! 🕐 *At least 1 hr. 2801 Westwood Dr. (parking is hard to spot after dark; use Highland Dr. & keep your eyes peeled).* ☎ *702/257-3030. www.treasureslasvegas.com. No unescorted women. Topless. $30 cover. Lap dances $20 & up. Sun–Thurs 4pm–6am; Fri–Sat 4pm–9am.*

Treasures is among the classiest of Sin City's famous strip clubs.

Las Vegas for **Elopers**

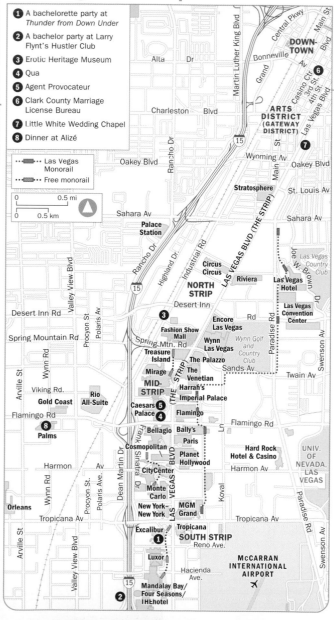

1 A bachelorette party at *Thunder from Down Under*

2 A bachelor party at Larry Flynt's Hustler Club

3 Erotic Heritage Museum

4 Qua

5 Agent Provocateur

6 Clark County Marriage License Bureau

7 Little White Wedding Chapel

8 Dinner at Alizé

Las Vegas Monorail
Free monorail

0   0.5 mi
0   0.5 km

DOWNTOWN

ARTS DISTRICT (GATEWAY DISTRICT)

Stratosphere

Palace Station

Circus Circus
Riviera
NORTH STRIP
Las Vegas Hotel
Las Vegas Convention Center

Fashion Show Mall
Encore Las Vegas
Wynn Las Vegas
Wynn Golf and Country Club

Treasure Island
The Palazzo
Mirage
The Venetian
MID-STRIP
Harrah's
Imperial Palace

Rio All-Suite
Gold Coast

Caesars Palace
Flamingo

Palms

Bellagio
Paris
Cosmopolitan
Planet Hollywood
CityCenter
Hard Rock Hotel & Casino

Monte Carlo
New York-New York
MGM Grand

UNIV. OF NEVADA, LAS VEGAS

Orleans

Excalibur
Tropicana
SOUTH STRIP
Reno Ave.

Luxor

Mandalay Bay Four Seasons/ IHGhotel

McCARRAN INTERNATIONAL AIRPORT

Las Vegas Country Club

Martin Luther King Blvd
Central Pkwy
Main St
Bonneville
Grand
Casino Ctr
3rd St
4th St
Las Vegas Blvd

Alta   Dr

Charleston   Blvd

Rancho Dr

Wyoming Av
Main St
Oakey Blvd

Oakey Blvd

St. Louis Av

Sahara Av

Sahara Av

Joe W. Brown

Paradise Rd

Desert Inn Rd

Spring Mountain Rd

Desert Inn   Rd

Spring Mtn. Rd
Sands Av.

Twain Av

Valley View Blvd
Procyon St
Polaris Av
Industrial Rd
Highland Dr

Wynn Rd

Arville St
Viking Rd.

Flamingo Rd

Flamingo Rd

Harmon   Av

Harmon Av

Wynn Rd

Dean Martin Dr
Frank Sinatra Dr
Procyon St
Polaris Ave.

Koval

Swenson Av

Paradise Rd

Tropicana Av

Tropicana Av

Arville St

Valley View Blvd

Hacienda Ave.

LAS VEGAS BLVD (THE STRIP)

THE STRIP

I**t's quite easy to get married in Vegas. Too easy.** There is little, apart from good sense, to prevent you from getting married to a total stranger, and given those free drinks handed out to anyone playing the slots, after a short time you might not even have much of that. If you want to join the more than 100,000 couples who have walked down the aisle before you, here's a traditional 24-hour tour of Vegas-style wedding action. START: **Brides-to-be should drive or take a taxi to Excalibur; grooms should head for Caesars Palace.**

The Aussie hunks in Excalibur's Thunder from Down Under are a very popular diversion for women.

❶ A bachelorette party at *Thunder from Down Under.*

Gals, check out the hunky action at this Aussie male strip revue, featuring some of the cheekiest—and I mean that in all ways—performers you can imagine. Hilarious as well as handsome, they know how to work a room. ⏱ *80 min. In Excalibur, 3850 Las Vegas Blvd. S.* ☎ *702/597-7600. www.thunderfromdownunder. com. Must be at least 18 years old. Ages 18–20 must be accompanied by an adult. Gentlemen welcome. General admission $41 (plus tax). VIP admission $61 (plus tax). Shows Sun–Thurs 9pm; Fri–Sat 9 & 11pm.*

❷ A bachelor party at Larry Flynt's Hustler Club. Really

understanding brides-to-be won't mind if their men head for this mammoth, four-story temple to excesses of the flesh, which claims to be the biggest strip club in Vegas (for whatever that's worth). The Hustler brand means that this ain't no seedy dive, which may be comforting to some future wives. ⏱ *At least 1 hr. 6007 Dean Martin Dr.* ☎ *702/795-3131. www.hustlerclubs.com. $30 cover. Lap dances $30. Open nightly 8pm–4am.*

❸ Erotic Heritage Museum.

The soon-to-be betrothed can get some background on various, uh, "possibilities" for their wedding night at this fascinating facility celebrating all manners of human sexuality. Exhibits include everything from ancient deflowering devices to modern adult entertainment and are equal parts sexy, sleazy, and sobering. ⏱ *45 min. 4275 Industrial Rd.* ☎ *702/369-6442. www.erotic heritagemuseumlasvegas.com. Admission $15. Kids 17 & under must be accompanied by an adult. Open Sun, Tues–Thurs 11am–4pm; Fri–Sat noon–10pm.*

Erotic Heritage Museum.

The luxe Qua spa is the perfect place to relax after a night out on the town.

❹ Qua. As soon as you can drag yourself out of bed in the morning, head to this lush spa at Caesars Palace. Get a special treatment or just sit in the blissful Roman bath area, moving from ice room (where you can exfoliate with shaved ice), to sauna, to plunge pools of varying temperatures, before finally collapsing in a heated lounge chair. Qua's salon also does hair and makeup to make you picture-perfect. ⏲ *At least 1 hr. In Caesars Palace, 3570 Las Vegas Blvd. S. (on the 2nd level of the Augustus Tower).* ☎ *866/782-0655. www.quabathandspa.com. Full-body massage $140 & up. Reservations required for all treatments. Daily 6am–8pm.*

❺ Agent Provocateur. If you really did come to Vegas in a hurry,

Couples from all over the world come to the very convenient Clark County Marriage License Bureau to secure a license to get hitched.

and you want to wear something, ahem, special for your wedding night, check out this British import's line of classy but naughty lingerie. ⏲ *30 min. In The Forum Shops at Caesars Palace.* ☎ *702/696-7174. www.agent provocateur.com. See p 69.*

❻ Clark County Marriage License Bureau. Ready to go? You can't until you've made sure what you are about to do is legal. Get your license here. It's no longer open round-the-clock, which is probably just as well, but the entire process should take no more than an hour—and possibly as little as 10 minutes. Once you have that important piece of paper, you're good to go—there's no set waiting period. ⏲ *10 min.–1 hr. Busiest days are Fri–Sat; slowest times are early morning Mon–Fri. 201 Clark Ave.* ☎ *702/671-0600. www.co.clark. nv.us. Must be 18 or older with valid proof of age & a Social Security number. Couples must be male-female. License $60. Open daily 8am–midnight, including holidays.*

Wedding Tip

If you want something a little more traditional . . . or outrageous for your big day, see p 119 for a run-down of my favorite wedding chapels in Las Vegas.

❼ Little White Wedding Chapel. Hotel chapels tend to be

It should come as no surprise that a city that holds as many weddings as this one does has plenty of hotel options for that must-have romantic honeymoon. Many hotels offer special packages for newlyweds, so ask when you book. For my favorite properties in Vegas, including some ultraromantic possibilities, see p 122.

prettier and more traditional, but if you came to Vegas for the kitsch, your search will be best fulfilled by this famous wedding factory. It was good enough for Michael Jordan, Demi Moore and Bruce Willis, and Britney Spears (though "good" in these cases may be a debatable term). Plus, for those particularly in a hurry, it has a drive-up window. *10 min.–1 hr., depending on how busy they are & if you made a reservation in advance. 1301 Las Vegas Blvd. S. (btw. E. Oakley & Charleston boulevards).* ☎ *800/545-8111 or 702/382-5943. www.alittlewhite chapel.com. Base chapel rate $55; add-ons (everything from garters to Elvis) & complete packages are available. Open 24 hrs.*

8 ★★★ **Dinner at Alizé.** Hold your wedding feast at the city's most romantic restaurant, with nearly floor-to-ceiling windows on three sides, and a virtually unobstructed view of the city and desert.

For a romantic dinner in Las Vegas, you can't beat Alizé.

Though surely you won't take your eyes off each other. *2 hr. See p 87 for more details on the restaurant.*

If you like your weddings kitschy and fast, the Little White Wedding Chapel is the best place to get married in Vegas.

Las Vegas **with Kids**

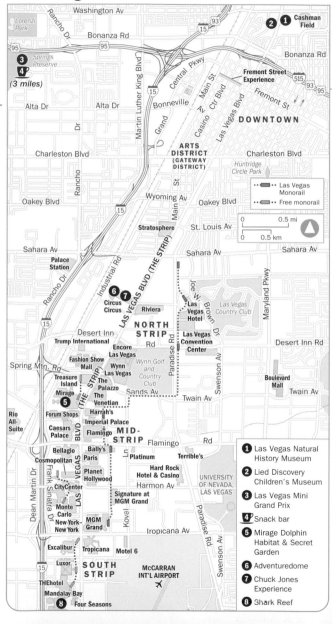

1 Las Vegas Natural History Museum

2 Lied Discovery Children's Museum

3 Las Vegas Mini Grand Prix

4 Snack bar

5 Mirage Dolphin Habitat & Secret Garden

6 Adventuredome

7 Chuck Jones Experience

8 Shark Reef

Don't kid yourself; Vegas isn't for children. The city markets itself strongly as a haven for distinctly adult pursuits and entertainment. This is obvious when you look at the sides of several of the casino hotels, often featuring multistory adverts for girlie shows in the form of shapely, nearly bare bottoms. But there are some activities appropriate for the younger set, so if you have kids in tow, your vacation won't come up a loser in the short run. START: **Drive to the Las Vegas Natural History Museum and park in the museum lot.**

❶ ★ **Las Vegas Natural History Museum.** Hardly high tech, this throwback to the era of dioramas of taxidermy animals comes off as small-town when compared to more venerable—and well-funded—institutions found in New York or Los Angeles. But your dinosaur-crazy kid will enjoy it, and you'll enjoy the relaxed pace. Among the hands-on, interactive exhibits is an installation that allows participants to experience life as a nocturnal critter—and not in the Vegas way! ⏱ 1½ hr. 900 Las Vegas Blvd. N. (at Washington Ave., adjacent to Cashman Center). ☎ 702/384-3466. www.lvnhm.org. Admission $10 adults, $8 seniors, students & military; $5 kids 3–11; free for kids 2 & under. Daily 9am–4pm.

The relaxed Las Vegas Natural History Museum is loaded with life-size fossils and animal exhibits.

❷ ★★ **Lied Discovery Children's Museum.** An excellent facility that provides tons of sugar (all kinds of playful, clever, interactive exhibits) to help the medicine—that is, education about physics, nature, the human body, history, and more—go down. Kids are probably savvy enough to realize it's good for them, but by the time they are launching tennis balls into the air, they probably won't care they are

Both kids and parents love the interactive exhibits at the Lied Discovery Children's Museum.

also learning about air pressure. There is even a special section for the 5-and-under set. ⏱ *2 hr. 833 Las Vegas Blvd. N. (½ block south of Washington Ave., across the street from Cashman Field).* ☎ *702/382-3445. www.ldcm.org. Admission $9.50 adults; $8.50 seniors, military & kids 1–17. Open Tues–Fri 9am–4pm; Sat 10am–5pm; Sun noon–5pm. Closed Mon, except school holidays.*

❸ ★★★ Las Vegas Mini-Grand Prix. Now that the kids have gotten a little education, let 'em have some fun! This attraction is part arcade, part go-kart racetrack; though the former is well stocked, it's the latter that holds the most appeal. Not only is it a rare outdoor nonwater-related activity, but your offspring can also work off nervous energy on four different tracks. ⏱ *2 hr. 1401 N. Rainbow Rd. (just off U.S. 95 N.)* ☎ *702/259-7000. www.lvmgp.com. Rides $7 each or $20 for 1 hr. on all rides. Must be at least 36 in. (91cm) tall to ride. Sun–Thurs 10am–10pm; Fri–Sat 10am–11pm.*

The pizzas at the **❹ snack bar** are triple the size and half the price of those you'll find in your hotel or on the Strip. And pretty tasty, too! *In Mini-Grand Prix, 1401 N. Rainbow Rd.* ☎ *702/259-7000. $.*

❺ ★★★ Mirage Dolphin Habitat & Secret Garden. Siegfried & Roy's show may have come to an abrupt and rather ignominious end, but the furry stars of their show are still on display in this lush, intimate setting, which allows for some fairly up-close encounters with white tigers and the like. The best part is the dolphin habitat, a 2.5-million-gallon (9.4-million-liter) tank where these most delightful of mammals frolic. Trainers dote on them, stimulating their charges. If you are really lucky, you might be around for a session of ball. Very little pleases kids more than trying to catch a wet ball flipped to them by a dolphin snout. ⏱ *1 hr. See p 16,* ❺.

❻ ★ Adventuredome. One of the coolest things about this amusement park is the fact that it is indoors and therefore cool even on the hottest of Las Vegas days. Although not huge by park standards, the relatively small space is packed with a roller coaster, a log flume, various twisty/turny/stomach-churning–style rides, carnival and arcade games, 4-D theaters, a miniature golf course, and more. *Warning:* There are clowns running around this particular circus, so the coulrophobic should take a sedative first. ⏱ *1–2 hr. In Circus Circus, 2880 Las Vegas Blvd. S.* ☎ *702/794-3939. www.adventuredome.com. Rides*

Future Formula One stars can get their speed on at the delightful Las Vegas Mini-Grand Prix.

A double-loop roller coaster takes center stage at Adventuredome.

$5–$8 each; all-day pass $17–$27. Mon–Thurs 11am–6pm; Fri–Sun 10am–midnight.

7 ★★ **Chuck Jones Experience.** Jones was the animation brain behind such classic Looney Tunes characters as Bugs Bunny and Wile E. Coyote, and this 10,000-square-foot (929 sq.-m) interactive facility showcases his art and his legacy in a way that both children and nostalgic adults can appreciate. You can make your own cartoons, try on some wacky character voices, see classic 'toons, and check out an extensive collection of Jones's art. Acme anvil not included. ⏱ *30 min. In Circus Circus, 2880 Las Vegas Blvd. S.* ☎ *702/734-0410. www.chuckjones experience.com. Admission $20 adults, $12 kids 17 & under, seniors 65 & up, and students $15. Daily 10am–10pm.*

8 ★ **Shark Reef.** Guests travel through a tunnel that runs through the middle of this giant aquarium, designed to look like a sunken ancient temple. The sharks (plus other finny friends) glide smoothly and somewhat sinisterly up and around you. It's engaging, but pricey for what you get. It doesn't take much time to navigate, which is probably just as well, because you—if not the kids—will probably be fairly tuckered out by this point. ⏱ *45 min. The aquarium is in a remote area of the casino hotel, a difficult trek for those with mobility problems. In Mandalay Bay, 3950 Las Vegas Blvd. S.* ☎ *702/632-4555. www.mandalaybay.com. Admission $18 adults, $12 kids 5–12, free for kids 4 & under. Sun–Thurs 10am–8pm; Fri–Sat 10am–10pm. Last admission 1 hr. prior to close.*

No Children Allowed!

When I said Vegas doesn't throw out the welcome mat to families, I wasn't kidding. Be advised that many hotels will not allow children who aren't staying on their property through the front door (they'll demand a room key as proof of occupancy). And don't even think about allowing your children to linger anywhere near a casino floor . . . they'll be shooed away pretty quickly. This tour will keep your youngsters happy for a day in the city, but as a long-term family vacation destination, Vegas falls short of ideal. If you have little ones, I strongly advise you to look elsewhere for a long break.

Las Vegas for **Thrill Seekers**

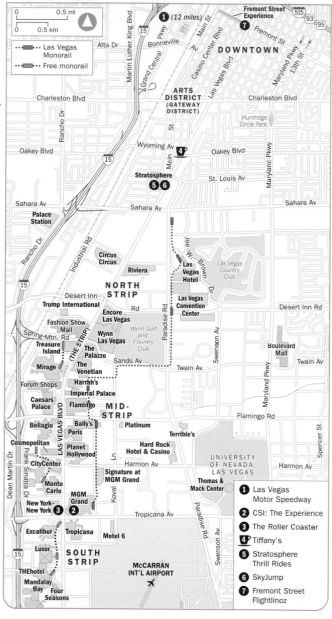

Scale	
0	0.5 mi
0	0.5 km

···■··· Las Vegas Monorail
···■··· Free monorail

Martin Luther King Blvd
Alta Dr
Bonneville Av
Grand Central Pkwy
① (12 miles)
Main St
Casino Center Blvd
Las Vegas Blvd
Fremont St
Fremont Street Experience ⑦
515
93
95
DOWNTOWN
Maryland Pkwy
13th St

Charleston Blvd
ARTS DISTRICT (GATEWAY DISTRICT)
Charleston Blvd
Huntridge Circle Park

Rancho Dr
Oakey Blvd
Wyoming Av **④ Ⓣ**
Main St
Oakey Blvd
St. Louis Av
Maryland Pkwy

Stratosphere ⑤⑥

Sahara Av
Palace Station
Sahara Av
Sahara Av
Sahara Av

Rancho Dr
Industrial Rd
15
Circus Circus
Riviera
Joe W. Brown Dr
Las Vegas Hotel
Las Vegas Country Club

NORTH STRIP
Las Vegas Convention Center
Paradise Rd

Desert Inn Rd
Trump International
Desert Inn Rd
Desert Inn Rd

Fashion Show Mall
Spring Mtn. Rd
Treasure Island
Encore Las Vegas
Wynn Las Vegas
Wynn Golf and Country Club
Sands Av
Swenson Av
Boulevard Mall
Twain Av

Mirage
The Palazzo
The Venetian
(THE STRIP)
Twain Av

Forum Shops
Harrah's
Imperial Palace
MID-STRIP

Caesars Palace
Flamingo
Flamingo Rd
Spencer St

Bellagio
Bally's
Paris
Platinum
Flamingo Rd

Dean Martin Dr
Frank Sinatra Dr
LAS VEGAS BLVD
Cosmopolitan
Planet Hollywood
Terrible's
Hard Rock Hotel & Casino
Harmon Av
UNIVERSITY OF NEVADA, LAS VEGAS
Harmon Av
Maryland Pkwy

CityCenter
Signature at MGM Grand
Koval Ln
Harmon Av

Monte Carlo
New York–New York ③
MGM Grand ②
Thomas & Mack Center
Paradise Rd

Excalibur
Tropicana
Motel 6
Tropicana Av
Swenson Av

15
Luxor
SOUTH STRIP
Koval Ln
THEhotel
Mandalay Bay
Four Seasons
McCARRAN INT'L AIRPORT

①	Las Vegas Motor Speedway
②	CSI: The Experience
③	The Roller Coaster
④ Ⓣ	Tiffany's
⑤	Stratosphere Thrill Rides
⑥	SkyJump
⑦	Fremont Street Flightlinoz

The thrills in Vegas don't come solely from games of chance. While efforts to sustain full-blown amusement parks have failed, there are still plenty of rides, and other what-a-rush-type activities scattered about the city. Many of the hotels, in an effort to lure business, have some kind of attraction designed to make some of us nauseous and others exhilarated. If you have balance or nerve issues, this ain't the tour for you. START: **Drive to Las Vegas Motor Speedway.**

For speedy thrills, racing fans flock to the Las Vegas Motor Speedway to watch the pros rev their engines.

❶ ★★ **Las Vegas Motor Speedway.** Just about anything with wheels that goes really, really fast can be found here in one form or another. A $200-million, state-of-the-art motor-sports entertainment complex, this 176,000-seat facility serves up drag racing and super-speed courses in the viewing department. If participation is more your thing, get your speed fix at the go-kart tracks, driving schools, and other attractions. ⏲ *At least 2 hr. 7000 Las Vegas Blvd. N. (directly across from Nellis Air Force Base; take I-15 N to Speedway exit 54).* ☎ *702/644-4443 for ticket information. www.lvms.com. Tickets $10–$75. Race days vary.*

❷ ★★ **kids** **CSI: The Experience.** This good exercise in forensics will give your brain a workout—think mental thrill (uncommon in Vegas) more than a physical one. The 3-D whodunit (best for ages 12 and up) puts you in the middle of a crime scene investigation studying DNA, fingerprints, and more as you make your way through an interactive lab and get to the bottom of one of three crimes. Think Colonel Mustard in the library with the candlestick, times 1,000. ⏲ *At least 1 hr. At MGM Grand, 3799 Las Vegas Blvd. S. (at Tropicana Ave.).* ☎ *877/660-0660 or 702/891-7006. www.mgmgrand.com. Admission $28 adults, $21 kids 4–11. Daily 9am–9pm.*

❸ **kids** **The Roller Coaster.** I consider this "classic" Las Vegas, not because it harkens back to the Rat Pack days, but because it's one of the few remnants of the family-friendly era. More than a decade

For the city's biggest adrenaline rush, plummet toward the earth on the Stratosphere's SkyJump.

ago, the attitude was "why *not* put the Coney Island–themed roller coaster (originally known as the Manhattan Express) right through the lobby and around the outside of the hotel?" Why not, indeed? In any case, it's indisputable that the coaster (which pours on the adrenaline with a 144-ft./44m drop, plus various inversions and twists) does replicate riding in the New York City cabs its cars resemble—with all that that entails. 🕐 *About 10 min., depending on the lines. In New York–New York, 3790 Las Vegas Blvd. S.* ☎ *800/689-1797. www.newyorknewyork.com. Must be at least 54 in. (137cm) tall to ride. Single-ride pass $14; all-day pass $25. Sun–Thurs 11am–1pm; Fri–Sat 10:30am–midnight.*

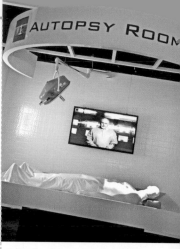

Follow the evidence at simulated crime scenes at CSI: The Experience.

There's no better place in town for good ole American comfort food of the old-school variety (think burgers, shakes, and breakfast) than 💲 **Tiffany's.** Open around the clock, it's a cheap but great diner in a city where such things are vanishing entirely too quickly. *1700 Las Vegas Blvd. S. (at East Oakey Blvd.).* ☎ *702/444-4459. $.*

⑤ ★★ Stratosphere Thrill Rides. The Stratosphere Tower is the tallest building west of the Mississippi. That's 1,149 feet (350m) up, for those keeping track. So naturally, one puts thrill rides on the top of it. The **Big Shot** takes you up the final 160 feet (49m) or so of the spire before letting you free-fall back down again. Once your heart is back where it belongs, you can then try the **X-Scream,** a giant teeter-totter that teeters and totters over the edge of the 100-story tower. Try not to throw up on the smart people who stayed safely below on the Strip,

Soar high above the Strip on the Stratosphere's very appropriately named Insanity.

From its cab-themed cars to its adrenaline-inducing drops, the Roller Coaster perfectly captures New York's breakneck speed.

okay? Finally, there is **Insanity**—an appropriate moniker, given that the very thought of this ride elicits an "are you nuts?" from me—which whirls you around 1,000 feet (305m) in the air. ⏱ *About 45 min., depending on the lines. In Stratosphere Las Vegas, 2000 Las Vegas Blvd. S. ☎ 702/380-7777. www.stratosphere hotel.com. Rides $12–$13, plus fee to ascend tower ($16 adults, $12 seniors & hotel guests, $10 kids 4–12, free for kids 3 & under). Discount multiride & all-day packages available. Sun–Thurs 10am–1am; Fri–Sat & holidays 10am–2am. Hours vary seasonally. Must be at least 48 in. (122cm) tall to ride.*

6 ★★ **SkyJump.** If the rides at the top of the Stratosphere Tower are too tame for you, why not check out the ride to the bottom of it? Yes, these days they actually allow you to jump off the 108th floor of the tower, albeit with a lot of safety equipment firmly in place. This is not a bungee jump, but rather a

"controlled descent" that allows the truly crazy (as far as I'm concerned) to plummet face first 855 feet (261m) straight down at speeds up to 40 mph (64kmph). It's worth noting that if you change your mind once you get up there, they don't offer refunds, but they will put your face on a "Chicken" T-shirt. ⏱ *At least 45 min. In the Stratosphere, 2000 Las Vegas Blvd. S. ☎ 702/99-TOWER (998-6937). www.skyjump lasvegas.com. $105 per jump, includes tower admission. Sun–Thurs 10am–1am; Fri–Sat 10am–2am.*

7 ★★ **Fremont Street Flightlinez.** Compared to SkyJump, this zip line above Fremont Street in Downtown Las Vegas is practically a kiddy ride, but only serious adrenaline junkies will complain. The ride takes you several hundred feet along the Viva Vision canopy at speeds up to 35 mph (56kmph), offering some spectacular views of the Glitter Gulch neon at night—that is if you can keep your eyes open, of course. ⏱ *20 min. plus wait time. 425 E. Fremont St. ☎ 702/410-7999. www.fremontstreetflightline.com. $15 before 6pm, $20 after 6pm. Open Sun–Thurs noon–midnight; Fri–Sat noon–2am.*

Zipping down Fremont Street beneath the Viva Vision canopy is an unforgettable Vegas experience.

Las Vegas for **Culture Lovers**

1. Clark County Heritage Museum
2. Pinball Hall of Fame
3. National Atomic Testing Museum
4. 18b Arts District/ Arts Factory
5. Bar+Bistro
6. Nevada State Museum
7. Smith Center for the Performing Arts

Acultural capital Vegas is not. When things fall out of favor here, the city tends to blow them up rather than preserve them for posterity. But there are a number of museums and galleries (most housed in unpromising strip malls or within hotels) that enshrine everything from the sublime to the ridiculous. And there are even some oases in this desert city of sin, where you can stop and (literally) smell the roses. START: **Drive to the Clark County Heritage Museum and park in lot.**

An old-fashioned train depot is just one of the many historic buildings preserved at the Clark County Heritage Museum.

① ★★ Clark County Heritage Museum. Charming and cheap, this surprisingly large facility is a collection of restored historic buildings from significant points in Vegas history. There is a train depot, a print shop, a mine, a ghost town, and much more to remind us that up until the days of Bugsy Siegel, Vegas was just another Wild West town, trying to make it in the desert. An exhibit center features changing displays on different eras in local history. On the downside, the museum is not particularly close to anything, and because most of it is outside, summer is not an optimum time for a visit unless you go early in the day. ⏱ 1 hr. 1830 S. Boulder Hwy., East Las Vegas. ☎ 702/455-7955. www.accessclarkcounty.com. Admission $1.50 adults, $1 seniors & kids 3–15, free for kids 2 & under. Daily 9am–4:30pm.

② ★★ Pinball Hall of Fame. In most museums they frown on you for playing with their works of art. Here, they encourage it. Hundreds of working pinball machines and arcade games (Ms. PAC-MAN, Space

Invaders, and so forth) from the 1940s through the 1990s have been lovingly restored and are just waiting for your quarters. Even if you don't actually play, you can appreciate these machines as pieces of pop art, shining a light on our culture through the generations with their themes, bells, and whistles. ⏱ 1 hr. 1610 E. Tropicana Ave. ☎ 702/597-2627. www.pinballmuseum.org. Free admission; game prices vary. Sun–Thurs 11am–11pm; Fri–Sat 11am–midnight.

③ ★★★ National Atomic Testing Museum. Sixty miles (97km) from Vegas is a large swath of desolate desert, the perfect place for the testing of nuclear weapons—which is exactly what the government did on that spot for 40 years. Once upon a time, aboveground blasts were a tourist attraction. Such naiveté is part of the complicated political, historical, scientific, and moral legacy of the nuclear testing program, and this excellent museum is as much dedicated to trying to sort it all out as it is to preserving this troubled part of Vegas heritage. Look among the excellent displays for the motion-simulator theater that attempts to demonstrate what it feels like to ride out a test blast in a bunker. ⏱ 1½ hr. See p 15, ②.

④ 18b Arts District/Arts Factory. Spanning roughly 18 blocks (hence the name) between the Strip and Downtown, the Las Vegas Arts District is not as cohesive an arts experience as you'll find in other cities. Here, the pawn stores and bail bondsmen seem to outnumber the galleries, but there are some diamonds among the rough, including some exciting exhibit spaces, fun retro furniture stores, antiques, and more. The epicenter of the district is the Arts Factory, an artists' collective housing galleries, boutiques, a cafe, and a bar. Start there and explore the surrounding neighborhood. Don't miss the First Friday street fair featuring art, food, and live entertainment. 🕐 1–2 hr. 101–107 E. Charleston Ave. ☎ 702/383-3133. www.theartsfactory.com. Mon–Sat 9am–6pm; First Fri of the month until 10pm.

5 **Bar+Bistro**, at the Arts Factory, has a surprisingly extensive and eclectic menu that incorporates European, Middle Eastern, and American flavors. A highlight: the Meat Lovers Pizza, with pancetta, chorizo, and roasted chicken. A work of art! 107 E. Charleston Ave. #155. ☎ 702/202-6060. www.theartsfactory.com. $$.

6 ★ **kids** **Nevada State Museum.** Opened in 2011 after years of delays, this interactive and entertaining facility was worth the wait. The state's history is on display, from ancient flora and fauna to the modern casino age with stops at the Wild West, aboveground nuclear testing, and Hoover Dam along the

Indulge in old-school fun at the Pinball Hall of Fame.

The Smith Center for the Performing Arts is the city's first-rate cultural center.

way. It's all presented in a lively, tech-friendly way that all but the most disaffected of youth will appreciate. 🕐 30 min. 309 S. Valley View Blvd. ☎ 702/486-5205. www.nevadaculture.org. Admission $9.95 adults, free for kids 18 & under. Fri–Mon 10am–6pm.

7 ★★ **Smith Center for the Performing Arts.** End your day of culture with a night inside the city's first real stab at creating a home for the performing arts that doesn't include French acrobats. Reynolds Hall is the centerpiece; it's a 2,050-seat, state-of-the-art concert hall that hosts everything from symphonies to such Broadway touring shows as Mary Poppins and Wicked. Two smaller theaters stage more intimate concerts and plays, including community-based performances for grown-ups and kids. It's a fantastic complex that is both totally unexpected in a city like Las Vegas and exactly what it needs. 🕐 2 hr. 361 Symphony Park Ave. ☎ 702/982-7805. www.thesmithcenter.com. Ticket prices and showtimes vary; consult the website for up-to-date offerings. ●

3 The Best
Neighborhood Walks

South Strip

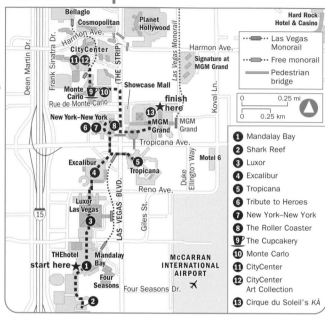

1. Mandalay Bay
2. Shark Reef
3. Luxor
4. Excalibur
5. Tropicana
6. Tribute to Heroes
7. New York–New York
8. The Roller Coaster
9. The Cupcakery
10. Monte Carlo
11. CityCenter
12. CityCenter Art Collection
13. Cirque du Soleil's *KÀ*

Of the three major sections of the Strip, this is probably the one with the most variety and the greatest concentration of over-the-top Vegas hotels. Wacky theme hotels are sadly giving way to good-taste resort hotels, which, though grand, are starting to seem a bit cookie-cutter. Not these babies. **START: Mandalay Bay's main lobby.**

1 Mandalay Bay. This hotel's Southeast Asia theme is more subdued than its gleaming gold exterior might lead you to believe. There are still statues, foliage, and tropical birds, but the property's appeal lies more in the whole package. Check out the 11-acre (4.5-hectare) Mandalay Beach pool area from the casino windows; it's a winner. And

Previous page: Dale Chihuly's Fiori di Como *glass sculpture adorns the ceiling of the Bellagio's lobby.*

do wander down the hotel's restaurant row, where design whimsy is still in effect. Evidence: There's a **statue of Lenin** (covered in fake pigeon droppings, and beheaded) outside **Red Square** (p 95), whose interior is covered with the ephemeral trappings of Bolshevik and Stalinist highs and lows. Only in Vegas. ⏱ *30 min., if you don't stop to eat. 3950 Las Vegas Blvd. S. (at Hacienda Ave.).* ☎ *702/632-7000. www.mandalaybay.com.*

2 ★ kids Shark Reef. Don't think this is Animal Planet's "Shark

A headless statue of Lenin marks the entrance to Mandalay Bay's stylish Red Square restaurant.

Week" come to life. This is really just a beautifully designed (and expensive) aquarium, though not a particularly large one. But because you travel via a glass tunnel that passes right through the exhibits, it does give you the illusion of joining the fish. It's more peaceful than stimulating, but it's decidedly cool to get that up close and personal with a shark or to see a piranha feed. ⏱ *45 min., unless you are hypnotized by fish-watching. See p 33,* ⑦.

③ **Luxor.** This Egyptian repro has sadly been downgraded in the theme department (the *Titanic*'s here instead of King Tut!), but enough of the old scheme remains to warrant a trip inside. Do tip your hat to the 30-foot (9m) sphinx that guards the entrance. *See p 46 for a walking tour of this hotel.*

④ **kids Excalibur.** Named for the mythical sword of King Arthur, this cute and colorful hotel's medieval theme is no longer the outsize wonder that it once was. It does, however, retain some of the more kid-friendly options in Vegas (including some multisensory simulator

rides, one of them featuring SpongeBob SquarePants). For a picture-perfect view of the castle, take the faux drawbridge passage out of the hotel, use the overhead walkway to Tropicana, and turn around. ⏱ *20 min. 3850 Las Vegas Blvd. S.* ☎ *800/937-7777 or 702/597-7700. www.excalibur.com.*

⑤ **Tropicana.** Opened in 1957, the so-called Tiffany of the Strip had suffered from years of neglect, but new owners arrived in 2009 and dumped more than $100 million in an extreme makeover that has put the old gal back in the game. The sunny, South Beach theme is a delight, but there are still nods to the hotel's past; check out the 4,000 square-foot (372-sq.-m) stained-glass ceiling over the casino floor, which was integrated into the remodeling. ⏱ *20 min. 3801 Las Vegas Blvd. S.* ☎ *702/739-2222. www.troplv.com.*

⑥ **Tribute to Heroes.** At the base of New York–New York's 150-foot-tall (46m) Statue of Liberty, this granite structure holds a permanent collection of notes, pins, and other mementos left outside the hotel post-9/11 to honor the victims and those who so valiantly worked at the tragic site. It's a rare somber

This lionfish is one of the many denizens of the deep you'll find at Shark Reef.

Excalibur is the city's tacky but entertaining take on the Arthurian legend.

note amid the Strip's carefully orchestrated irreverence. ⏱ *15 min. Outside New York–New York. See* ⑦.

⑦ New York–New York. The audacious Manhattan exterior—12 skyscrapers (one-third the size of the originals), including a 47-story Empire State Building, the New York Public Library, Ellis Island, and more—is riveting. It makes me sorry that Vegas hotels now trend toward good taste. Be sure to cross over the ⅛th-size (300-ft.-tall/91m) replica of the Brooklyn Bridge to stroll the hotel's interior, which is sadly less theme intensive than it used to be. It's also still one of the most confusing and crowded properties, but surely that's only one more faithful re-creation, this time of midtown during rush hour. ⏱ *30 min. 3790 Las Vegas Blvd. S.* ☎ *702/740-6969. www.newyorknewyork.com.*

⑧ 🧒 The Roller Coaster. This 203-foot-tall (62m) roller coaster has classic cars designed to look like old-fashioned checker cabs and swoops not only around the outside of the New York–New York complex (at speeds hovering around 67 mph/108kmph), but also right through the interior. Enthusiasts will note that it was the first coaster to feature a 180-degree "heartline" twist and turn.

⏱ *up to 1 hr., depending on the lines; ride is only 5 min. Go early in the morning to avoid crowds. See* ⑥. *Must be at least 54 in. (137cm) tall to ride. Single-ride pass $14; all-day pass $25. Open Sun–Thurs 11am–11pm; Fri–Sat 10:30am–midnight.*

If you need proof that the cupcake craze is still alive and kicking, stop by **⑨ ★★★ The Cupcakery,** for a sugar fix. The generous application of buttercream frosting and flavorful cakes will make you a believer. *In Monte Carlo.* ☎ *702/997-8657. www.thecupcakery.com. $. See* ⑪.

⑩ Monte Carlo. The $344-million project was supposed to be named the Grand Victoria, but MGM Grand objected, so instead, this 44-acre (18-hectare) resort was named after the city in which the Place du Casino (on which this hotel was modeled) resides. It ostensibly captures European elegance (and the grand entranceway on the Strip, loaded with classy statuary and arches, is a

New York–New York's famous whimsical exterior is dominated by a replica of Lady Liberty.

Modeled on its namesake's famous casino, the Monte Carlo is elegant, but a little bland when compared to its Strip neighbors.

great place for a snapshot), but it's not as theme intensive or detailed as its Strip brethren, which sort of makes it the Vegas equivalent of a wallflower. Though a nice wallflower, to be sure. ⏱ *15 min. 3770 Las Vegas Blvd. S. (btw. Flamingo Rd. & Tropicana Ave.).* ☎ *702/730-7777. www.montecarlo.com.*

⓫ ★★ CityCenter. Vegas entered the 21st century with the opening of this mammoth "community" of hotels, condo residences, and retail stores—a joint venture of MGM Mirage and Dubai World that cost almost $11 billion! Did they get their money's worth? It definitely has the bling factor (the retail complex earns its name, Crystals), the green factor (it earned Gold LEED certification for all its components—a big deal in a city not known for its environmental savvy), the culture factor (almost $40 million in public art; see below), the luxe factor (those hotels, including a Mandarin Oriental, aren't for the budget set), and it's actually good for strolling. Just be sure to wear your shades as you wander the well landscaped walkways—that glass and steel is sort of blindingly brilliant. ⏱ *30 min. See p 10.*

⓬ CityCenter Art Collection. No city can achieve greatness without great art, a concept the designers of

CityCenter took to heart. Scattered around the massive property are more than a dozen works including a sculpture by Vietnam Veterans Memorial designer Maya Lin; the famous "Reclining Connected Forms" by Henry Moore; a massive installation of colorfully painted canoes by Nancy Rubins; and more. Ask the concierge for a map or download the app for your smart phone. ⏱ *30 min. At CityCenter, 3730 Las Vegas Blvd. S.* ☎ *866/359-7757. www.citycenter. com. Free. Most works accessible 24 hrs.*

⓭ ★★★ 🧒 Cirque du Soleil's KÀ. This stellar Cirque creation is a superb mix of production values, stage, showmanship, storytelling, and derring-do. And unlike the other Cirque shows in town, this one has a story line (a simple tale about separated royal siblings trying to reunite with one another). The incredible moving stage puts other mechanical theatrical gee-whiz gimmicks to shame, while simultaneously providing just the right literal and figurative platform for Cirque artistry. ⏱ *1½ hr. In MGM Grand, 3799 Las Vegas Blvd. S.* ☎ *866/740-7711 or 702/531-3826. www.cirquedusoleil.com. Shows Tues–Sat 7 & 9:30pm. No shows Sun–Mon. See p 114.*

Luxor Las Vegas

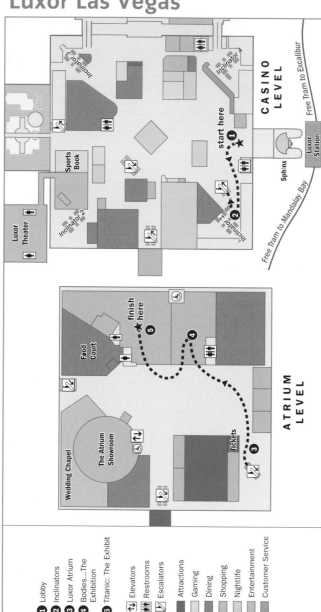

start here

CASINO LEVEL

Free Tram to Excalibur

Free Tram to Mandalay Bay

Sphinx

Luxor Station

Inclinator 3

Inclinator 4

Pool

Sports Book

Inclinator 2

Inclinator 1

Luxor Theater

ATRIUM LEVEL

finish here

Food Court

Wedding Chapel

The Atrium Showroom

Tickets

1 Lobby
2 Inclinators
3 Luxor Atrium
4 Bodies...The Exhibition
5 Titanic: The Exhibit

Elevators
Restrooms
Escalators

Attractions
Gaming
Dining
Shopping
Nightlife
Entertainment
Customer Service

A perfect example of the city's move to scale down themes that should be embraced. In this case, it's a 30-story, black-glass pyramid—a three-quarter-scale replica of the famous one at Giza—but then again, Luxor's Sphinx has its nose intact. This South Strip stalwart (it opened in 1993 and was named for the ancient city of Thebes, aka Luxor) is one of the best examples of late-20th-century postmodern architecture—unfortunately, the 21st century hasn't been as kind as much of the interior has been stripped of its fun Egyptian theme. START: **Valet park your car (it's free) at the hotel, at 3900 Las Vegas Blvd. S. (btw. Reno and Hacienda aves.).**

Touring Tip

For more information on the Luxor, check out my hotel review on p 130.

1 Lobby. This Art Deco/Egyptian Revival space is dominated by two giant Ramses statues (ostensibly guarding the entrance to that Holy of Holies, the casino). Part of the point of the original Egyptian architecture was to remind mere mortals of their insignificance; it works just as well for the difference between monolithic casino hotels and the average slot player.

2 Inclinators. Sneak on the best free ride in town, the hotel's "inclinators"—the high-speed elevators that slant up at a 39-degree angle to deliver guests to their rooms. (In theory they're for guests only, but you can often jump on.)

3 Luxor Atrium. This is one of the largest atriums in the world, occupying almost 29 million cubic feet (821,189 cubic m). From here you can gaze on the vast inner space of the pyramid and recite "Ozymandias" to yourself ("look on my works, ye mighty, and despair!").

4 ★★ Bodies . . . The Exhibition. Instead of the old Luxor mummies you now get this strangely fascinating and controversial collection of dissected body parts and stripped down cadavers

The Grand Staircase is just one of many perfect re-creations at Titanic: The Artifact Exhibition.

demonstrating the human body's mechanics. It's pretty educational, if not for the faint of stomach. ⏱ *45 min. Admission $32 adults, $30 seniors, $24 kids 4–12, free for kids 3 & under. Daily 10am–10pm. Last admission 9pm.*

5 ★ Titanic: The Artifact Exhibition. A can't miss for buffs of the 1912 disaster thanks to its relics and atmospheric re-creations of the ship's ill-fated voyage. ⏱ *45 min. Admission $32 adults, $30 seniors, $24 kids 4–12, free for kids 3 & under. Daily 10am–10pm. Last admission 9pm.*

Mid-Strip

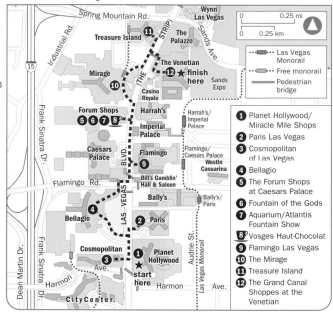

1. Planet Hollywood/Miracle Mile Shops
2. Paris Las Vegas
3. Cosmopolitan of Las Vegas
4. Bellagio
5. The Forum Shops at Caesars Palace
6. Fountain of the Gods
7. Aquarium/Atlantis Fountain Show
8. Vosges Haut-Chocolat
9. Flamingo Las Vegas
10. The Mirage
11. Treasure Island
12. The Grand Canal Shoppes at the Venetian

Here's the most crowded part of the Strip, though some of the larger casino hotels take up a great deal more space than may first appear. That's because this is, for the most part, the luxury-resort-hotel-on-steroids portion of Vegas. In between are leftovers from Vegas's tacky era. With a few exceptions, most items of interest will be inside, where there are all kinds of distractions designed to keep visitors within the property rather than straying to competitors.
START: Southernmost entrance to Planet Hollywood, by Pink's Hot Dogs.

① Planet Hollywood/Miracle Mile Shops. On April 17, 2007, the historic but fiscally troubled Aladdin (the original incarnation of which hosted Elvis and Priscilla's wedding) officially became the Planet Hollywood Resort & Casino, and work began on obliterating its *Arabian Nights* theme in favor of LA sophistication (or what passes for it). And its famed Desert Passage mall has become the Miracle Mile Shops, which has mostly rid itself of

its Middle East Kasbah in favor of something that is sort of high tech and a lot generic (though there is a touch of glitz there, too). Too bad; I like my themes along with my retail therapy. ⏱ *About 1 hr., depending on how dedicated a shopper you are. 3667 Las Vegas Blvd. S. ☎ 702/785-5555. www.planethollywood resort.com or www.miraclemileshops lv.com. Hotel open 24 hrs; mall open Sun–Thurs 10am–11pm, Fri–Sat 10am–midnight.*

Planet Hollywood's Miracle Mile Shops is one of the best hotel shopping arcades on the Strip.

② Paris Las Vegas. After admiring the mash up of landmarks of Paris outside, take a stroll within, where the feet of the Eiffel Tower replica rest on the casino floor, itself watched over by a ceiling painted to resemble a Parisian spring day. Revolutionary-era facades ring the casino area, and lead to **Le Boulevard,** the hotel's cobblestone shopping area. The original plan was for the smell of fresh bread to waft through here, complete with the occasional dash of a bike rider ferrying fresh baguettes to the eateries. That attention to detail has been lost, but the Disneyland version of Paris is still in place. It's not so much romantic as it is amusing—but heavily themed is the way Vegas ought to be; and this $785-million fantasyland certainly fits the bill. *See p 11,* **⑤**.

③ ★★★ Cosmopolitan of Las Vegas. This will probably be the last megaresort to open in Vegas for the foreseeable future. Most of that has to do with the country's economic woes, but some of it likely involves the unlikely probability that any new hotel could possibly top this one. The Cosmo is outrageous by design, eschewing the typical "theme" in favor of a cutting-edge, modern style that manages to be as visually arresting as those places with re-creations of famous landmarks. The vertical layout places the casino on the first floor, shopping on the second, restaurants on the third, and the pool and nightclub above that, so be sure to take some time to explore—you just might find some surprises, like a "hidden" pizza place tucked away in a corner. *See p 10,* **⑧**.

④ Bellagio. The opening of this lightly themed behemoth in the fall of 1998 marked the beginning of the end for the Vegas theme trend and the start of the march toward hotel elegance. *See p 52 for a walking tour of the hotel.*

⑤ The Forum Shops at Caesars Palace. The first great absurd hotel shopping mall in Vegas, and still the One to See. Walk down corridors designed to look like the streets of ancient Rome—if new and gleaming—with a sky-painted ceiling

A stunning three-story chandelier is just one of the Cosmopolitan's design hallmarks.

The Fountain of the Gods inside The Forum Shops may not be divine, but it is quite kitschy diversion.

overhead that tricks you into thinking it's broad daylight when it's really approaching midnight. The 160-store sprawling complex includes a more modern-looking (though just as liberally adorned with Roman statues) expansion featuring a three-story atrium accessed by a spiral-shaped escalator. It's a hoot even if you don't care about shopping. *Daily 10am–11pm. See p 69.*

6 kids Fountain of the Gods. This fountain appears to sport the same faux marble statue copies that pop up all over Caesars—until Bacchus, in his drunken glory, comes to creaky animatronic life and delivers a somewhat muffled speech about the wonders of decadence and living it up. The other statues concur. There are some laser effects to try to make it more up-to-date, but it remains cheesy and hokey. It's what passed for a marvel in old Vegas. It's amazing it's still there. ⏱ *8 min. In The Forum Shops at Caesars Palace, section D on the casino level. See 5. Free shows on the hour 10am–11pm.*

7 kids Aquarium/Atlantis Fountain Show. More elaborate and ambitious than the Fountain of the Gods, this show tells the "story" of the fall of Atlantis. Look for an actual story line, bigger special effects, and correspondingly bigger crowds. For the low tech and less

demanding, behind the fountains is a nifty (and free) 50,000-gallon (189,271L) saltwater aquarium. With luck, you'll arrive during one of the regular (and entertaining) fish feedings. *In The Forum Shops at Caesars Palace, section F on the casino level. See 5. Free 8-min. fountain shows on the hour 10am–11pm. Aquarium daily feedings 1:15 & 5:15pm.*

Get a shot of energy at **8 Vosges Haut-Chocolat**, which, in addition to exotic chocolate-based candy confections, offers a cocoa bar (my favorite: the white chocolate with lavender and lemon myrtle) and fancy ice cream. *In The Forum Shops at Caesars Palace, 3570 Las Vegas Blvd. S. (section H on the street level). ☎ 702/836-9866. www. vosgeschocolate.com. $.*

9 Flamingo Las Vegas. When mobster Bugsy Siegel's $6-million Art Deco–ish baby was born in 1946, all the staff (even the janitors!) wore tuxedos. Siegel met an infamous end in 1947, and none of the Flamingo's original structure

It's not what it was back in Bugsy's day, but the Flamingo is still a Strip mainstay worth seeing.

The atmosphere at Treasure Island nowadays is more tropical than pirate, though there's still booty to be won here.

remains. The Flamingo no longer rules the Strip roost, but its free wildlife sanctuary (yes, there are flamingos) and gardens are still beautiful and worth a gander. ⏱ *20 min. 3355 Las Vegas Blvd. S. (btw. Sands Ave. & Flamingo Rd.).* ☎ *800/732-2111 or 702/733-3111. www.flamingo lasvegas.com.*

⑩ The Mirage. Built on the site of the old Castaways hotel, The Mirage made Steve Wynn's rep as the king of Las Vegas hoteliers when it opened in 1989. Say "hi" to the scary-looking statues in front of the resort commemorating magicians Siegfried & Roy, who performed almost 6,000 shows here before Roy Horn was seriously injured onstage in 2003 after a disastrous encounter with one of the famous duo's beloved white tigers. *See p 13,* **⑪**.

⑪ Treasure Island. When it opened in 1993, this $450-million property was designed to attract families with a Disneyesque Caribbean pirates theme. That idea walked the plank in 2003, and the property was turned into an adult-oriented resort with nary a trace of theme. And its once kid-friendly free pirate battle now features sexed-up sirens. Yo Ho Hum.

⑫ The Grand Canal Shoppes at The Venetian. Every bit as over-the-top as The Forum Shops, but less cheesy, provided you don't automatically sneer at architectural reproductions (which are wonderfully rendered). Given how well executed the place is—including a rather cunning scaled-down replica of St. Mark's Square and canals with actual gondoliers—and that there are even period costumed performers who actually sing and otherwise interact with customers, it qualifies as a mall as theme park experience, and I mean that in a good way. ⏱ *45 min., longer if you actually shop. 3355 Las Vegas Blvd. S.* ☎ *702/414-4500. www.thegrandcanal shoppes.com. Sun–Thurs 10am–11pm; Fri–Sat 10am–midnight.*

Let a gondolier serenade you beneath a fake blue sky as you sail past the stores and restaurants of The Grand Canal Shoppes at The Venetian.

Bellagio

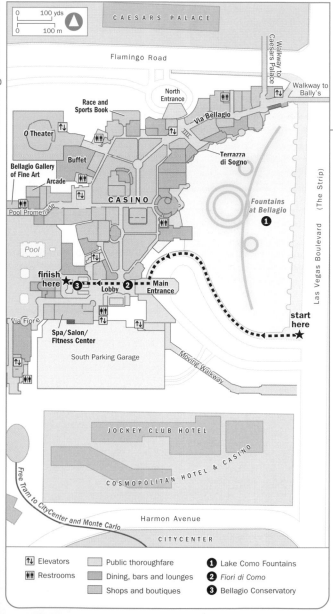

CAESARS PALACE

Flamingo Road

North Entrance

Race and Sports Book

Via Bellagio

O Theater

Terrazza di Sogno

Buffet

Bellagio Gallery of Fine Art

Arcade

CASINO

Pool Promenade

Fountains at Bellagio ❶

Pool

Las Vegas Boulevard (The Strip)

finish here ★ ❸

Lobby

❷

Main Entrance

start here ★

Via Fiore

Spa/Salon/ Fitness Center

South Parking Garage

Moving Walkway

JOCKEY CLUB HOTEL

Free Tram to CityCenter and Monte Carlo

COSMOPOLITAN HOTEL & CASINO

Harmon Avenue

CITYCENTER

↑↓ Elevators	Public thoroughfare	❶ Lake Como Fountains
♦♦ Restrooms	Dining, bars and lounges	❷ *Fiori di Como*
	Shops and boutiques	❸ Bellagio Conservatory

0 — 100 yds
0 — 100 m

Whe n it opened in 1998 on the site of the old Dunes hotel, this $1.6-billion brainchild of casino magnate Steve Wynn (who's since moved on to properties named for himself) was the most expensive ever built. This is the luxury resort that ushered in the new adults-only elegance epoch in Vegas. It's not quite the relaxing oasis that ads for the hotel make it out to be, but it is probably the closest thing Vegas has to a European casino hotel. And this expensive resort is, ironically, home to some of the best freebies in the city. START: **Valet-park your car (it's free) at the hotel, at 3600 Las Vegas Blvd. S. (at the corner of Flamingo Rd.), then walk to the sidewalk in front of the hotel.**

Touring Tip

For more information on Bellagio, check out my hotel review on p 126; for dining opportunities in the hotel, check out chapter 6.

1 Lake Como/Fountains. It's too bad that, after having gone to so much trouble to create this beautiful 8 acre (3.2-hectare) reproduction of Lake Como, Bellagio does not allow visitors into the scenic provincial Italian village strung along the lake's banks. Still, it remains a top spot for shutterbugs. If you haven't seen one of the fountain shows that take place on the lake yet you're past noon, wait for one—you won't regret it. *See p 11,* **9***, for more on the fountain shows.*

2 *Fiori di Como.* This $10-million Dale Chihuly glass sculpture adorns the ceiling of the reception area. When it was commissioned in 1998, this extravagant floral creation, measuring 30×70 feet (9.1×21m) and containing 2,000 handblown flowers, was the largest glass sculpture in the world. Nearly 5 tons (4.5 metric tons) of steel affix the sculpture to the ceiling.

3 ★★★ Bellagio Conservatory. The botanical theme is continued in the hotel's 14,000-square-foot (1,300 sq.-m) indoor garden, basking beneath a 55-foot-tall (17m) glass ceiling. As the plants and flowers are freshened daily, and decorations regularly changed in their entirety to correspond to seasons and holidays (Easter and Chinese New Year bring particularly spectacular displays), and given that access to this oasis of life and color is entirely free, this is surely one of the great follies in a town otherwise totally dedicated to commerce. The hotel's yearly bill for all this floral goodness? Close to $10 million. **Note:** The fountain that stands just outside the conservatory entrance is over 100 years old. ⏱ *15 min. 3600 Las Vegas Blvd. S. (at the corner of Flamingo Rd.).* ☎ *702/693-7111. www.bellagio.com.*

The rotating floral displays inside the Bellagio Conservatory are among the city's best free attractions.

Downtown

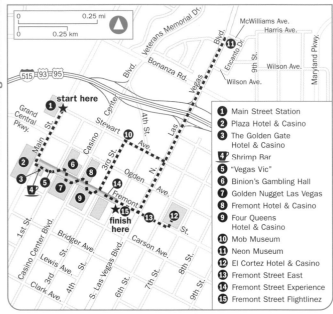

start here

- **1** Main Street Station
- **2** Plaza Hotel & Casino
- **3** The Golden Gate Hotel & Casino
- **4** Shrimp Bar
- **5** "Vegas Vic"
- **6** Binion's Gambling Hall
- **7** Golden Nugget Las Vegas
- **8** Fremont Hotel & Casino
- **9** Four Queens Hotel & Casino
- **10** Mob Museum
- **11** Neon Museum
- **12** El Cortez Hotel & Casino
- **13** Fremont Street East
- **14** Fremont Street Experience
- **15** Fremont Street Flightlinez

finish here

The former "Glitter Gulch" and glamour spot of Las Vegas, this smaller stretch of correspondingly decreased-in-size hotels and casinos is overlooked in favor of the flashy deal down south. Too bad—you can cover the whole thing so easily, thanks to pedestrian-only Fremont Street; the crowds are usually friendlier; and the minimum bets are cheaper. **START: Entrance to Main Street Station; if you're driving, park in one of the many lots off Fremont Street and walk to the hotel.**

1 Main Street Station. Start your tour off in early-20th-century San Francisco . . . Vegas style, at this lovely property. As you stroll through, note the many Victorian decor elements, from the wrought-iron railings to the antique brass casino cages. Ask at the lobby for the casino's worthwhile self-guided tour of its lovely antiques collection. The males in your party should check out the men's room on the main casino floor—that slab of rock

holding up the urinals is a genuine piece of the Berlin Wall. *200 N. Main St.* ☎ *800/713-8993 or 702/387-1896. www.mainstreetcasino.com.*

2 Plaza Hotel & Casino. Let's be honest: Although iconic with its retro '70s lighting and glass dome in the front, the Plaza has become a bit of a dump. It's amazing what $30 million or so can do. A top-to-bottom makeover has turned grimy into gorgeous with furnishings and fixtures from a

The Plaza Hotel & Casino's ultra-Vegas exterior has been featured in many a cinematic production.

defunct multibillion-dollar Strip hotel project. It still has a great old-Vegas vibe, but with a modern flair that makes it one of the best hotels in Downtown Vegas. *1 Main St.* 📞 *702/386-2110. www.plazahotelcasino.com.*

❸ The Golden Gate Hotel & Casino.
This four-story building is Sin City's oldest hotel, dating back to 1906 (it opened as the Hotel Nevada), when room and board cost $1 a day. In one incarnation, it was the Sal Sagev (spell each word backward for the inside joke) hotel. Today, the exterior facade reflects the original building's roots. *1 Fremont St.* 📞 *702/385-1906. www.goldengatecasino.com.*

4 🍴 The Golden Gate Hotel & Casino's 99¢ shrimp cocktail, the symbol of bargain Las Vegas, originated back in 1959 (it cost only 50¢ then); in the ensuing decades, the hotel has served over 30 million of them. The price jumped to $1.99 in 2008, and the treat served today is just bay shrimp, but it's actually a pretty good snack, and a Vegas must. *In the Golden Gate Hotel & Casino, 1*

Fremont St. 📞 *702/385-1906. www.goldengatecasino.com. $.*

❺ Vegas Vic.
This 40-foot-tall (12m) neon cowboy, one of the city's most recognized icons, went up for the first time in 1951 and has suffered many an indignity since. He lost his voice (he once offered up a "howdy partner" to visitors) when actor Lee Marvin (in town to shoot *The Professionals*) complained in 1966 that he was too loud and had him silenced. His arm used to wave, and that doesn't work anymore either. Then his hat was partially cut off to make way for the canopy for the Fremont Street Experience in 1994. And that ever-present cigarette ain't too popular nowadays either. But he (and across-the-street neighbor "Sassy Sally"—you can't miss her) is one of the last bastions of Old Vegas, and you should tip your hat to him. *25 Fremont St.*

Vegas Vic, arguably the most famous neon sign in Las Vegas.

Hard-core gamblers still flock to Binion's, though the World Series of Poker is no longer played here.

⑥ Binion's Gambling Hall. This hall, formerly the Horseshoe Casino, dates back to 1951, when it was combined with the Apache Hotel by legendary casino operator Benny Binion (1904–89). One of the most venerable gambling establishments in Vegas, and, up until 2005, the home of the World Series of Poker (which began life in 1970), Binion's is pretty desiccated, but it is still where hard-line gamblers go to play. The place isn't nearly as dazzling as its lurid history (former owner Ted Binion's stripper girlfriend was tried for his murder in 1998, a story that includes a vault filled with treasure buried in the desert), but 2008 did see the return of its famed $1 Million Dollar Display. *128 Fremont St.* ☎ *702/382-1600. www.binions.com.*

⑦ Golden Nugget Las Vegas. Its 1946 construction date makes this one of Vegas's oldest extant casinos; but renovations have kept it looking fresh, and it's one of the indisputable stars of Downtown. It's had its moments of fame, notably

when it became casino magnate Steve Wynn's first local purchase in 1973, and then during its brief run in 2004 as the setting of a short-lived reality series called *The Casino,* which documented the antics of later owners. But its biggest claim to fame nowadays resides in its lobby: The **Hand of Faith,** the world's largest gold nugget, was found in Australia and weighs in at nearly 62 pounds (28kg). *129 Fremont St.* ☎ *702/385-7111. www. goldennugget.com.*

⑧ Fremont Hotel & Casino. This 15-story hotel debuted in 1956 as Nevada's tallest building. It's also where Mr. Las Vegas, Wayne Newton, got his start in Sin City. For that alone it gets a *danke schoen. 200 Fremont St.* ☎ *702/385-3232. www. fremontcasino.com.*

⑨ Four Queens Hotel & Casino. Opened in 1966, this venerable property was named in homage to the original builder's four daughters. Today the giant 3.2-acre (1.3-hectare) property occupies an

Stop in at the Golden Nugget Las Vegas to rub the solid gold Hand of Faith for luck.

The Hand of Faith Nu

entire city block right in the heart of Downtown and is notable in that it's home to Downtown's only major club, the Canyon Club, and a usually crowd-free discount ticket booth for all the major shows. *202 Fremont St.* ☎ *702/385-4011. www.fourqueens.com.*

⑩ ★★★ Mob Museum. Much of Vegas was built by infamous mob figures like Bugsy Siegel, so where better to have a museum dedicated to exploring the influence of the Mafia in America. Three floors of endlessly fascinating exhibits are housed in a lovingly restored court-house that was one of the locations of the mob-related Kefauver Hearings in the '50s. Photos, video, touch-screen displays, and artifacts are cool (they have the actual St. Valentine's Massacre wall!) but it's the high-tech experiences that are the most fun, from the 3-D images in the courtroom playing out the hearings to the simulated "bad guy" target practice feature and beyond. By far the most entertaining museum in Vegas. ⏱ *at least 1 hr. 300 Stewart Ave. (at 3rd St.). www. themobmuseum.org.* ☎ *702/229-2734. Admission $18 adults, $12 kids 5–17, $14 seniors. Open Sun–Thurs 10am–7pm; Fri–Sat 10am–8pm.*

⑪ Neon Museum. Though Vegas is still all about the bright lights, the introduction of computer-generated signage has meant the slow death of a great art form, the city's iconic neon signs. These have been gradually phased out, condemned as hokey and old-fashioned, and would have been consigned to trash heaps had this nonprofit not stepped in. A permanent home for the neon art is due to open in mid-2012; until then you can see restored signs on Fremont Street and get a tour of the famed Neon Museum Boneyard where other treasures from Vegas days of yore are waiting to be restored.

The old Hacienda's horse and rider is one of the most famous signs in the Neon Museum.

⏱ *30 min. 770 Las Vegas Blvd. N. (at McWilliams Ave.). www.neon museum.org. Boneyard tours $15. Hours vary; call for times.*

⑫ El Cortez Hotel & Casino. When it opened in 1941 (at a then-whopping cost of $245,000   gotta love inflation), this small hotel was Downtown's largest and most luxurious resort. So good was it that Bugsy Siegel bought it in 1946, but he later dumped it in order to finance his dream of the Strip. It's been renovated and gutted over the years, but you'll still spot some of the original Spanish-flavored details. And wave to the top of the hotel tower while you're here; former owner Jackie Gaughan, a local legend, lives at the tippy top! *600 Fremont St. www.elcortezhotelcasino. com.* ☎ *702/385-5200.*

⑬ Fremont Street East. Just east of Las Vegas Boulevard is a revitalized stretch of Fremont Street that features a number of fun and funky bars, art galleries, restored vintage neon signs, and some friendly low-limit gambling in the form of El Cortez (see **⑫**). Once a no-man's land ruled by less-than-savory characters, the area is now as safe as the Strip and best visited

Fremont Street during the day: The canopy over the pedestrian zone helps protect shoppers and gamblers from the hot Nevada sun.

in the evening when the saloons are up and running and the neon is brightly lit. ⏱ *30 min. Fremont St. (btw. Las Vegas Blvd. & 6th St.).*

⑭ ★★ kids Fremont Street Experience. Sauntering down Fremont Street is the closest you can get these days to the archetypal Vegas (because buildings and corresponding lighted signs are set so much closer together). Nowadays, most visitors come for the giant 90-foot-high (27m) canopy erected over the pedestrian mall, which displays a genuinely impressive light-and-sound show (the whole thing appropriately named "Viva Vision"). Several different shows play in rotation, including ones based on Area 51, KISS, and Queen. Good views are available just about anywhere on the mall, as all it requires is neck craning, but if you want to get a little closer to the action, stand on a balcony at Fitzgerald's or in that hotel's branch of McDonald's. ⏱ *10 min. Fremont St. (btw. Main St. & Las Vegas Blvd.). www.vegasexperience. com. Free admission. Shows nightly every hour, dusk–midnight.*

⑮ ★ Fremont Street Flightlinez. If you want to get *really* close to the Fremont Street Experience,

why not take a little ride underneath it? This zip line attraction runs under the giant canopy and gives intrepid souls a glimpse of Glitter Gulch from a totally different perspective. Certainly not for the faint of heart but also not as scary as it seems from the ground. ⏱ *20 min. (depending on how long the line is). 425 Fremont St. #160. ☎ 702/410-7999. www. fremontstreetflightline.com. $15 before 6pm; $20 after 6pm. Open Sun–Thurs noon–midnight; Fri–Sat noon–2am (weather permitting).* ●

Fremont Street is best toured at night, when it's lit up in all of its neon- and laser-enhanced glory.

Shopping Best Bets

Best Place for Tacky Vegas Souvenirs
Bonanza Gift & Souvenir Shop, *2460 Las Vegas Blvd. S. (p 67)*

Best Classy but Naughty Underthings
Agent Provocateur, *In The Forum Shops at Caesars Palace, 3570 Las Vegas Blvd. S. (p 64)*

Best Sweets & Pastries
Jean-Phillppe Patlsserle, *In Bellagio, 3600 Las Vegas Blvd. S. (p 67)*

Best Jewelry
Tiffany & Co., *In Crystals at CityCenter, 3720 Las Vegas Blvd. S. (p 71)*

Best Theme Mall
The Grand Canal Shoppes, *In The Venetian, 3355 Las Vegas Blvd. S. (p 70)*

Best Art
Emergency Arts, *520 E. Fremont St. (p 67)*

Best Place for Books on Gambling
Gambler's Book Club, *5473 S. Eastern Ave. (p 64)*

Best Place to Buy the Makings for Your Own Casino
Gambler's General Store, *800 S. Main St. (p 68)*

Best Outlets
Fashion Outlets Las Vegas, *32100 Las Vegas Blvd. S. (p 66)*

Best Mall
Fashion Show, *3200 Las Vegas Blvd. S. (p 72)*

Best Toys
The Toy Shack, *In Neonopolis, 450 E. Fremont St., no. 117 (p 72)*

Best Pret a Porter
Prada, *In Via Bellagio at Bellagio, 3600 Las Vegas Blvd. S. (p 66)*

Best Museum Shop
National Atomic Testing Museum Store, *755 E. Flamingo Rd. (p 68)*

Best High-Fashion Casual
Juicy Couture, *In The Forum Shops at Caesars Palace, 3570 Las Vegas Blvd. S. (p 65)*

Best Place for Antiques
Retro Vegas, *1131 S. Main St. (p 63)*

For designer duds and accessories, it's hard to beat Prada.

Previous page: A window display at Agent Provocateur, the city's best lingerie shop.

Shopping **on the Strip & Downtown**

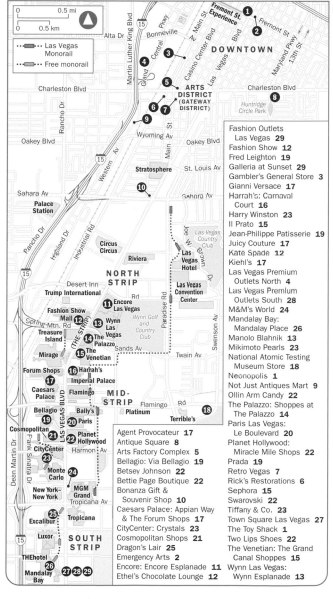

Shopping **off the Strip**

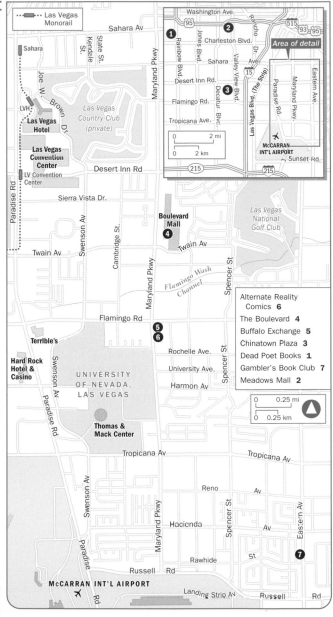

- - - Las Vegas Monorail

Area of detail

Washington Ave.

Sahara Av

Rainbow Blvd.

Jones Blvd.

Charleston Blvd.

Sahara

Valley View Blvd.

Desert Inn Rd.

Flamingo Rd.

Tropicana Ave.

Decatur Blvd.

Paradise Rd.

Maryland Pkwy.

Eastern Ave.

Las Vegas Blvd. (The Strip)

Rancho Dr.

McCARRAN INT'L AIRPORT

Sunset Rd.

0   2 mi
0   2 km

Sahara

State St.

Kendale St.

Joe W. Brown Dr.

LVH

Las Vegas Hotel

Las Vegas Convention Center

LV Convention Center

Maryland Pkwy

Paradise Rd

Las Vegas Country Club (private)

Desert Inn Rd

Sierra Vista Dr.

Swenson Av

Cambridge St.

Boulevard Mall

Twain Av

Twain Av

Las Vegas National Golf Club

Flamingo Wash Channel

Spencer St

Maryland Pkwy

Flamingo Rd

Terrible's

Hard Rock Hotel & Casino

Swenson Av

Paradise Rd

UNIVERSITY OF NEVADA, LAS VEGAS

Thomas & Mack Center

Rochelle Ave.

University Ave.

Harmon Av

Spencer St

Alternate Reality Comics **6**
The Boulevard **4**
Buffalo Exchange **5**
Chinatown Plaza **3**
Dead Poet Books **1**
Gambler's Book Club **7**
Meadows Mall **2**

0   0.25 mi
0   0.25 km

Tropicana Av

Tropicana Av

Swenson Av

Maryland Pkwy

Spencer St

Eastern Av

Paradise Rd

Reno   Av

Hacienda   Av

Rawhide   St

Russell   Rd

McCARRAN INT'L AIRPORT

Landing Strip Av

Russell   Rd

Las Vegas Shopping A to Z

Antiques

Antique Square DOWNTOWN
It's the smallest of the city's three antiques malls, but careful shoppers can uncover a plethora of treasures, including comics, vintage Las Vegas matchbooks, postcards, ashtrays, and other souvenirs of bygone casinos. *2020 E. Charleston Blvd.* ☎ *702/471-6500. AE, MC, V. Map p 61.*

★ Not Just Antiques Mart

WEST OF THE STRIP   Virtually every square inch of the 12,000 square feet (1,115 sq. m) in this antiques minimall is filled with stuff, from furniture to clothes to bric-a-brac and beyond. The trash-to-treasure ratio is good, but the size means you're going to have to hunt for the best finds. *1422 Western Ave. (btw. Wyoming Ave. & Charleston Blvd.). ☎ 702/384-4922. www.notjustantiques mart.com. AE, MC, V. Map p 61.*

★★★ Retro Vegas DOWNTOWN
Stunningly designed mid-century

Retro Vegas is crammed with vintage Vegas memorabilia.

modern and Danish furnishings dominate the space here, but it's the cool, swinging Vegas memorabilia, art, and antiques (from ashtrays to chandeliers) that will have you shouting "Vegas, Baby!" *1131 S. Main St. (just south of Charleston Blvd.).* ☎ *702/384-2700. www.retrovegas.com. AE, MC, V. Map p 61.*

★★ Rick's Restorations DOWNTOWN   You don't have to be a fan of the History Channel's *American Restoration* to get a kick out of the loving reincarnations of everything from old slot machines to Coca-Cola coolers. The stars of the show are on-site and will sign autographs after a free tour. *1112 S. Commerce St. (just south of Charleston Ave.).* ☎ *702/366-7030. www.ricks restorations.com. AE, DISC, MC, V. Map p 61.*

Beauty Products & Accessories

★★★ Kiehl's MID-STRIP   This 150-year-old cosmetics line isn't quite as limited in access as it used to be, thanks to a buy-out from a much larger cosmetics company. But the line's skin and hair products, particularly the popular Lip Balm #2, still make any store visit a treat. *In The Forum Shops at Caesars Palace, 3500 Las Vegas Blvd. S.* ☎ *702/784-0025. www.kiehls.com. AE, DC, MC, V. Map p 61.*

★ Sephora MID-STRIP   False eyelashes! Nail polish! Perfume! Lipstick! Toenail clippers! If you need a beauty item, you'll find it here. And if you want to wow them at the tables or get ready for a night of club hopping, have your face made up for free by a staff member. *In The Grand Canal Shoppes at The Venetian, 3355 Las Vegas Blvd. S.*

☎ 702/735-3896. www.sephora. com. AE, DISC, MC, V. Map p 61.

Books & Stationery
★ Alternate Reality Comics

EAST OF THE STRIP   As the name suggests, the emphasis here is on underground comics, but the stock is comprehensive enough to include mainstream titles. *4110 S. Maryland Pkwy., no. 8.* ☎ *702/736-3673. www.alternaterealitycomics.net. AE, DISC, MC, V. Map p 61.*

★★ Dead Poet Books WEST OF
THE STRIP   Even in Vegas, I love a musty old bookstore, and the owners here are particularly literary types. *937 W. Rainbow Blvd.* ☎ *702/ 227-4070. MC, V. Map p 62.*

★ Gambler's Book Club EAST
OF THE STRIP   I keep telling you, you can't beat the system. And yet, this shop swears that you can. Or at least that one of their thousands of titles knows how and will tell all. *5473 S. Eastern Ave.* ☎ *702/382- 7555. www.gamblersbookclub.com. AE, MC, V. Map p 62.*

Clothing & Shoes
★★★ Agent Provocateur MID-

STRIP   This British lingerie line, favored by Kate Moss and other slinky celebs, is for those who want some art and style in their seduction wear. The black silk satin Nikita line and the lacy Love styles definitely fit the bill; some of their stuff has to be

Kiehl's is not as exclusive as it once was, but it is still an excellent place to pick up cosmetics.

seen to be believed. *In The Forum Shops at Caesars Palace, 3570 Las Vegas Blvd. S.* ☎ *702/696-7174. www.agentprovocateur.com. AE, MC, V. Map p 61.*

Betsey Johnson MID-STRIP Playful, sexy, strong, and boldly feminine fashions—flouncy dresses with bright floral prints, lacy tops, vibrant knits and velvet skirts, and curve-displaying garments—have been Betsey Johnson's signature styles since the mid-1980s. *In the Miracle Mile Shops at Planet Holly- wood, 3663 Las Vegas Blvd. S.* ☎ *702/731-0286. www.betsey johnson.com. AE, MC, V. Map p 61.*

★★ Bettie Page Boutique MID-
STRIP   Can you leave Sin City without paying homage to the pin-up? No, you can't. And this shop—done up in leopard, no less—sells a rather cute line of Page-inspired '50s-style dresses, corsets, hosiery, and more. It's a hoot. *In the Miracle Mile Shops at Planet Hollywood, 3663 Las Vegas Blvd. S.* ☎ *702/636- 1100. www.bettiepageclothing.com. AE, MC, V. Map p 61.*

★ Buffalo Exchange EAST OF
THE STRIP   This vintage chain store relies a lot on consignment, so the selection varies. The hip staff has good taste, though the stock edges more toward recent decades rather than rare finds from the '40s. *4110 S. Maryland Pkwy. (at Flamingo Rd.).* ☎ *702/791-3960. www.buffalo exchange.com. MC, V. Map p 62.*

★★★ Gianni Versace MID-STRIP
This designer line, synonymous with opulent celebrity-endorsed high fashion, manages to be both cutting edge and classic, with attention paid to detail and fabric. *In The Forum Shops at Caesars Palace, 3500 Las Vegas Blvd. S.* ☎ *702/932- 5757. www.versace.com. AE, MC, V. Map p 61.*

One of several art installations inside CityCenter's Crystals.

★ **Juicy Couture** MID-STRIP
Single-handedly responsible for the ubiquity of velour sweat suits, not to mention the word "Juicy" along backsides. To be fair, the designers tapped into the casual wear zeit-geist by making some genuinely cute clothes. *In The Forum Shops at Caesars Palace, 3570 Las Vegas Blvd. S.* ☎ *702/365-5600. www.juicy couture.com. AE, MC, V. Map p 61.*

Literary lovers will find lots of good buys at Dead Poet Books.

★★★ **Kate Spade** MID-STRIP
Bright colors and sleek styles with a modern vibe have made this line of handbags, luggage, stationery, and accessories hip from the Hamptons to Hollywood. *In Fashion Show, 3200 Las Vegas Blvd. S.* ☎ *702/691-9968. www.katespade.com. AE, DISC, MC, V. Map p 61.*

★★★ **Manolo Blahnik** NORTH
STRIP Revealing just the right amount of "toe cleavage," this store's expensive, sexy, and strappy sandals and stiletto-heeled shoes were enshrined in pop culture by *Sex and the City. In Wynn Esplanade at Wynn Las Vegas, 3131 Las Vegas Blvd. S.* ☎ *702/770-3477. www. manoloblahnik.com. AE, DC, DISC, MC, V. Map p 61.*

★ **Ollin Arm Candy** CENTER
STRIP "One woman's trash is another woman's treasure" is the motto at this store, where recycled and found materials are turned into high fashion. Check out the purses made of old candy wrappers and seat belts, which are just as stylish (and certainly more fun) than your average handbag. *In the Miracle Mile Shops at Planet Hollywood, 3667 Las Vegas Blvd. S.*

The boutiques inside the Cosmopolitan Shops sell everything from fashion to high-end foodstuffs.

☎ 702/260-3223. www.ollinarm candy.com. Map p. 61.

★★★ **Prada** MID-STRIP Its clothes are the opposite of Vegas: timeless, classy, and simple. Equally elegant are the shoes and accessories. *In Via Bellagio at the Bellagio, 3600 Las Vegas Blvd. S.* ☎ 702/866-6886. www.prada.com. AE, DC, DISC, MC, V. Map p 61.

★ **Two Lips Shoes** MID-STRIP Cute flats and satin Mary Janes share

Two Lips Shoes is a great place to pick up fashion-forward footwear on the cheap.

space with hip high-heeled sandals and leather pumps—all fashion forward and reasonably priced. Some are even well padded enough to add comfort to your style. *In the Miracle Mile Shops at Planet Hollywood, 3663 Las Vegas Blvd. S.* ☎ 702/737-0369. www.twolipsshoes.com. AE, DISC, MC, V. Map p 61.

Factory Outlets
★★★ **Fashion Outlets Las Vegas** PRIMM A 40-minute schlep from the city, but worth it for dedicated bargain hunters: You get inside shopping (air conditioning!), plus Ralph Lauren, Tommy Hilfiger, Williams-Sonoma, and Banana Republic outlets, among others. *32100 Las Vegas Blvd. S.* ☎ 702/874-1400. www.fashionoutletlasvegas. com. AE, DISC, MC, V. Map p 61.

Las Vegas Premium Outlets North DOWNTOWN The high-end names here—Armani, Dolce & Gabbana, Calvin Klein—make this most conveniently located outlet center enticing for dedicated bargain hunters, but amateurs may not have the stamina to endure the open-air facility on hot days. *875 S. Grand Central Pkwy. (at I-15).* ☎ 702/474-7500. www.premiumoutlets.com. AE, DISC, MC, V. Map p 61.

Las Vegas Premium Outlets South EAST OF THE STRIP A 2011 remodeling of this mall has only increased its appeal, which was already high because of the everyman outlets (Ann Taylor, Izod, Reebok) and the cool, indoor carousel. *7400 Las Vegas Blvd. S. (at Warm Springs Rd.).* ☎ 702/896-5599. www.premiumoutlets.com. AE, DISC, MC, V. Map p 61.

Food & Chocolate
★ **Ethel's Chocolate Lounge** NORTH STRIP This fun store/ lounge/cafe—run by famed local confectioner Ethel M—is a top spot

for a blood-sugar pick-me-up. Flavors for the fancy chocolates run the gamut from pomegranate to cinnamon to cheesecake! *In Fashion Show, 3200 Las Vegas Blvd. S.* ☎ *702/796-6662. www.ethelm.com. AE, DC, DISC, MC, V. Map p 61.*

★★★ Jean-Philippe Patisserie

MID-STRIP   Come for the chocolate fountain, stay for the award-winning pastries (including a brioche-oozing *dulce de leche*) and maybe some authentic gelato, and then leave with a box full of expensive truffles. Repeat as necessary. *In the Bellagio, 3600 Las Vegas Blvd. S.* ☎ *702/693-8788. www.jpchocolates.com. AE, DC, DISC, MC, V. Map p 61.*

★ kids M&M's World SOUTH

STRIP   Walls filled with tubes of unusually colored M&Ms and themed merchandise. It's totally gimmicky until you realize what an awesome assortment you can make by mixing hot pink with black. *In the Showcase Mall, 3785 Las Vegas Blvd. S. (just north of MGM Grand).* ☎ *702/740-2504. AE, DISC, MC, V. Map p 61.*

Gift Shops
★★ Arts Factory Complex

DOWNTOWN   You'll find more than neon cityscapes and desert scenes on display and for sale in this two-story complex (once a crematorium), where a number of painters, photographers, and sculptors maintain studios and galleries. *107 E. Charleston Blvd.* ☎ *702/383-3113. www.theartsfactory.com. AE, MC, V. Map p 61.*

★★ Bonanza Gift & Souvenir

Shop NORTH STRIP   The self-proclaimed "world's largest gift shop." All I can say for sure is that it is indeed big, contains everything from dice earrings to "Indian" goods, and has never let me down when I'm looking for the perfect tacky souvenir. *2460 Las Vegas Blvd. S.* ☎ *702/385-7359. www.worldslargestgiftshop.com. AE, DISC, MC, V. Map p 61.*

kids Dragon's Lair SOUTH STRIP

Crystal balls, magic wands, dragon figurines, and magically themed knickknacks to help bring out your inner wizard. *In the Castle Walk at Excalibur, 3850 Las Vegas Blvd. S.* ☎ *702/597-7850. AE, DISC, MC, V. Map p 61.*

★★★ Emergency Arts DOWN-

TOWN   If you are looking for a truly unique souvenir, this former medical building houses dozens of artists and galleries, selling one-of-a-kind

Want to taste a gray M&M? Hot pink? Both? M&M's World is the place to do it.

For the perfect tacky Vegas souvenir, look no further than the immense Bonanza Gift & Souvenir Shop.

pieces. Don't miss the funky vintage record store and charming cafe. *520 E. Fremont St.* ☎ *702/409-5563. www.emergencyartslv.com. AE, MC, V. Map p 61.*

★ **Gambler's General Store** DOWNTOWN Eight thousand square feet (743 sq. m) filled with all manner of gambling-related merchandise. It's *the* place to purchase that most splendid of Vegas souvenirs, your very own antique (or modern) slot machine. Or you could settle for a book on blackjack. *800 S. Main St.* ☎ *702/382-9903. www. gamblersgeneralstore.com. AE, DISC, MC, V. Map p 61.*

★ **Il Prato** MID-STRIP Need a mask for Mardi Gras? A gown fit for Carnivale? This Venetian-themed gift shop stocks items ranging from beautiful masks and marionettes to detailed miniatures and fine stationery. The prices will make you wince, but the quality is there. *In The Grand Canal Shoppes at The Venetian, 3355 Las Vegas Blvd. S.* ☎ *702/733-1201. www.ilpratousa. com. AE, DC, DISC, MC, V. Map p 61.*

★★★ **National Atomic Testing Museum Store** MID-STRIP The museum is as serious as its subject matter, but its shop is where absurdity—atomic tests used to be tourist attractions—is allowed to sneak in, in the form of Albert Einstein action figures, fallout shelter signs, and other bomb- and blast-themed trinkets. *755 E. Flamingo Rd.* ☎ *702/ 794-5151. www.atomictesting museum.org. AE, DISC, MC, V. Map p 61.*

★ **Swarovski** MID-STRIP Crystals (made by a company that has specialized in the finest of same for generations) adorn everything from purses to picture frames in this glittering shop. Costly? Yes. But it's high-quality bling. *In the Miracle Mile Shops at Planet Hollywood, 3663 Las Vegas Blvd. S.* ☎ *702/732-7302. www.swarovski.com. AE, DISC, MC, V. Map p 61.*

Hotel Shopping Arcades
★★ **Bellagio: Via Bellagio** MID-STRIP I can't even afford the small bit of oxygen it takes to walk this

Want a cool pair of fuzzy dice? Your own slot machine? If it's gambling related, then the Gambler's General Store has it.

short, but high-priced, luxury shopping promenade, marked by such names as Fendi, Hermès, and Chanel. But I sure do like pretending I can. *3600 Las Vegas Blvd. S. (at the corner of Flamingo Rd.).* ☎ *702/693-7111. www.bellagio.com. AE, DC, DISC, MC, V. Map p 61.*

★★★ Caesars Palace: Appian Way & The Forum Shops MID-STRIP

Every bit as much as an attraction as it is a shopping destination. Think Rodeo Drive—Christian Dior, Louis Vuitton, and so on—reimagined as the Via Veneto and other Italian cityscapes, plus some ridiculous talking statues. *3500 Las Vegas Blvd. S.* ☎ *702/731-7110. www. caesarspalace.com. AE, DISC, MC, V. Map p 61.*

★★ CityCenter: Crystals MID-STRIP

Break out your platinum card. Vegas's newest house of retail worship glitters with such high-end names as Zegna, Louis Vuitton, Cavalli, Tom Ford, and H. Stern. If your budget doesn't extend into the stratosphere, check out the three-story "tree house" and the art installations between Crystals and ARIA (p 76). *3720 Las Vegas Blvd. S.* ☎ *702/590-9299. www.crystalsat citycenter.com. AE, DISC, MC, V. Map p 61.*

Cosmopolitan Shops MID-STRIP

The boutiques may have names that are more familiar in Europe (All-Saints, Beckley) but the fashions, footwear, and gifts have global, albeit expensive, appeal. *3708 Las Vegas Blvd. S.* ☎ *702/698-7000. www.cosmopolitanlasvegas.com. AE, DISC, MC, V. Map p 61.*

Encore: Encore Esplanade

NORTH STRIP Eleven boutiques selling high-priced merchandise to the wealthy (or suddenly wealthy). Aside from major luxe brands (Chanel, Hermès, and the like), you'll find the Homestore with furnishings,

Won a slot jackpot and want some bling to celebrate the victory? Harry Winston is the place . . . but it better have been a big jackpot.

bath items, and such from the hotel in case you must take them home with you. *3121 Las Vegas Blvd. S.* ☎ *702/770-8000. www.encorelasve gas.com. AE, DISC, MC, V. Map p 61.*

Harrah's: Carnaval Court MID-STRIP

Notable for being the only outdoor hotel shopping mall on the Strip itself, this collection of stalls sells purses, hippie-style clothes, jewelry, and other inexpensive trinkets. *3475 Las Vegas Blvd. S.* ☎ *702/369-5000. www.harrahslv.com. AE, DC, DISC, MC, V. Map p 61.*

Mandalay Bay: Mandalay Place SOUTH OF THE STRIP

In appearance, Mandalay Place is more like an actual indoor mall than a hotel shopping arcade, but in content it has neither the rarified atmosphere of Via Bellagio or the Wynn Esplanade, nor the variety of The Forum Shops. But there is a men's shop called the Art of Shaving and a Nike Golf. That may be just enough. *3930 Las Vegas Blvd. S. (btw. Luxor & Mandalay Bay).* ☎ *702/632-9333. www.mandalaybay.com. AE, DC, DISC, MC, V. Map p 61.*

★★ The Palazzo: The Shoppes at The Palazzo MID-STRIP

It's

The Shoppes at The Palazzo is a primo mall for the serious (and wealthy) fashionista.

less fun than its sister, The Grand Canal Shoppes, but if you're a fashionista with money to burn go ahead and empty your wallet at Christian Louboutin, Michael Kors, Chloé, and the other luxe boutiques here. Anna Wintour would approve. *3327 Las Vegas Blvd. S.* ☎ *702/414-4525. www.theshoppesatthepalazzo.com. AE, DC, DISC, MC, V. Map p 61.*

Paris Las Vegas: Le Boulevard SOUTH STRIP   Ooo-la-la! It's *le petit Paree,* complete with cobblestone streets, quaint lampposts, replicas of the Pont Alexandre III and the Eiffel Tower, and shops carrying chic sunglasses, watches, and a host of premium foods and wines. *3655 Las Vegas Blvd. S.* ☎ *702/946-7000. www.parislv.com. AE, DC, DISC, MC, V. Map p 61.*

★★ Planet Hollywood: Miracle Mile Shops SOUTH STRIP The once sumptuous, exotically themed Desert Passage has been remodeled into a gizmo-equipped whiz-bang generic version of an upper-end American mall. The stores themselves stand out, but the experience ain't what it used to be. *3667 Las Vegas Blvd. S.* ☎ *702/866-0703. www.miraclemileshopslv.com. AE, DC, DISC, MC, V. Map p 61.*

★★ The Venetian: The Grand Canal Shoppes MID-STRIP   Stroll

through St. Mark's Square and wander along a faux Grand Canal replete with serenading gondoliers. *Trompe l'oeil* clouds float past the "roofs" of the 15th-century-style "houses" that are home to stores fit for the Doge, including BCBG, Marshall Rousso, and Kenneth Cole. Performers who interact with shoppers while in period costume complete the experience. *3355 Las Vegas Blvd. S.* ☎ *702/414-4500. www.thegrand canalshoppes.com. AE, DC, DISC, MC, V. Map p 61.*

Wynn Las Vegas: Wynn Esplanade NORTH STRIP   Not as large as Via Bellagio, this marble-walled stroll features such dream-and-drool-inducing retailers as Cartier, Alexander McQueen, and Oscar de la Renta. *3131 Las Vegas Blvd. S.* ☎ *702/770-7000. www.wynnlasve gas.com. AE, DC, DISC, MC, V. Map p 61.*

Jewelry

★★★ Fred Leighton MID-STRIP Specializing in period estate jewelry—including expensive turn-of-the-20th-century and Art Deco baubles dripping with emeralds, sapphires, rubies, and other precious and semiprecious stones—this boutique showcases one-of-a-kind works of envy- and swoon-inducing art. This is where I would blow all my jackpots. *In Via Bellagio at the Bellagio, 3600 Las Vegas Blvd. S. ☎ 702/693-7050. www.fredleighton. com. AE, DC, MC, V. Map p 61.*

★★ **Harry Winston** SOUTH STRIP *The* diamond dealer for haute couture consumers. Winston's stones shine as brightly as the stars who wear them on red carpets. *In Crystals at CityCenter, 3720 Las Vegas Blvd. S. ☎ 702/262-0001. www.harrywinston. com. AE, DC, MC, V. Map p 61.*

★ **Mikimoto Pearls** SOUTH STRIP The originator of cultured pearls, Mikimoto has been creating the famous smooth white Akoyo pearl since 1893. The store also carries cultured South Sea pearls in shades of gray, pink, and cream. *In Crystals at CityCenter, 3720 Las Vegas Blvd. S. ☎ 702/730-4710. www.mikimoto america.com. AE, DC, DISC, MC, V. Map p 61.*

★★ **Tiffany & Co.** MID-STRIP There may be some who are unmoved by the power of Tiffany, even after Truman Capote and Miss Hepburn explained it to all, but I am not one of them. Even just a simple diamond seems to sparkle more brightly in a Tiffany setting, especially at this two-story, 10,000-square-foot (929 sq.-m) flagship shop. *In Crystals at CityCenter, 3720 Las Vegas Blvd. S. ☎ 702/545-9090. www.tiffany.com. AE, DC, DISC, MC, V. Map p 61.*

Malls

The Boulevard EAST OF THE STRIP Macy's, Sears, and JCPenney are the anchors at this mall, which has 140 retail stores, including Old Navy, the Body Shop, and Radio Shack. Out-of-state visitors can visit the Customer Service Center for special offers. *3528 S. Maryland Pkwy. (btw. Twain Ave. & Desert Inn Rd.). ☎ 702/735-7430. www.blvdmall.com. AE, DISC, MC, V. Map p 62.*

Chinatown Plaza WEST OF THE STRIP One of the most telling things about this overgrown, Chinese-themed strip mall is that the vast majority of the people shopping here are of Asian descent. Restaurants take up the bulk of the space (dim sum while you shop?) but there are also jewelry, fashion, art, and book stores galore. *4255 Spring Mountain Rd. (btw. Wynn Rd. & Arville St.). ☎ 702/221-8448. www.lvchinatown.com. AE, DISC, MC, V. Map p 62.*

Combine top-notch shopping and an ancient Roman theme with some tacky elements, and you get The Forum Shops, the quintessential Vegas shopping destination.

★★ Fashion Show MID-STRIP One of the strangest design elements ever seen in a shopping center—or anywhere else for that matter—is the giant twisted steel sculpture called *The Cloud*, which hovers above the entrance as part of a multimedia display featuring LED screens, flashing lights, and music. During the winter, fake snow drifts down on shoppers visiting the 240 shops, including Neiman Marcus, Macy's, Saks Fifth Avenue, and Nevada's only branch of Nordstrom. It's so very Vegas. *3200 Las Vegas Blvd. S. ☎ 702/369-8382. www.the fashionshow.com. AE, DISC, MC, V. Map p 61.*

★ The Galleria at Sunset WEST OF THE STRIP Along with Macy's, Dillard's, and JCPenney, this immense and well-stocked suburban mall is home to Forever 21, Hot Topic, Zales, and a slew of other mall standards. *1300 W. Sunset Rd. (at Stephanie St., just off I-15), Henderson. ☎ 702/434-0202. www. galleriaatsunset.com. AE, DISC, MC, V. Map p 61.*

★ Meadows Mall WEST OF THE STRIP This ultramodern mall combines a wide range of traditional mall shops, such as Victoria's Secret, Kay Jewelers, Sunglass Hut, and Foot Locker, with an anchor lineup of Macy's, Dillard's, Sears, and JCPenney. *4300 Meadows Lane. ☎ 702/878-3331. www.meadowsmall. com. AE, DISC, MC, V. Map p 62.*

Neonopolis DOWNTOWN At one point it was virtually abandoned, but this collection of boutiques, restaurants, and bars has gotten a new lease on life thanks to such stores as the Toy Shack and such eateries as the Heart Attack Grill. Be sure to take some time to check out the classic, restored neon signs that give the building its name. *450 E. Fremont St. (at Fourth St.). ☎ 702/232-5539.*

Vintage collectibles line the shelves at the Toy Shack.

www.neonopolislv.com. AE, DISC, MC, V. Map p 61.

★ Town Square Las Vegas SOUTH OF THE STRIP Each of this attractive outdoor mall's 22 buildings is designed in a different international style, luring shoppers and architecture buffs alike. The eclectic collection of retailers and restaurants includes Whole Foods, H&M, Guess, and a giant movieplex. *6605 Las Vegas Blvd. S. (south of Mandalay Bay). ☎ 702/269-5000. www. mytownsquarelasvegas.com. AE, DISC, MC, V. Map p 61.*

Toys

★★★ kids The Toy Shack DOWNTOWN There are plenty of new toys here, including one of the biggest collections of Hot Wheels I've ever seen, but it's the retro and collectible toys that are an irresistible lure for kids of all ages. Think of a toy you had when you were 12 and they probably have three of them (or can find it for you). *In Neonopolis, 450 E. Fremont St., no. 117. ☎ 702/ 538-8600. www.lasvegastoyshack. com. AE, MC, V. Map p 61. ●*

The Best **Casinos**

Casino Best Bets

Most **Glamorous**
Bellagio, *3600 Las Vegas Blvd. S.*
(p 77)

Most **Visually Stimulating**
Cosmopolitan of Las Vegas, *3708*
Las Vegas Blvd. S. (p 77)

Most **Visually Overwhelming**
The Venetian, *3355 Las Vegas Blvd.*
S. (p 82)

Best **Casino for Budget**
Gamblers
Main Street Station, *200 N. Main*
St. (p 79)

Best **Layout**
Red Rock Casino Resort Spa,
11011 W. Charleston Blvd. (p 81)

Least **Smoky**
Mandalay Bay, *3950 Las Vegas*
Blvd. S. (p 80)

Most **Comfortable Chairs**
Wynn Las Vegas, *3131 Las Vegas*
Blvd. S. (p 82)

Most **Airy**
Luxor, *3900 Las Vegas Blvd. S.*
(p 79)

Most **Likely to Become Lost In**
MGM Grand, *3799 Las Vegas Blvd.*
S. (p 80)

Best **Smoke-Free Poker**
Rooms
Bellagio, *3600 Las Vegas Blvd. S.*
(p 77); and The Mirage, *3400 Las*
Vegas Blvd. S. (p 80)

Best **Video Poker**
The Orleans, *4500 W. Tropicana*
Ave. (p 80)

Best **Fake Sky**
Paris Las Vegas, *3655 Las Vegas*
Blvd. S. (p 81)

Previous page: The casino floor at Planet
Hollywood.

The casino at the MGM Grand is the larg-
est in Las Vegas—you'll get lost at least
once.

Most **Confusing to Navigate**
Caesars Palace, *3570 Las Vegas*
Blvd. S. (p 77)

Most **Rock 'n' Roll**
Hard Rock Hotel & Casino, *4455*
Paradise Rd. (p 78)

Best **Classic Casino**
Binion's, *128 E. Fremont St. (p 77)*

Friendliest **Poker Tables**
MGM Grand, *3799 Las Vegas Blvd.*
S. (p 80)

Most **Distracting**
Circus Circus, *2880 Las Vegas Blvd.*
S. (p 77)

Best **Lit**
Encore Las Vegas, *3121 Las Vegas*
Blvd. S. (p 77)

Casinos **on the Strip**

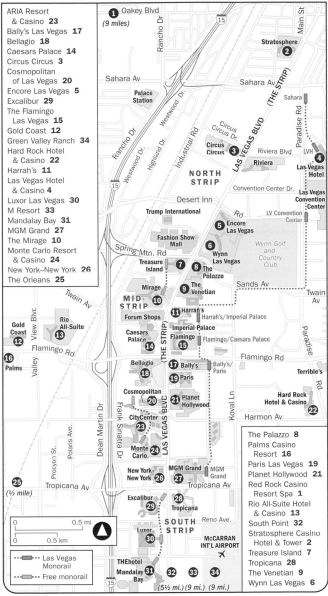

Oakey Blvd **1**
(9 miles)

Stratosphere **2**

Sahara Av

Sahara Av (THE STRIP)

Palace
Station

Sahara

Paradise Rd

LVH

Circus
Circus Dr.

Circus
Circus **3**

Riviera Blvd

Las Vegas
Hotel **4**

NORTH
STRIP

Riviera

Convention Center Dr.

Las Vegas
Convention
Center

Desert Inn

LV Convention
Center

Rd

Trump International

Encore
Las Vegas **5**

Wynn Golf
and
Country
Club

Fashion Show
Mall

Wynn
Las Vegas **6**

Spring Mtn. Rd

Treasure
Island **7**

The
Palazzo **8**

Sands Av

Mirage

The
Venetian **9**

Twain
Av

MID-
STRIP

The Mirage **10**

Harrah's **11**

Harrah's/Imperial Palace

Twain Av

Forum Shops

Imperial Palace

Gold
Coast **12**

Rio
All-Suite **13**

Caesars
Palace **14**

Flamingo **15**

Flamingo/Caesars Palace

Flamingo Rd

Flamingo Rd

Palms **16**

Bellagio **18**

Bally's **17**

Bally's/
Paris

Terrible's

Paris **19**

Hard Rock
Hotel & Casino **22**

Cosmopolitan **20**

Planet
Hollywood **21**

CityCenter

Harmon Av

ARIA **23**

Monte
Carlo **24**

New York–
New York **26**

MGM Grand **27**

MGM
Grand

Excalibur **29**

Tropicana **28**

Tropicana Av

25
(½ mile)

Tropicana Av

SOUTH
STRIP

Reno Ave.

Luxor **30**

McCARRAN
INT'L AIRPORT

THEhotel

Mandalay
Bay **31**

32   **33**   **34**

(5½ mi.) (9 mi.) (9 mi.)

0   0.5 mi
0   0.5 km

···■··· Las Vegas
          Monorail
···■··· Free monorail

Downtown Casinos

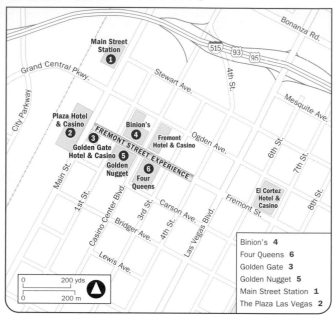

Binion's **4**
Four Queens **6**
Golden Gate **3**
Golden Nugget **5**
Main Street Station **1**
The Plaza Las Vegas **2**

Casinos A to Z

Rating Alert

When it comes to casinos, the general rule is "you love where you win, you hate where you lose." A casino could be stunning, and you'll still loathe it if you lose a bundle there. Because luck is so annoyingly unpredictable and casino choice so personal a selection, you won't find star ratings in this chapter. I hope you end up loving all of them.

ARIA Resort & Casino SOUTH STRIP The boldly modern design of this massive but easily navigable casino emphasizes wood, glass, metal, and fabric to create a visual feast. The slots are cutting-edge modern (and notoriously stingy), while the tables are usually full of eager gamblers. *3730 Las Vegas Blvd. S.* ☎ *702/590-7757. www. arialasvegas.com. Map p 75.*

Bally's Las Vegas MID-STRIP Something of an afterthought on the Strip, there's still a lot to like about this casino. Ceilings are high and machines are well spaced, so it doesn't feel crowded. Because it has less of a profile, the casino seems to try harder, and that results in a pleasant place to gamble. *3645 Las Vegas Blvd. S.* ☎ *702/739-4111. www.ballyslv.com. Map p 75.*

For a big thrill—if not the largest jack-pot—visit one of the casinos and play a giant slot machine like this one in Bally's.

Bellagio MID-STRIP   The fancy-pants casino in town. It's just a tiny bit intimidating for some, sophisti-cated and grown-up for others, and a little bit bland for me. It does get points for the high ceilings and the grid layout, which makes navigating this place less of a chaotic experience. *3600 Las Vegas Blvd. S. ☎ 702/693-7111. www.bellagio.com. Map p 75.*

Binion's DOWNTOWN   The for-mer home of the World Series of Poker (now at the Rio), Binion's is still the place serious gamblers go about their business, which isn't to say it's not fun, but rather a particu-lar kind of fun. Thanks to the newest in a long string of owners, the place looks a little less dingy. Lower table limits and good craps odds are big attractions. *128 E. Fremont St. ☎ 702/382-1600. www.binions.com. Map p 76.*

Caesars Palace MID-STRIP   A great big rambling mess of a casino (getting lost is a Vegas rite of pas-sage), but despite the sprawl, this is still an oh-so-Vegas place to gamble, with glitzy chandeliers and ginormous "Roman" statues. Some parts of the

casino are lighter and more airy, while other areas can be crazy crowded. Avoid the slots near the Colosseum before and after the big shows. *3570 Las Vegas Blvd. S. ☎ 702/731-7110. www.caesarspalace.com. Map p 75.*

Circus Circus NORTH STRIP Surely the most gimmick-laden casino in town, where the main action is covered by a Big Top in which various highflying circus per-formers do their thing virtually around the clock. Obviously, this is meant as a way to entertain the kids—many of whom pass through the area, making it exceedingly noisy and crowded—while adults spend their college tuition funds. *2880 Las Vegas Blvd. S. ☎ 702/734-0410. www.circuscircus.com. Map p 75.*

Cosmopolitan of Las Vegas MID-STRIP   In most casinos, the machines and games of chance are what draw the eye, but here the artistic, contemporary design of the room is almost as enticing. The sounds and sights can be a bit over-whelming, but the energy is undeni-able, plus the simple layout (long and narrow) is easy to navigate. *3708 Las Vegas Blvd. S. ☎ 702/698-7000. www.cosmopolitanlasvegas. com. Map p 75.*

Encore Las Vegas NORTH STRIP This pretty and unique space is small enough that it's easy to navigate and it's loaded with natural light, unlike the vampire-friendly confines of most casinos. Low rollers and those who like umpteen options for wager-ing their cash, however, should look elsewhere. *3121 Las Vegas Blvd. S. ☎ 702/770-8000. www.encorelas vegas.com. Map p 75.*

Excalibur SOUTH STRIP   It's adorned with suits of armor, stained-glass panels, heraldic banners, impressively massive iron chande-liers, and other castle-ready accou-terments. Unfortunately, the

The Cosmopolitan is one of the prettiest places to gamble in Vegas.

atmosphere is more cluttered than cool, and the theming appeared less intensive on my last visit, making it even less fun. *3850 Las Vegas Blvd. S.* ☎ *702/597-7777. www.excalibur. com. Map p 75.*

The Flamingo Las Vegas MID-STRIP   Updates over the past few years, including the addition of a Margaritaville-themed gaming area (think fake foliage and parrots), have allowed Bugsy's folly to stay competitive, but it mainly appeals to midmarket gamblers who are content with the bells and whistles on the slots. *3555 Las Vegas Blvd. S.* ☎ *702/733-3111. www.flamingolv. com. Map p 75.*

Four Queens DOWNTOWN   Sweetly anachronistic, the Four Queens is just the sort of Downtown casino—low limits and unintimidating crowds—that makes you wonder why you bothered with the behemoths on the Strip in the first place. *202 Fremont St.* ☎ *702/385-4011. www.fourqueens.com. Map p 76.*

Gold Coast WEST OF THE STRIP   I like this locals' favorite because it's one of the few in Vegas that has windows! It also has high ceilings, and a relatively high number of video-poker machines (and some of those may actually have odds favorable to you . . . the wonders never cease). *4000 W. Flamingo Rd.*

☎ *702/367-7111. www.goldcoast casino.com. Map p 75.*

Golden Gate DOWNTOWN   The oldest casino in Vegas, first opened in 1906, celebrates the history of the city with classic photos and memorabilia. There is plenty of gaming action from the slots and table games despite its small size. *1 Fremont St.* ☎ *702/385-1906. www. goldengatecasino.com. Map p 76.*

Golden Nugget DOWNTOWN   A classy Downtown casino made even better thanks to renovations by its latest owner. In looks and feel, it's the closest thing in the area to a Strip casino, though its table minimums thankfully don't ascend that far. *129 E. Fremont St.* ☎ *702/385-7111. www.goldennugget.com. Map p 76.*

Green Valley Ranch EAST OF THE STRIP   The low limits, copious video poker, and better-than-average payback appeal mainly to locals, but there is no reason why you shouldn't get in on the action. The casino is gorgeous with warm lighting, lots of Mediterranean stone accents, and comfy furnishings. And the staff is friendly, too. Sounds like a winner to me. *2300 Paseo Verde Pkwy., Henderson.* ☎ *702/617-7777. www.greenvalleyranchresorts.com. Map p 75.*

Hard Rock Hotel & Casino EAST OF THE STRIP   An admirable work of Boomer marketing, where rock music blares, and gamers play on tables designed like piano keyboards with chips emblazoned with musicians' faces. You drop change into Jimi Hendrix–brand slots or kick back in the sports book's reclining leather chairs. Too loud for some, it's the only place to gamble for others. *4455 Paradise Rd. ☎ 702/693-5000. www.hardrockhotel.com. Map p 75.*

Harrah's Las Vegas MID-STRIP Some complain about the crowds, the smoke, and the relatively tight confines, but others praise the slots, which are often considered to be the loosest on the Strip, and the fast, friendly casino staff. *3475 Las Vegas Blvd. S. ☎ 702/369-5000. www.harrahslv.com. Map p 75.*

Las Vegas Hotel & Casino EAST OF THE STRIP This classy casino is polished (check out those crystal chandeliers), but the main draw here is the enormous sports book—it's the world's largest and has a video wall that's second in size only to NASA's. *3000 Paradise Rd. ☎ 702/732 7111. www.hilton.com. Map p 75.*

Learning the Ropes

Hitting up a one-armed bandit (that's a slot machine in gaming lingo) isn't exactly brain surgery, but ignorance won't likely result in bliss if you sit at a poker or craps table when you don't know what you're doing. For a rundown of the major games in town, complete with basic strategy tips, check out the chapter, "The Savvy Gambler."

Luxor Las Vegas SOUTH STRIP The tallest casino ceiling on the Strip makes for a low-claustrophobia gambling situation, though I can't forgive them for de-Egyptifying it and making gambling here way less fun. *3900 Las Vegas Blvd. S. ☎ 702/262-4444. www.luxor.com. Map p 75.*

Main Street Station DOWNTOWN It's got high ceilings and a delightfully realized theme (turn-of-the-last-century San Francisco, with old-fashioned fans dropping down from a Victorian tin ceiling). The atmosphere, combined with lower-than-Strip limits, makes it a winner. *200 N. Main St. ☎ 702/387-1896. www.mainstreetcasino.com. Map p 76.*

The enormous sports book inside the Las Vegas Hotel & Casino lets bettors watch action from all over the globe.

Mandalay Bay SOUTH STRIP   Thanks to the higher-than-average ceiling, the spacious layout, and an attempt to create an elegant atmosphere, this is an appealing place to play. Its southern location means it's often not overwhelmingly crowded, but if there is an event at the hotel's arena or the House of Blues, expect a massive influx of additional players. *3950 Las Vegas Blvd. S. ☎ 702/632-7777. www. mandalaybay.com. Map p 75.*

MGM Grand SOUTH STRIP   The biggest of the big—171,500 square-feet (15,933-sq.-m) of gaming space—is getting a major makeover throughout 2012, designed to make it lighter, brighter, and more naviga-ble (getting lost here is a badge of honor). But big doesn't mean imper-sonal, and some of the friendliest poker tables are found here. *3799 Las Vegas Blvd. S. ☎ 702/891-7777. www.mgmgrand.com. Map p 75.*

The Mirage MID-STRIP   The old-school tortuous layout makes navi-gating here a little difficult (as do the crowds), but the vibe is good and the Asian-sleek decor is almost relaxing. *3400 Las Vegas Blvd. S. ☎ 702/791-7111. www.mirage.com. Map p 75.*

Monte Carlo Resort & Casino SOUTH STRIP   A remodel has toned down the gaudy but replaced it with lots of beige—not exactly exciting. That said, the ceilings are high, it's easy to navigate, and it's definitely one of the best-smelling casinos in town. *3770 Las Vegas Blvd. S. ☎ 702/730-7777. www. montecarlo.com. Map p 75.*

M Resort EAST OF THE STRIP This lively neighborhood casino mixes Strip-level amenities (check out the extensive use of mother of pearl on the walls and ceiling) with lower limits and lots of locals-friendly perks through their gener-ous players' reward club. *12300 Las Vegas Blvd. S. ☎ 702/797-1000. www.themresort.com. Map p 75.*

New York–New York SOUTH STRIP   The NYC theming here has been toned down (drat!) to a more generic look, which means that this massive gaming place now doesn't have as much of a fun factor to offset its too hectic, crowded, and distract-ing atmosphere. *3970 Las Vegas Blvd. S. ☎ 702/740-6969. www. newyorknewyork.com. Map p 75.*

The Orleans WEST OF THE STRIP A low claustrophobia level, good video-poker options, and cheaper table minimums lure locals and tour-ists seeking better odds than those available on the Strip. The Cajun and zydeco music they occasionally play

The stylish M Resort casino is a favorite with locals.

The casino at New York–New York provides plenty of noisy distractions for gamblers.

on the sound system makes it that much more fun. *4500 W. Tropicana Ave.* ☎ *702/365-7111. www.orleans casino.com. Map p 75.*

The Palazzo MID-STRIP My reaction to this blandly designed casino is a distinct yawn, but there are lots of gaming options, and a simple layout makes it easy to navigate. *3325 Las Vegas Blvd. S.* ☎ *702/607-7777. www.palazzo.com. Map p 75.*

Palms Casino Resort WEST OF THE STRIP Although the hotel and its long list of nightclubs cater to a young, party crowd, you'll usually find older locals in the colorfully decorated casino, drawn by the low-limit gaming and generous slot machine payouts. *4321 W. Flamingo Rd.* ☎ *702/942-7777. www.palms. com. Map p 75.*

Paris Las Vegas MID-STRIP One of the few casinos that's still reveling in its theme (a fact I applaud): It's set beneath a ceiling painted like an April day in Paris and is partly under the feet of the hotel's Eiffel Tower recreation. The 83,000-square-foot (7,711-sq.-m) gaming area is ringed by Disneyesque European facades. *3655 Las Vegas Blvd. S.* ☎ *702/946-7000. www.parislv.com. Map p 75.*

Planet Hollywood MID-STRIP An impressive interior showcases classic Hollywood glamour, and all the usual gambling suspects have been rounded up for your betting pleasure.

It's not exactly serene (and a little hard to navigate), but it's way calmer—and more fun—than it used to be. *3667 Las Vegas Blvd. S.* ☎ *702/ 736-0111. www.planethollywood resort.com. Map p 75.*

The Plaza Las Vegas DOWN-TOWN Once one of the dingiest major casinos in Vegas, an extreme makeover has made this a modern, fun, and relaxed place to play. The new light and bright decor make it a winner, plus they kept the things that made it worth visiting before, namely low limits and friendly dealers. *1 Main St.* ☎ *702/386-2110. www.plaza hotelcasino.com. Map p 76.*

Red Rock Casino Resort Spa WEST OF THE STRIP For sheer, nontheme design, this is the best-looking casino in town, utilizing natural woods, glass ornaments, and stone. Like the rest of the resort, it's a stunner. It's also a convivial place to play. *11011 W. Charleston Blvd.* ☎ *702/797-7777. www.redrock station.com. Map p 75.*

Rio All-Suite Hotel & Casino MID-STRIP The 85,000-square-foot (7,897-sq.-m) main casino is dark and claustrophobic; stick to the section in the Masquerade Village area, which has much higher ceilings and is way more pleasant. And don't get distracted by those scantily costumed waitresses . . . who might break into song and dance every

The Plaza Las Vegas, one of Downtown's cheeriest places to gamble.

now and then. *3700 W. Flamingo Rd.* ☎ *702/252-7777. www.riolasvegas. com. Map p 75.*

South Point WEST OF THE STRIP This is one instance where high ceilings and an open layout can actually be a downer, leaving gamblers feeling a bit exposed in the big barn of a space. You may, however, get over that feeling quickly when you see how low the gaming limits are and how frequently the slots hit. *9777 Las Vegas Blvd. S.* ☎ *702/796-7111. www. southpointcasino.com. Map p 75.*

Stratosphere Casino Hotel & Tower NORTH STRIP You'll get more bang for your buck at this low-limit haven, which is often less crowded than many of its Strip cohorts. People who play above 25-cent denominations will have a hard time finding something to do, but video-poker aficionados will be thrilled. *2000 Las Vegas Blvd. S.* ☎ *702/380-7777. www.stratosphere hotel.com. Map p 75.*

Treasure Island MID-STRIP They've completely obliterated the dripping-with-plunder pirate theme that used to make this place fun, and all that remains is a nice casino. For most of you, that will be enough. *3300 Las Vegas Blvd. S.*

☎ *702/894-7111. www.treasure island.com. Map p 75.*

Tropicana SOUTH STRIP If you haven't visited this classic Strip casino lately you won't believe your eyes. What had become a textbook example of faded glory has been lovingly upgraded with a bright and sunny South Beach theme and plenty of modern gaming action. *3801 Las Vegas Blvd. S.* ☎ *702/739-2222. www.troplv.com. Map p 75.*

The Venetian MID-STRIP A theme-happy casino—check out the Venetian art on the ceilings!—that still exudes class. It's hard to navigate, but because the smoke factor is very low and I hit it big here once, I love it. *3355 Las Vegas Blvd. S.* ☎ *702/414-1000. www.venetian. com. Map p 75.*

Wynn Las Vegas NORTH STRIP A large but simple layout and the overall classy gestalt are pluses, but on the minus side, table limits are expensive and it's not all that exciting either. No matter; the machines (tight as they may be) run from nickels on up, so park yourself in the most comfortable slot seats in town and save the tables for Downtown. *3131 Las Vegas Blvd. S.* ☎ *702/770-7100. www.wynnlasvegas.com. Map p 75.* ●

Dining Best Bets

Best **Coffee Shop**
★★ Peppermill $ 2985 Las Vegas Blvd. S. (p 94)

Best **Burger**
★★ KGB: Kerry's Gourmet Burgers $ In Harrah's, 3475 Las Vegas Blvd. S. (p 92)

Best **Cupcakes**
★★ The Cupcakery $ In Monte Carlo, 3770 Las Vegas Blvd. S. (p 90)

Best **Sushi**
★★★ Shibuya $$$ In MGM Grand, 3799 Las Vegas Blvd. S. (p 96)

Best **Place to Blow All Your Jackpot Winnings**
★★★ Joël Robuchon $$$$ In MGM Grand, 3799 Las Vegas Blvd. S. (p 92)

Best **Thai**
★★★ Lotus of Siam $ In the Commercial Center, 953 E. Sahara Ave. (p 93)

Best **Cajun/Creole**
★★ Lola's: A Louisiana Kitchen $$ 241 W. Charleston Ave. (p 93)

Best **View**
★★ Mix $$$ In Mandalay Place at Mandalay Bay, 3950 Las Vegas Blvd. S., no. 2 (p 94)

Best **Breakfast**
★★★ Hash House a Go Go $ In Imperial Palace, 3535 Las Vegas Blvd. S. (p 91)

Best **Off-Strip Dining**
★★★ Raku $ 5030 W. Spring Mountain Rd. (p 95)

Best **Italian**
★★★ Bartolotta Ristorante di Mare $$$ In Wynn Las Vegas, 3131 Las Vegas Blvd. S. (p 88)

Previous page: A gourmet dish from the highly regarded kitchen of L'Atelier Joël Robuchon.

Best **Steak**
★★★ Strip House $$$ In Planet Hollywood, 3667 Las Vegas Blvd. S. (p 97)

Most **Romantic**
★★★ Alizé $$$ In Palms Casino Resort, 4321 W. Flamingo Rd. (p 87)

Best **Buffet**
★★★ Wynn Las Vegas Buffet $$ In Wynn Las Vegas, 3131 Las Vegas Blvd. S. (p 98)

Best **Bistro**
★★★ Bouchon $$ In The Venetian, 3355 Las Vegas Blvd. S. (p 88)

Best **Inexpensive Meal**
★★★ Capriotti's $ 322 W. Sahara Ave. (p 89)

Best **Mexican**
★★ Tacos & Tequila $$ In Luxor, 3900 Las Vegas Blvd. S. (p 97)

Best **Barbecue**
★★ Gilley's $$ In Treasure Island, 3300 Las Vegas Blvd. S. (p 90)

Best **Greek**
★★★ Estiatorio Milos $$$ In Cosmopolitan of Las Vegas, 3708 Las Vegas Blvd. S. (p 90)

A peppercorn burger is just one of the tasty offerings served at Burger Bar.

South Strip Restaurants

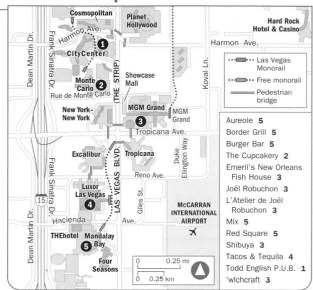

Aureole **5**
Border Grill **5**
Burger Bar **5**
The Cupcakery **2**
Emeril's New Orleans
  Fish House **3**
Joël Robuchon **3**
L'Atelier de Joël
  Robuchon **3**
Mix **5**
Red Square **5**
Shibuya **3**
Tacos & Tequila **4**
Todd English P.U.B. **1**
'wlchcraft **3**

Mid-Strip Restaurants

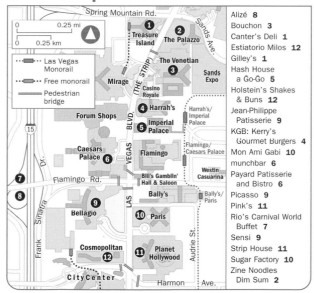

Alizé **8**
Bouchon **3**
Canter's Deli **1**
Estiatorio Milos **12**
Gilley's **1**
Hash House
  a Go-Go **5**
Holstein's Shakes
  & Buns **12**
Jean-Philippe
  Patisserie **9**
KGB: Kerry's
  Gourmet Burgers **4**
Mon Ami Gabi **10**
munchbar **6**
Payard Patisserie
  and Bistro **6**
Picasso **9**
Pink's **11**
Rio's Carnival World
  Buffet **7**
Sensi **9**
Strip House **11**
Sugar Factory **10**
Zine Noodles
  Dim Sum **2**

The Best Dining

Las Vegas Restaurants

0 — 0.5 mi
0 — 0.5 km

···■■··· Las Vegas Monorail
···■■··· Free monorail

Bartolotta Ristorante di Mare **8**
Capriotti's **3**
Dona Maria Tamales **1**
Lola's: A Louisiana Kitchen **2**
Lotus of Siam **4**
Peppermill **6**
Raku **9**
Sinatra **7**
Society Café Encore **7**
The Steak House **5**
Todd's Unique Dining **10**
Wynn Las Vegas Buffet **8**

See "Mid-Strip Restaurants" map

See "South Strip Restaurants" map

Downtown Restaurants

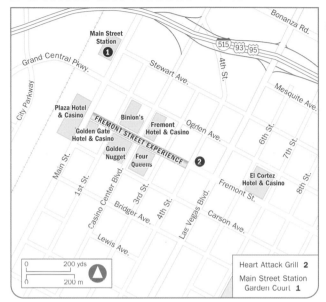

Main Street Station ❶

Grand Central Pkwy.

Bonanza Rd.

Stewart Ave.

515 93 95

4th St.

Mesquite Ave.

Plaza Hotel & Casino

Binion's

FREMONT STREET EXPERIENCE

Fremont Hotel & Casino

Ogden Ave.

Golden Gate Hotel & Casino

Golden Nugget

Four Queens

❷

6th St.

7th St.

El Cortez Hotel & Casino

8th St.

City Parkway

Main St.

1st St.

Casino Center Blvd.

3rd St.

Bridger Ave.

4th St.

Las Vegas Blvd.

Fremont St.

Carson Ave.

Lewis Ave.

| 0 | 200 yds |
| 0 | 200 m |

Heart Attack Grill **2**

Main Street Station Garden Court **1**

Las Vegas Restaurants A to Z

★★★ **Alizé** MID-STRIP *FRENCH*
Perhaps the most dazzling space in
Vegas, in that the space itself is simple, but the setting—floating above
Vegas and the desert at the top of
the Palms—is not. Sit next to one of
the floor-to-ceiling windows and
bask. The food is just as ethereal,
though the fish is sometimes dry;
stick to meat and you'll be happy. *In
Palms Casino Resort, 4321 W. Flamingo Rd.* ☎ *702/951-7000. www.
alizelv.com. Reservations strongly
recommended. Entrees $36–$75;
5-course tasting menu $105;
7-course tasting menu $125. AE,
MC, V. Dinner daily. Map p 85.*

★★ **Aureole** SOUTH STRIP *NOU-
VELLE AMERICAN* The food here is
American regional haute, but many
also come for the height—the

*A custom-flavored cupcake from the Cup-
cakery is one of the city's best treats.*

Border Grill is renowned for its twists on traditional Mexican cuisine.

four-story glass wine tower, where bottles are fetched by enticing cat-suited "wine angels" in harnesses. It's a Vegas-style gimmick, but the cuisine is strong enough to stand on its own. *In Mandalay Bay, 3950 Las Vegas Blvd. S. ☎ 702/632-7401. www.aureolelv.com. Reservations suggested. Prix-fixe dinner $75; tasting menu $95. AE, MC, V. Dinner daily. Map p 85.*

★★★ **Bartolotta Ristorante di Mare** NORTH STRIP *ITALIAN* Award-winning chef Paul Bartolotta gets his fish flown in daily from the Mediterranean and then cooks it simply, classically, and divinely. You can choose from a variety that may well include species hitherto unfamiliar to you, or have an excellent pasta dish instead. The restaurant also has a rare outdoor dining area, complete with modern art. *In Wynn Las Vegas, 3131 Las Vegas Blvd. S. ☎ 888/352-3463 or 702/248-3463. Reservations recommended. Entrees $30–$57; family-style tasting $145 per person; Grand Seafood Feast $155 per person. AE, DC, DISC, MC, V. Dinner daily. Map p 86.*

★★ **Border Grill** SOUTH STRIP *MEXICAN* The Food Network's Two Hot Tamales, Mary Sue and

Susan, learned Mexican home-style cooking south of the border and put their own twist on traditional dishes. It's not the place to go for plain old tacos—though you can, if you like—and you should skip the often bland fish dishes. *In Mandalay Bay, 3950 Las Vegas Blvd. S. ☎ 702/632-7403. www.bordergrill.com. Reservations recommended. Entrees $19–$36. AE, DC, DISC, MC, V. Lunch & dinner daily. Map p 85.*

★★★ **Bouchon** MID-STRIP *BISTRO* You won't find famed owner-chef Thomas Keller in the kitchen, but you also won't be disappointed. There's a deep satisfaction that comes from consuming this superlative bistro's regional French cooking in all its deserved glory. *In The Venetian, 3355 Las Vegas Blvd. S. ☎ 702/414-6200. www.bouchonbistro.com. Reservations strongly recommended. Entrees $26–$45; oyster bar $18–$110. AE, DC, MC, V. Breakfast & dinner daily; brunch Sat–Sun. Map p 85.*

★★ **Burger Bar** SOUTH STRIP *DINER* A little costly for "just" a burger, but diners get to build their own custom creation from a menu

The magnificent decor at Bartolotta Ristorante di Mare serves as a proper backdrop to its equally delectable Italian cuisine.

containing dozens of topping options, so the markup is nearly worth it. It can be fun and creative (though I think there is no good reason to have truffles *and* lobster on your burger). Skip the Kobe beef— it's too much money for a meat that doesn't make a good patty anyway. *In Mandalay Place at Mandalay Bay, 3930 Las Vegas Blvd. S.* ☎ *702/632- 9364. www.burger-bar.com. Entrees $9–$60. AE, DISC, MC, V. Lunch & dinner daily. Map p 85.*

★★ **Canter's Deli** MID-STRIP *DELI* A semireplica of a Los Angeles institution, though minus the ageless waitstaff and with a menu only one-fifth the size of the original's. Still, the pastrami is authentic and so is the brisket, and it smells like a real deli. Plus, black-and-white cookies! *In Treasure Island, 3300 Las Vegas Blvd. S.* ☎ *702/894-7111. Entrees $6–$16. AE, DISC, MC, V. Lunch & dinner daily. Map p 85.*

★★★ **Capriotti's** NORTH STRIP *DELI* A rare combination for Vegas: something affordable and delicious. Capriotti's makes

You can't do much better for bistro cooking in Vegas than Thomas Keller's Bouchon.

enormous submarine sandwiches that inspire such loyalty that many an out-of-town customer has planned their entrance and exit from Vegas around a stop here. Try the Slaw B. Joe, the Bobby, or design your own; opt for the "large" of anything and you can easily feed two. *322 W. Sahara Ave.*

Dining Tips

Vegas is not the bastion of low-priced dining that many travelers imagine it is. You can eat well or you can eat cheap, but it's not often that you can do both (though I do give you a number of options in this chapter that fit the bill). Even the vaunted buffet doesn't offer as much bang for the buck as it used to if you want food that is more than forgettable. So if you want to please your palate without emptying your wallet, here are a couple of options:

1. **Hit the primo restaurants at lunch.** Prices in this chapter, unless otherwise specified, are for dinner entrees. Prices at lunch are often discounted 20% to 50%.

2. **Get off the Strip.** Restaurants that don't have to shell out big bucks for the real estate they sit on tend to have lower prices. Plus, restaurants that depend on locals are more invested in keeping their quality up and their prices from reaching the height of the stratosphere.

☎ 702/474-0229. www.capriottis. com. All sandwiches under $13. AE, DISC, MC, V. Lunch & dinner daily. Map p 86.

★★ **The Cupcakery** SOUTH STRIP *CUPCAKES* The best cupcakes in Vegas and very possibly the best cupcakes in the entire country are found at this delightful bakery, where generous helpings of buttercream frosting top rich cakes in an ever-changing mix of custom flavors. A personal favorite: Oh My Gosh Ganache. Trust me. *In Monte Carlo, 3770 Las Vegas Blvd. S.* ☎ *702/730-7777. www.thecupcakery.com. Cup-cakes $3–$4. AE, DISC, MC, V. Open daily. Map p 85.*

★★ **Dona Maria Tamales** NORTH STRIP *MEXICAN* Classic Mexican food that's heavy on the lard, heavy on the sauces, heavy on the crowds (especially at lunch), and light on the wallet. You definitely want to try the tamales, but the enchiladas and chiles rellenos are excellent, too. *910 Las Vegas Blvd. S.* ☎ *702/382-6538. www.donamariatamales.com. Entrees $8–$17. AE, DC, DISC, MC, V. Break-fast, lunch & dinner daily. Map p 86.*

★ **Emeril's New Orleans Fish House** SOUTH STRIP *CREOLE* Not as reliable as the original in New Orleans, and the fish dishes are often the least impressive. But a Creole-spiced rib-eye has Emeril's infamous kick, and the decadent lobster cheesecake is like nothing you've ever tried before. *In MGM Grand, 3799 Las Vegas Blvd. S.* ☎ *702/891-7374. www.emerils.com. Reserva-tions recommended. Entrees $28–$46 (more for lobster). AE, DC, DISC, MC, V. Lunch & dinner daily. Map p 85.*

★★★ **Estiatorio Milos** MID-STRIP *GREEK* Great Greek cuisine is rare in Vegas so thank goodness for Milos and its delectable, regional favorites, which focus heavily on seafood that you usually can't get unless you are within walking dis-tance of the Mediterranean Sea. Start with the fried eggplant and zucchini appetizer and you'll want to scream "opah!" and throw a dish on the floor. *In Cosmopolitan of Las Vegas, 3708 Las Vegas Blvd. S.* ☎ *702/698-7930. www.milos.ca. Reservations recommended. Entrees $39–$65. AE, DC, DISC, MC, V. Lunch & dinner daily. Map p 85.*

★★ **Gilley's** MID-STRIP *BARBECUE* If all you came here for was their award-winning chili, packed with ten-der chunks of beef and bursting with flavor, it would be totally worth it. But while you're here, check out the rest of the menu filled with hearty and

Dine on terrific seafood paired with great views at Estiatorio Milos.

The classic Mexican cuisine at Dona Maria Tamales is beloved by young and old alike.

tasty down-home favorites from amazing barbecue to juicy burgers, all at a reasonable price. *In Treasure Island, 3300 Las Vegas Blvd. S. ☎ 702/894-7111. www.gilleyslasvegas.com. Entrees $9–$25. AE, DISC, MC, V. Lunch & dinner daily. Map p 85.*

★★★ **Hash House a Go Go** MID-STRIP *BREAKFAST* A suitably goofy concept restaurant, where breakfast is taken to the limit as salmon and cream cheese are worked into the hash, the pancakes are the size of a large pizza, and the waffles have bacon baked right into them. Dinner brings other excellent options, but you want to make the pilgrimage here for breakfast. Prices aren't dirt-cheap, but everything is meant to be shared. *In Imperial Palace, 3535 Las Vegas Blvd. S. ☎ 702/254-4646. www.hashhouseagogo.com. Entrees $9–$20. AE, MC, V. Breakfast, lunch & dinner daily. Map p 85.*

★ **Heart Attack Grill** DOWN-TOWN *BURGERS* Vegas was built on the concept of excess, so why not try a Quadruple Bypass Burger at this hospital-themed eatery. Said burger's more than a pound of meat and bacon totaling over 8,000 calories; eat it and you get a free wheelchair ride to your car. The burgers are only okay, but the butterfat milkshakes are deliciously artery clogging. *450 E. Fremont St. ☎ 702/254-0171. www.heartattackgrill.com. Entrees $8–$15. Cash only. Lunch & dinner daily. Map p 87.*

★★ **Holstein's Shakes & Buns** MID-STRIP *BURGERS* Of course it's the burgers here that draw the most attention (and for good reason; they are fabulous), but pay attention to the wide-ranging menu that includes sausages (from Chicago Dogs to bratwurst) and nonbeef options (tandoori chicken to spiced lamb). And don't forget the milkshakes, which you can get "spiked" from the bar. *In Cosmopolitan of Las Vegas, 3708 Las Vegas Blvd. S. ☎ 702/698-7940. www.holsteinslv.com. Entrees $13–$17. AE, DISC, MC, V. Lunch & dinner daily. Map p 85.*

★★★ **Jean Philippe Patisserie** MID-STRIP *CAFE/BAKERY* The product of an award-winning pastry chef, the Patisserie first attracted notice for its immense chocolate fountain and then inspired deep devotion with such fare as a *dulce*

In the battle for best buffet in Vegas, the Wynn wins.

de leche–stuffed brioche, serious gourmet chocolates, authentic gelato, and much more. It also serves sandwiches and crepes both savory and sweet, making this a perfect spot for a light meal. *In Bellagio, 3600 Las Vegas Blvd. S.* ☎ *702/693-8788. All items $3.50–$12. AE, DC, DISC, MC, V. Open daily. Map p 85.*

★★★ **Joël Robuchon** SOUTH STRIP *FRENCH* Knowledgeable foodies worldwide were all atwitter when much-lauded master chef Robuchon was coaxed out of early retirement and into this lush fine-dining venture. It will be a pricey

experience, but you shouldn't expect to pay less for great art—and that's what Robuchon offers, masterpieces on a plate, all served with multi-Michelin-starred attention and care. *In MGM Grand, 3799 Las Vegas Blvd. S.* ☎ *702/891-7925. www.joel-robuchon.net. Reservations strongly recommended. 5-course tasting menu $195; 16-course tasting menu $425. AE, DC, DISC, MC, V. Dinner daily. Map p 85.*

★★ **KGB: Kerry's Gourmet Burgers** MID-STRIP *BURGERS* The competition for best burgers in Vegas is tough, but after you eat the divine bovine (or turkey or lamb or chicken) served here at Kerry Simon's casual eatery you will probably declare a winner. I know I did. *Warning:* The slow-cooked, pulled-pork Sloppy Joe may tempt you away from a burger, and you won't regret a messy minute of it. *In Harrah's, 3475 Las Vegas Blvd. S.* ☎ *702/369-5065. Entrees $10–$15. AE, DISC, MC, V. Lunch, dinner & late-night dining daily. Map p 85.*

★★★ **L'Atelier de Joël Robuchon** SOUTH STRIP *FRENCH* This is the casual, counter-seating version of the formal restaurant run by legendary chef Joël Robuchon. Prices here are lower, the vibe is lively rather than reverent, and the food

Getting a Table

The growing reputation of Vegas as a foodie haven means that getting a table at the best spots is a lot harder than it used to be. If you can, make reservations in advance or you may find that spot you had your heart set on totally booked throughout your stay. And note that at places that don't take reservations (especially in the casino hotels), you may find yourself standing in line for a while to get inside (unless you gamble enough to get a pass that will get you in faster—see p 148 for details on comps).

not only is just as good as over at the main facility but is also some of the finest French food in the world. Plan enough time and appetite to sample as many of the delicate, playful, fanciful creations as you can. *In MGM Grand, 3799 Las Vegas Blvd. S. ☎ 702/891-7358. www.joel-robuchon.com. Reservations strongly recommended. Average check $60–$115 per person. AE, DC, DISC, MC, V. Dinner daily. Map p 85.*

★★ Lola's: A Louisiana Kitchen

WEST OF THE STRIP *CAJUN/CREOLE* True NOLA natives scoff at the idea that "real" Louisiana cooking can be found outside of the state, but Chef Lola, a native herself, brings the bayou to the desert in this charming little bistro. The jambalaya is perfect and the po' boys are served on genuine Leidenheimer bread, flown in from the Big Easy. Doesn't get much more real than that. *241 W. Charleston Ave., no. 101 ☎ 702/227-5652. www.lolaslasvegas.com. Entrees $6–$18. AE, DISC, MC, V. Lunch & dinner Mon–Sat. Map p 86.*

★★★ Lotus of Siam

EAST OF THE STRIP *THAI* Its legend rests on its coronation, some years ago, by *Gourmet* magazine as the best Thai food in North America. Really? I haven't tried them all, but I have journeyed to this strip mall hole-in-the-wall restaurant and was glad. Be sure to ask for the special-items menu to get the full effect of the authenticity. *In the Commercial Center, 953 E. Sahara Ave. ☎ 702/735-3033. www.saipinchutima.com.*

For masterful French cuisine in an equally inspired setting, look no further than Joël Robuchon.

One of the divine pastries sold at Jean Philippe Patisserie: Each is worth every calorie.

Reservations strongly recommended for dinner. Entrees $9–$24; lunch buffet $9. AE, DISC, MC, V. Lunch Mon–Fri; dinner daily. Map p 86.

★★★ kids Main Street Station Garden Court

DOWNTOWN *BUFFET* Like pretty much everything else in Vegas, the classic buffet—and by that I mean mounds of food for budget prices—is gradually getting edged out in favor of flashy-looking high-cost places. This place has found the sweet spot of value, serving really quite good buffet staples for value prices. *In Main Street Station, 200 N. Main St. ☎ 702/387-1896. Breakfast $8; lunch $9; dinner $12–$19; Sat–Sun champagne brunch $12. Free for kids 3 & under. AE, DC, DISC, MC, V. Breakfast, lunch & dinner daily. Map p 87.*

★★ Mix SOUTH STRIP *FRENCH AMERICAN* With its white decor and 15,000-bulb chandelier (cost: $500,000), the interior of Chef Alain Ducasse's ultramod restaurant feels bubbly like champagne. But it's the 360-degree views from the 64th floor of Mandalay Bay that will really make you dizzy. The menu is a balanced mix of meat, game, and seafood, each with its own subtle French twist. Though the food's decadent, you'll leave feeling satisfied but not uncomfortable. *In Mandalay Place at Mandalay Bay, 3950 Las Vegas Blvd. S.* ☎ *877/632-1766 or 702/632-9500. Reservations suggested. Average check $90 per person. AE, MC, V. Dinner daily. Map p 85.*

★★ Mon Ami Gabi MID-STRIP *BISTRO* Along with a delicious steak and *pommes frites,* Mon Ami Gabi delivers some of the best first-floor views in Las Vegas. The French bistro is located at the foot of the fake Eiffel Tower and across from Bellagio's fountain show. Despite a minor identity crisis (Am I in Paris? Italy? A drug-addled *Fear and Loathing* dream?), this is prime territory to enjoy Las Vegas's frenetic beauty,

The best Strip-side dining in Vegas is at Mon Ami Gabi; the bistro fare is great too.

as well as a good, affordable meal. *In Paris Las Vegas, 3655 Las Vegas Blvd. S.* ☎ *702/944-4224. www. monamigabi.com. Entrees $13–$40. AE, DC, DISC, MC, V. Breakfast, lunch & dinner daily. Map p 85.*

★★ kids munchbar MID-STRIP *DINER* Don't be fooled by the name—the food here is much more substantial than the munchie moniker implies. The menu is small but complete with everything from fish tacos to terrifically juicy burgers. Kids will love the Pizzadilla, a pizza in quesadilla form, and adults will enjoy the full bar. *In Caesars Palace, 3570 Las Vegas Blvd. S.* ☎ *702/731-7778. www.munchgroup.com. Entrees $9–$17. AE, DISC, MC, V. Lunch, dinner & late-night dining daily. Map p 85.*

★★★ Payard Patisserie and Bistro MID-STRIP *BISTRO/BAKERY* The invisible chocolate-scented come-hither finger will guide you through Caesars to Payard, owned by renowned pastry chef François Payard. Though famous for its sweets, this is actually the go-to spot for a power breakfast. The eggs Florentine are hearty, the chocolate croissants decadent, and the crepes are calling your name. *In Caesars Palace, 3570 Las Vegas Blvd. S.* ☎ *877/346-4642. Entrees $14–$27. AE, DC, DISC, MC, V. Breakfast & lunch daily. Map p 85.*

★★ Peppermill NORTH STRIP *COFFEE SHOP* When a high-end coffee shop collides with a swanky '70s lounge, the Peppermill happens. Fake cherry trees and servers in floor-length regalia add to the strangely colorful spot—think Denny's on LSD—that's open 24 hours a day. The food is overpriced but reliable, from the 24-hour breakfast and burgers to the hearty steaks. *2985 Las Vegas Blvd. S.* ☎ *702/735-4177. www.peppermilllasvegas.com.*

Entrees $10–$30. AE, DISC, MC, V.
Open 24 hrs. Map p 86.

★★★ **Picasso** MID-STRIP *FRENCH*
Julian Serrano is one of the few
celebrity chefs in town who actually
works in his own kitchen. Meals are
multicourse tasting menus, which
rotate regularly, but for your sake, I
hope it includes the Maine lobster
with corn trio, including a corn flan
that is like consuming sunshine. It's
hard to compete with the many
Picassos hanging on the walls, but
Serrano manages it. *In Bellagio,
3600 Las Vegas Blvd. S.* ☎ *877/234-
6358 or 702/693-8105. Reservations
recommended. 4-course menu $113;
5-course degustation $123. AE, DC,
DISC, MC, V. Dinner Wed–Mon. Map
p 85.*

Dine on excellent French cuisine while
surrounded by millions of dollars worth
of art at Picasso.

★★ kids **Pink's** MID-STRIP *HOT
DOGS*   The lines here are shorter
than the block-long queues found at
the legendary original Los Angeles
location, but it doesn't mean the
dogs are any less desirable. They
are cooked to perfection with the
classic "snap" when you bite into
them, and the outrageous toppings
(from chili to pastrami) will require
lots of napkins. *In Planet Hollywood,
3667 Las Vegas Blvd. S.* ☎ *702/785-
5555. Entrees $4–$10. AE, DISC, MC,
V. Lunch, dinner & late-night dining
daily. Map p 85.*

★★★ **Raku** WEST OF THE STRIP
JAPANESE   Curious where celebrity
chefs such as Joël Robuchon eat?
The answer is Raku, a tiny restaurant serving some of the most inno-
vative food in town. The Japanese
small plates range from soups and
skewers to Kobe beef liver and
Kurobuta pork cheek and are made
even more delicious when seasoned
with the house-made salt (seaweed,
shitake mushroom, and green–tea
flavored) and soy sauce. *5030 W.
Spring Mountain Rd., no. 2.* ☎ *702/
367-3511. www.raku-grill.com. Small*

plates $1.50–$16. AE, MC, V. Dinner
Mon–Sat. Map p 86.

★★ **Red Square** SOUTH STRIP
CONTINENTAL/RUSSIAN   When I
think of this restaurant, it's usually
because of the hilarity of its over the
top interior—a post–Communist
Party riot of Bolshevik and Soviet-era
gewgaws. Then I think of the Ice bar
and the impressive vodka selection,
one of the largest in the world. Then
I remember that the food, especially
the Roquefort-crusted filet mignon, is
really quite good. And I wonder why
I don't think of that first. Then I
remember the headless statue of
Lenin out front and get distracted all
over again. *In Mandalay Bay, 3950
Las Vegas Blvd. S.* ☎ *702/632-7407.
www.chinagrillmgt.com. Reservations
recommended. Entrees $27–$39. AE,
DC, MC, V. Dinner daily. Map p 85.*

★★ **Rio's Carnival World Buffet** MID-STRIP *BUFFET*   Locals have
long voted this the best in Vegas; I
say that, qualitywise, it's probably
better than ever, if not the best. The
cuisines offered are pretty global
(Mexican, Chinese, Brazilian, Italian,

The Soviet theme at Red Square may cause a double take, but nobody complains about the Russian cuisine—or the world-class collection of vodkas.

and more), and there's even a diner setup for burgers, fries, and milkshakes. Best of all, the desserts (usually disappointing at Vegas buffets) are worth blowing your diet on. *In Rio All-Suite Hotel & Casino, 3700 W. Flamingo Rd.* ☎ *702/252-7777. www.riolasvegas.com. Breakfast $19; lunch $22; dinner $30; Sat–Sun champagne brunch $30. AE, DC, MC, V. Breakfast, lunch & dinner daily. Map p 85.*

★★ **Sensi** MID-STRIP *ECLEC-TIC* Usually a place with "a little of this, a little of that" is an example of the adage "jack of all trades and master of none." But despite featuring Italian, American, grilled, and Asian-influenced dishes, Sensi is successful across the entirety of its eclectic menu. The lunchtime bento box is a popular item. *In Bellagio, 3600 Las Vegas Blvd. S.* ☎ *702/693-7223. Entrees $28–$60. AE, MC, V. Lunch & dinner daily. Map p 85.*

★★★ **Shibuya** SOUTH STRIP *ASIAN/SUSHI* A must for sushi fans and sake connoisseurs alike. Rejoice over such signature dishes as *toro tartare* and wild miso salmon, or order the divine tasting menu. The sommelier will gladly pair each course with sake by the glass (the list is the largest in the U.S., and much of it is exclusive to Shibuya) to complete the experience. *In MGM Grand, 3799 Las Vegas Blvd. S.*

☎ *702/891-3100. Reservations highly recommended. Average check $75 per person. Dinner daily. AE, DC, DISC, MC, V. Map p 85.*

★★★ **Sinatra** NORTH STRIP *ITAL-IAN* The Chairman of the Board theme is thankfully subtle, allowing you to focus on the fresh flavors of the Italian cuisine from chef Theo Schoenegger. Everything tastes as though it was caught or harvested moments before it arrived at your table, including some of Frank's favorites like spaghetti with clams and *osso buco. In Encore Las Vegas, 3121 Las Vegas Blvd. S.* ☎ *702/248-3463. www.encorelasvegas.com. Reservations highly recommended. Entrees $26–$52. AE, DC, DISC, MC, V. Dinner daily. Map p 86.*

★★ **Society Café Encore** NORTH STRIP *AMERICAN* The Belle Epoque–meets–South Beach aesthetic matches the old-meets-new twist on food at Society, with its sliders (filet mignon, charred tuna, and sloppy joe), lobster rolls, and mac-and-cheese bites with truffle dipping sauce. At first glance, Society appears to be Encore's coffee shop; at first bite, it's clear why it was recently named one of "The Best New Restaurants in America" by *Esquire. In Encore Las Vegas, 3131 Las Vegas Blvd. S.* ☎ *702/248-3463. www. encorelasvegas.com. Entrees $15–$40. AE, DISC, MC, V. Breakfast, lunch & dinner daily. Map p 86.*

★ The Steak House NORTH STRIP
STEAK Stifle your cynicism and hear me out: The Steak House at Circus Circus *is* good. It's one of the last true vintage steakhouses in town, with cushy booths, dark wood, and dry-aging beef hanging on display as you enter. The no-nonsense, affordable steakhouse fare—steaks, prime rib, crab legs, chicken—is more delicious than you would ever expect from an age-stained clown-filled casino. *In Circus Circus, 2880 Las Vegas Blvd. S.* ☎ *702/794-3767. Entrees $23–$70. AE, DISC, MC, V. Dinner daily. Map p 86.*

★★★ Strip House MID-STRIP
STEAK The cheeky, PG-13 bordello theme is what may lure you inside, but it's the steaks that will make you stay. Flavorful and juicy, the cuts of meat are aged, cured, and cooked to perfection, making this a standout in the crowded steakhouse field in Vegas. Be sure to start with the garlic bread with Gorgonzola fondue—you will want a second order. *In Planet Hollywood, 3667 Las Vegas Blvd. S.* ☎ *702/737-5200. www. planethollywoodresort.com. Entrees $30–$65. AE, DISC, MC, V. Dinner daily. Map p 85.*

Sensi's bento box is a popular and tasty lunch option.

★★ Sugar Factory MID-STRIP
AMERICAN If you can tear your eyes away from the giant candy shop just a few feet away, you'll be delighted by an eclectic and extensive menu that has more than a dozen pages of breakfast (the crepes are fantastic), lunch, and dinner options from sandwiches to steak. The Strip-side dining room offers great people-watching opportunities, but you will probably still have your eye on that candy shop. Go ahead and indulge! *In Paris Las Vegas, 3655 Las Vegas Blvd. S.* ☎ *702/331-5100. www.sugarfactory. com. Entrees $10–$25. AE, DISC, MC, V. Daily 24 hrs. Map p 85.*

★★ Tacos & Tequila SOUTH STRIP *MEXICAN* Vegas might be the only city where you can reasonably expect to find great Mexican food inside of a giant pyramid. Tacos & Tequila goes beyond the goopy enchilada standbys, offering light and fresh ceviches (tuna, mahimahi, and shrimp), memorable *carnitas*, and eclectic tacos (falafel, spicy Mexican pork, and so forth). With more than 100 tequilas to choose from expect a spirited crowd. *In Luxor, 3900 Las Vegas Blvd. S.* ☎ *702/262-5225. www.tacosandtequilalv.com. Entrees $13–$25. AE, DISC, MC, V. Lunch & dinner daily. Map p 85.*

★★★ Todd English P.U.B.
SOUTH STRIP *PUB FARE* Celebrity chef English brings his lofty epicurean talents to a more down-to-earth level at this fantastic brewpub. Create your own sandwiches from a laundry list of ingredients or trust them to make a juicy burger or savory potpie. The British faves, like bangers and mash and shepherd's pie, give the place an authentic pub flair. *In Crystals at CityCenter, 3720 Las Vegas Blvd. S.* ☎ *702/489-8080. www.toddenglishpub.com. Entrees $13–$28. AE, DC, DISC, MC, V. Lunch & dinner daily. Map p 85.*

★★★ Todd's Unique Dining

EAST OF THE STRIP *GOURMET* The Strip is packed with great gourmet restaurants, so why would I send you to the suburbs for this one? Chef Todd Clore changes his menu almost daily based upon the freshest ingredients he can find, and the dishes he puts together are veritable works of art at prices that are substantially lower than what you'll pay on the Strip. Choosing an entree will be a Sophie's choice, but the braised boneless short rib is a signature dish for good reason. *4350 E. Sunset Rd., Henderson.* ☎ *702/259-8633. www. toddsunique.com. Reservations recommended. Entrees $20–$30. AE, DC, DISC, MC, V. Dinner Mon–Sat. Map p 86.*

★ 'wichcraft SOUTH STRIP *SAND-WICHES*

Too often "sandwich" is synonymous with "boring." Not so at Tom Colicchio's 'wichcraft, where the *Top Chef* judge layers intrigue between slices of bread. Soups, salads, and panini are offered too. It's pricier than your typical chain sub shop, but sink your teeth into the Sicilian tuna with fennel, black olives, and lemon on baguette, and you'll understand why. *In MGM Grand, 3799 Las Vegas Blvd. S.* ☎ *702/891-1111. Sandwiches* $7–$12. AE, DC, DISC, MC, V. Lunch daily. Map p 85.

★★★ Wynn Las Vegas Buffet

NORTH STRIP *BUFFET* It may be the most expensive buffet in town, but it's also the best. Hands down. After all, there is Indian food, Kansas City–style barbecue, Southern specialties, ceviche, jerk chicken, and a dessert station that for once isn't a waste of calories. *In Wynn Las Vegas, 3131 Las Vegas Blvd. S.* ☎ *702/770-3463. Breakfast $20; lunch $24; dinner Sun–Thurs $35, Fri–Sat $40; brunch Sat Sun $32–$39. AE, DC, DISC, MC, V. Breakfast, lunch & dinner Mon–Fri; brunch & dinner Sat–Sun. Map p 86.*

★★ Zine Noodles Dim Sum MID-STRIP *CHINESE*

Chinatown flavors collide with Strip luxury. The tastes here are so authentic that *Chinese News* named Zine one of the top 100 Chinese restaurants in the U.S. You won't find Americanized classics. such as General Tso's chicken, but when you try the soy-flavored beef chow fun, Peking duck, and *siu mai* (steamed shrimp and pork dumpling) you certainly won't be missing it. *In Palazzo, 3325 Las Vegas Blvd. S.* ☎ *877/883-6423 or 702/607-2220. Entrees $14–$34. AE, DISC, MC, V. Lunch & dinner daily. Map p 85.* ●

Sushi fans and sake lovers are catered to at Shibuya, where the general Asian cuisine is nothing to sneeze at.

Nightlife Best Bets

Best Cocktail Lounge
★★ Petrossian, In *Bellagio, 3600 Las Vegas Blvd. S.* (p 105)

Best Retro Scene
★ Peppermill's Fireside Lounge, *2985 Las Vegas Blvd. S.* (p 104)

Best Place to Celebrity Watch
★★ Tao Nightclub, In *The Venetian, 3355 Las Vegas Blvd. S.* (p 108); and ★★★ PURE, In *Caesars Palace, 3570 Las Vegas Blvd. S.* (p 107)

Best Gay Bar
★★ Krave, In *Planet Hollywood, 3667 Las Vegas Blvd. S.* (p 109)

Best Place to Make a Fool of Yourself
★ Coyote Ugly, In *New York–New York, 3790 Las Vegas Blvd. S.* (p 103)

Best Downtown Nightlife
★★★ Insert Coin(s), *512 E. Fremont St.* (p 104)

Best View
★★ ghostbar, In the *Palms, 4321 W. Flamingo Rd.* (p 103)

Best Country Bar
★★ Gilley's, In *Treasure Island, 3300 Las Vegas Blvd. S.* (p 105)

Best Microbrews
★ Triple 7 Brew Pub, In *Main Street Station, 200 N. Main St.* (p 105)

Best Grown-Up Nightclub
★★ PURE, In *Caesars Palace, 3570 Las Vegas Blvd. S.* (p 107)

Best Neighborhood Punk Rock Hangout
★★★ Double Down Saloon, *4640 Paradise Rd.* (p 103)

Friendliest Club on the Strip
★ Tabu, In *MGM Grand, 3799 Las Vegas Blvd. S.* (p 108)

Best Piano Bar
★★ The Bar at Times Square, In *New York–New York, 3790 Las Vegas Blvd. S.* (p 103)

Best Strip Club
★★★ Treasures, *2801 Westwood Dr.* (p 110)

It's a tourist trap, but Coyote Ugly is packed every night by visitors eager to see its bar-dancing waitresses. Previous page: The bars in Las Vegas are renowned for mixing a wide array of fabulous cocktails.

Las Vegas Nightlife

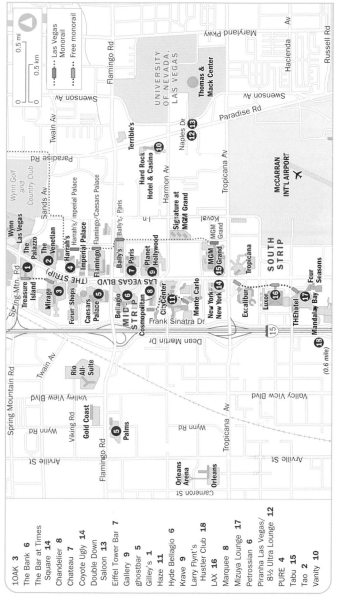

1OAK **3**
The Bank **6**
The Bar at Times Square **14**
Chandelier **8**
Chateau **7**
Coyote Ugly **14**
Double Down Saloon **13**
Eiffel Tower Bar **7**
Gallery **9**
ghostbar **5**
Gilley's **1**
Haze **11**
Hyde Bellagio **6**
Krave **9**
Larry Flynt's Hustler Club **18**
LAX **16**
Marquee **8**
Mizuya Lounge **17**
Petrossian **6**
Piranha Las Vegas/ 8½ Ultra Lounge **12**
PURE **4**
Tabu **15**
Tao **2**
Vanity **10**

Nightlife North & West of the Strip

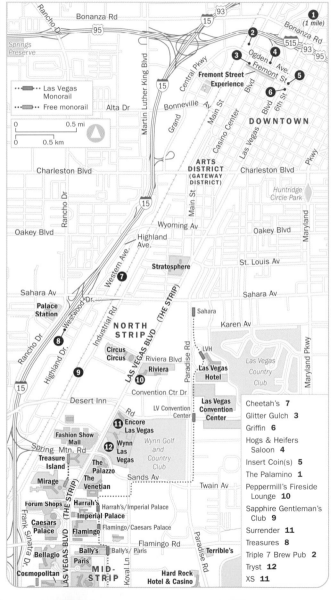

Cheetah's **7**

Glitter Gulch **3**

Griffin **6**

Hogs & Heifers Saloon **4**

Insert Coin(s) **5**

The Palamino **1**

Peppermill's Fireside Lounge **10**

Sapphire Gentleman's Club **9**

Surrender **11**

Treasures **8**

Triple 7 Brew Pub **2**

Tryst **12**

XS **11**

Las Vegas Nightlife A to Z

Bars

★★ The Bar at Times Square

SOUTH STRIP   If one piano is good, two must be better. Dueling pianos rule this lively lounge, smack in the middle of Vegas's homage to the Big Apple. If you make requests, try to give the poor performers more to do than just play Billy Joel. *In New York–New York, 3790 Las Vegas Blvd. S. ☎ 702/740-6969. $10 cover after 8pm Fri–Sat. Map p 101.*

★★★ Chandelier MID-STRIP   A

three-story chandelier houses three separate but equally fun bars, a casual casino lounge, a mixology haven, and a sleek ultralounge, all located in the center of the hotel's action. Not only is it a fun place to get a cocktail, but it's also great for people-watching. *In Cosmopolitan of Las Vegas, 3708 Las Vegas Blvd. S. ☎ 702/698-7000. Map p 101.*

★ Coyote Ugly SOUTH

STRIP   Part tourist trap, part genuinely good fun (as if that combo doesn't describe the whole city). You know the gimmick: The waitresses get up on the bar and dance around. A little frat boy, or even pedestrian-guy-trying-for-naughty-thrills, sure, but no less fun for all that. *In New York–New York, 3790 Las Vegas Blvd. S. ☎ 702/740-6969. www.coyoteuglysaloon.com. Cover varies, usually $10 after 9pm. Map p 101.*

★★★ Double Down Saloon

EAST OF THE STRIP   Local iconoclasts (from Manic Panic punks to strippers to even some famous faces) love this perfect dump, where the jukebox has selections ranging from Zappa to Rev. Horton Heat, the bartenders push something called Ass Juice, and signs remind patrons that "you puke, you clean." *4640*

Paradise Rd. (at Naples Dr.). ☎ 702/791-5775. www.double downsaloon.com. Map p 101.

★ Eiffel Tower Bar SOUTH

STRIP   Look down on everyone (just like a real Parisian—I'm kidding . . . mostly) from this chic and elegant room on the 11th floor of the Eiffel Tower. Drop by this date-impressing bar for a sophisticated and relatively affordable drink if your attire meets the business-casual dress code. *In Paris Las Vegas, 3655 Las Vegas Blvd. S. ☎ 702/948-6937. Map p 101.*

★★ ghostbar WEST OF THE

STRIP   Hovering over the city, this beautifully designed space-age bar boasts a stunning setting and some of the most superb views around. It's usually crammed with beautiful people paying absurd prices for drinks. If you've had one shot too many or generally suffer from vertigo, avoid the glass floor that's set

The Double Down Saloon is the best dive bar in Vegas.

If you're feeling daring, add your own bra to the collection that hangs above the bar at the boisterous Hogs & Heifers Saloon.

over the pool area, which is many stories below. *Note:* At press time, ghostbar announced it would undergo a major renovation. *In the Palms, 4321 W. Flamingo Rd. (just west of the Strip).* ☎ *702/942-6832. www.ghostbar.com. Cover varies, usually $20 & up. Map p 101.*

★★ **Griffin** DOWNTOWN   As part of the burgeoning Fremont Street East district, this funky little bar has a subtle castle decor (think stone walls and a fireplace) but it's the relaxed, low-pressure vibe that makes it worth visiting. *511 E. Fremont St.* ☎ *702/382-0577. Map p 102.*

★ **Hogs & Heifers Saloon** DOWNTOWN   That's "hogs" as in bikes. The movie *Coyote Ugly* was actually based on the original NYC Hogs & Heifers, and for a copy, this works pretty well. The most boisterous and partying place in Downtown. *201 N. Third St. (btw. Ogden & Stewart aves.).* ☎ *702/676-1457. www. hogsandheifers.com. Map p 102.*

★★★ **Insert Coin(s)** DOWNTOWN   Part bar, part dance club, part video-game arcade, this fun and funky tavern features dozens of restored arcade games (from Ms.

PAC-MAN to Asteroids), plus popular and retro console games available at the bar and in VIP booths. Despite the high-score competition, the vibe is distinctly laid-back, and the crowd ranges from young hipsters to middle-aged nostalgia seekers. *512 E. Fremont St.* ☎ *702/477-2525. www. insertcoinslv.com. Map p 102.*

★ **Mizuya Lounge** SOUTH STRIP Almost every hotel has a casino lounge, but this one in Mandalay Bay is one of the best for its casual atmosphere and energetic live entertainment. If you want to dance but the trendy clubs intimidate you, come here instead. *In Mandalay Bay, 3950 Las Vegas Blvd. S.* ☎ *702/ 632-7777. Map p 101.*

★ **Peppermill's Fireside Lounge** NORTH STRIP   Hilariously wrong and wonderful, this bar is a mélange of '80s fuchsia fluorescent lights, a '70s fire pit (the star attraction), and fake bougainvillea. Cozy up in the cushy pit or get a snack at the adjoining coffee shop. The enormous-size drinks just add to the fun. *2985 Las Vegas Blvd. S.* ☎ *702/735-7635. Map p 102.*

Cozy up to a fire pit at Peppermill's Fireside Lounge, where the interior wows, as do the large drinks.

★★ **Petrossian** MID-STRIP
Located right off the Bellagio lobby, and thus taking advantage of that space's impressive beauty, Petrossian is visually one of the prettiest places to drink in the city. Its cocktails don't come cheap, but they come with much knowledge—bartenders are required to attend continuing education classes—and are made with the finest ingredients; thus true cocktailians will tell you it's better to pay somewhat more for something so very right. *In Bellagio, 3600 Las Vegas Blvd. S.* ☎ *702/693-7111. Map p 101.*

★ **Triple 7 Brew Pub** DOWN-TOWN Its first demographic appeal is to microbrew buffs, though anyone longing to drink somewhere in Downtown that isn't smoky and noisy (except for the dueling piano acts) will find this something of a haven; glass walls separate it from the casino, cutting out much of that chaos. They also serve solid bar food. *In Main Street Station, 200 N. Main St.* ☎ *702/387-1896. Map p 102.*

Dance Clubs

★★ **The Bank** MID-STRIP It's for a "discerning audience with higher sensibilities." That translates as rich, exclusive, and uppity—though its top-of-the-line everything nearly justifies the stratospheric prices. You can bank on it being packed every night, but we think this trend is a bust. *In Bellagio, 3600 Las Vegas Blvd. S.* ☎ *702/693-8300. www.bellagio.com. Cover varies, usually $30 & up. Map p 101.*

★ **Chateau** MID-STRIP The main difference between this high-energy nightclub and all the others in town is the outdoor patio overlooking the Bellagio Fountains and the fact that you can enter without going through the hotel. Whether that's enough to make you put up with long lines, a

Hit Downtown's Triple 7 Brew Pub for a microbrew and a chance to drink in relatively peaceful surroundings.

high cover, and expensive drinks is up to you. *In Paris Las Vegas, 3655 Las Vegas Blvd. S.* ☎ *702/776-7770. www.chateaunightclublv.com. Cover varies. Map p 101.*

★ **Gallery** MID-STRIP The space is done up as a baroque art gallery, only with photos of scantily clad women in the lighted frames instead of something boring like a Picasso. The energy is infectious, and the vibe is less intimidating than at some clubs, but it still requires that you dress to impress. *Note:* The cover charge here includes admission to the adjacent Pussycat Dolls Saloon, which is exactly what you would think a club with that name would be. *In Planet Hollywood, 3667 Las Vegas Blvd. S.* ☎ *702/818-3700. www.gallerylv.com. Cover varies. Map p 101.*

★★ **Gilley's** MID-STRIP The saloon portion of this restaurant offers up the kind of down-home, boot-scootin' kicks that made it famous in the movie *Urban Cowboy*. Line dance lessons, a mechanical bull, and "Cowboy Karaoke" make this a root-tooting good time. And

The Bank is a popular nighttime refuge for the rich, famous, and trendy.

yes, the famous Gilley Girls will pose for pictures with you and your buddies. *In Treasure Island, 3300 Las Vegas Blvd. S.* ☎ *702/894-7111. www.gilleyslasvegas.com. Cover varies. Map p 101.*

★ **Haze** SOUTH STRIP   Strange "human aquariums" with models in various states of repose, plus a unique, moving light-and-sound system may make you feel like you're in a haze at this ultratrendy nightclub. Expect to wait in epically long lines and pay a lot for the privilege. *In ARIA, 3730 Las Vegas Blvd. S.* ☎ *702/693-8300. www.hazelv.com. Cover varies. Map p 101.*

★ **Hyde Bellagio** MID-STRIP   The unique thing at this Bellagio nightspot is that the vibe is very different depending on when you show up: a relaxed hotel lounge early; a hip hangout spot a little later; a full-fledged nightclub into the wee hours. Regardless of which incarnation you get, the lakeside patio offers the best views of the Bellagio Fountains in town. *In Bellagio, 3600 Las Vegas Blvd. S.* ☎ *702/693-8700. www. hydebellagio.com. Cover varies. Map p 101.*

★ **LAX** SOUTH STRIP   You might need a flashlight to properly see the swank supper club decor at this hugely popular if dim nightclub. It caters to an aggressively young and hip clientele (including plenty of celebs—Christina Aguilera was an investor before it got bought by a nightclub company) with multiple bars and an ultra-high-tech dance floor. *In Luxor Las Vegas, 3900 Las Vegas Blvd. S.* ☎ *702/242-4529. www.laxthenightclub.com. Cover varies. Map p 101.*

★★★ **Marquee** MID-STRIP   The competition for hottest club in Vegas changes on an almost weekly basis, but this multiroom space at the Cosmo wins raves, fans, and long lines for its high-energy party atmosphere. If the main room isn't doing it for you, try the more intimate Boombox ultralounge, the relatively quiet Library (complete with books and billiards), or the outdoor pool club area. *In the Palms, 4321 W. Flamingo Rd.* ☎ *702/492-3960. Cover varies. Map p 101.*

★ **1OAK** MID-STRIP   The nightclub 1OAK replaced, JET, was only a few

Scantily clad dancers constitute the "artwork" at the high-energy Gallery.

A celeb clientele frequents the always-packed dance floor at the ultra-cool 1Oak.

years old, which tells you how competitive the nightclub game is in Vegas. The original version of this club in New York's meatpacking district is a celebrity magnet; this one may not be as glam, but still appeals to the see-and-be-seen set with an upscale decor, a slamming dance floor, and fancy drinks. BTW, 1OAK = 1 Of A Kind. *In The Mirage, 3400 Las Vegas Blvd. S.* ☎ *702/791-7111. www.1oaklv.com. Cover varies. Map p 101.*

★★★ **PURE** MID-STRIP   With two stories and 36,000 square feet

(3,345 sq. m.) of white/ivory/silver design, intense crowding, hot sounds, and pure madness, this remains one of the most popular clubs in town. Lines to get in are long; tales of A-list celebrity embarrassment within are even longer. *In Caesars Palace, 3570 Las Vegas Blvd. S.* ☎ *702/731-7110. www.purelv. com. Cover varies. Map p 101.*

★★ **Surrender** NORTH STRIP
The interior of this sleek and sexy club is small by Vegas standards, but it opens up onto the massive Encore pool club area, turning the entire

You Are What You Wear

We may all be taught not to judge a book by its cover, but that's what pretty much every nightclub (and even the strip clubs) in town is going to do. Most of the clubs have precise dress codes, banning the obvious gang attire, but also, in some cases, collarless shirts, sneakers, baseball caps, shorts, jeans, sandals, and more. When in doubt, call ahead, but you might want to pack something fashionable and metrosexual just to be sure.

Don't let the Zen decor fool you—the hip don't wait to get into Tao Nightclub for peace and quiet, but for its pounding dance music.

thing into a slamming hot spot under the stars for the mostly younger party set. *In Encore Las Vegas, 3121 Las Vegas Blvd. S.* ☎ *702/770-7300. www.surrendernightclub.com. Cover varies. Map p 102.*

★ **Tabu** SOUTH STRIP   You'll hear the word "ultralounge" a lot in Vegas. All it means is "fancier than a bar, smaller than a nightclub." This is one of the best of an admittedly choice (if often interchangeable) lot. Which might sound like I'm damning it with faint praise, but it really is smooth. *In MGM Grand, 3799 Las Vegas Blvd. S.* ☎ *702/891-7183. Cover varies. Map p 101.*

★★ **Tao Nightclub** MID-STRIP   A gorgeously designed space that seems to span forever, encompassing an ultralounge, restaurant, and nightclub—all of which covers a couple of floors. The decor is Zen Asian, which is absurd, because thanks to the anxious crowds hoping to gain entrance, the flashing lights, and the pounding music, this celeb fave is anything but peaceful. *In The Venetian, 3355 Las Vegas Blvd. S.* ☎ *702/388-8588. www.taolasvegas. com. Cover varies. Map p 101.*

★★ **Tryst** NORTH STRIP   It's a bit more sophisticated and mellow than its club brethren . . . but this is

Getting in the Door

Club hopping in Vegas isn't a very practical affair, given the number of hours you may spend in line to get past the velvet rope guarding the entrance to the top nightspots. You're best off picking a club and then sticking around for the evening. To help increase the amount of time you spend on the dance floor, be sure to dress appropriately (see "You Are What You Wear," above), be on time if you've made a reservation, and try to have at least one woman (preferably showing some cleavage) in your party (ladies rule on club lines). Ask your hotel concierge if he or she can get you onto the club's guest list, or call the club yourself. If all else fails, you can try a discreet tip ($20 or more) to the doorman.

Vegas, so that's all relative. It is a pretty sexy space, notable also for the 90-foot (27m) waterfall and the patio that opens over a lagoon; it's rare to have a shot at fresh air in a Vegas club. *In Wynn Las Vegas, 3131 Las Vegas Blvd. S.* ☎ *702/770-3375. www.trystlasvegas.com. Cover varies. Map p 102.*

★★ **Vanity** EAST OF THE STRIP The Hard Rock Hotel is famous for its hard-partying vibe, and nowhere is it more apparent than here at their premiere nightclub. The indoor/outdoor space is swank check out that massive LED crystal chandelier—but personal space is definitely at a minimum and the competition to get in is fierce. *In the Hard Rock Hotel, 4455 Paradise Rd.* ☎ *702/693-5555. www.vanitylv. com. Cover varies. Map p 101.*

★★★ **XS** NORTH STRIP The "encore" of Tryst (see above) is aptly named in that it definitely ups the wow and energy factor over its sister club. It's notable for being more grown-up and sophisticated than the club norm—thanks to decent lighting, you can see the crowds you'll be bumping into on the dance floor and immense outdoor patio. *In Encore Las Vegas, 3121 Las Vegas Blvd. S.* ☎ *702/770-0097. www.xslasvegas.com. Cover varies. Map p 102.*

Gay Bars

★★ **Krave** MID-STRIP The first gay club to open on the Strip, but open enough to attract a mixed crowd—unlike most other joints, its go-go dancers come in both genders. That's probably the key; the club wants to promote itself more as "alternative" than anything sexuality specific, but the result is a fine place to party regardless of your orientation. *In Planet Hollywood, 3667 Las Vegas Blvd. S. (entrance on Harmon).* ☎ *702/836-0830. www.kravelasvegas.com. Cover varies. Map p 101.*

Music celebs, such as Wyclef Jean, are a fixture at ultra-trendy Haze.

★ **Piranha Las Vegas/8½ Ultra Lounge** EAST OF THE STRIP One building, two distinct gay hot spots. Piranha is a high-energy dance club with a walk-through aquarium that is sadly no longer filled with live piranhas (apparently there's a law against that—who knew?). The 8½ side is cool and groovy, with lots of space to relax. Lines for both are long, prices are high, and you need to dress to impress. *4633 Paradise Rd. (at Naples Dr.).* ☎ *702/791-0100. www.piranhavegas.com. Cover varies, usually $20. Map p 101.*

Strip Clubs

★ **Cheetah's** WEST OF THE STRIP Here's your classic, sporty, frat-boy strip-club vibe, small and cheesy but also friendly. Not as up-to-the-minute wow as newer places, but a lot less pressure because of it. *2121 Western Ave.* ☎ *702/384-0074. Topless. $30 cover after 8pm until early morning. Map p 102.*

★ **Glitter Gulch** DOWNTOWN The last bastion of Old Vegas, though an updated version of it. Not great for the bashful, but perfect for

the merely curious. *20 Fremont St.*
☎ *702/385-4774. Topless. 2-drink
minimum (drinks $10 & up). Map
p 102.*

★ **Larry Flynt's Hustler Club**
WEST OF THE STRIP   Four floors
and more than 70,000 square feet
(6,503 sq. m) of Sin City–style pleasures collide in this garish temple
perfectly suited to the style of both
its owner and the magazine it is
named after. You probably aren't
looking for good taste when going
to a strip club, but if you are, you
won't find it here. *6007 Dean Martin
Dr.* ☎ *702/795-3131. Topless. $30
cover. Map p 101.*

★ **The Palomino** NORTH STRIP
Smart owners of this all-nude facility
gave the lower level a minor face-lift
(farewell, red-flocked wallpaper;
hello, flatscreen monitors) and then
turned the upstairs over to male
strippers on weekends. (Yes, they
get totally naked as well.) Expect a
very gender-mixed crowd with an
urban vibe. *1848 Las Vegas Blvd. N.*
☎ *702/642-2984. Totally nude. $20
cover. Map p 102.*

*Technically, Krave is a gay club, but it's a
popular party place with people of all
orientations.*

*Tryst is popular with celebs, who like to
hang out beneath the sexy club's
waterfall.*

★★★ **Sapphire Gentleman's Club** NORTH STRIP
This modern
and friendly facility is billed as the
largest strip club in the world. The
girls are less clad than the Strip's
ubiquitous go-go dancers, but really
just by a scant degree. Oh, and
ladies have their very own male
strippers to leer at. *3025 S. Industrial.* ☎ *702/796-0000. Unescorted
women allowed. Topless. $30 cover
after 6pm. Map p 102.*

★★★ **Treasures** WEST OF THE
STRIP   A mélange of Victorian sporting house—the way a real "gentlemen's club" should look, if you ask
me—and high-tech accouterments
(look at the effects on the stage,
including the neon stripper pole).
You pay for this comfort and style,
but its class also makes it a comfortable first-time strip-club experience.
2801 Westwood Dr. ☎ *702/257-
3030. No unescorted women. Topless. $30 cover. Map p 102.* ●

Arts, Entertainment & Weddings Best Bets

Best **Cirque Production**
★★★ *KÀ, In MGM Grand, 3799 Las Vegas Blvd. S. (p 114)*

Best **Cirque Production Set on Water**
★★★ *O, In Bellagio, 3600 Las Vegas Blvd. S. (p 115)*

Best **Non-Cirque Production Set on Water**
★★ *Le Rêve, In Wynn Las Vegas, 3131 Las Vegas Blvd. S. (p 116)*

Best **Cirque Bargain**
★★★ *Mystère, In TI Las Vegas, 3300 Las Vegas Blvd. S. (p 114)*

Best **Cirque Imitator**
★★★ *Absinthe, In Caesars Palace, 3750 Las Vegas Blvd. S. (p 114)*

Smartest Show in Town
★★★ *Penn & Teller, In the Rio, 3700 W. Flamingo Rd. (p 117)*

Best **High-Tech Performance Art**
★★★ *Blue Man Group, In Monte Carlo, 3770 Las Vegas Blvd. S. (p 114)*

Best **Magic**
★★ *Criss Angel Believe, In Luxor, 3900 Las Vegas Blvd. S. (p 115)*

Best **Celebrity Impersonators**
★ *Legends in Concert, In Harrah's, 3475 Las Vegas Blvd. S. (p 116)*

Best **Beefcake** Show
★★ *Thunder from Down Under, In Excalibur, 3850 Las Vegas Blvd. S. (p 117)*

Best **Afternoon Show**
★★★ *Mac King, In Harrah's, 3475 Las Vegas Blvd. S. (p 117)*

Best **for Broadway Fans**
★★ *Jersey Boys Vegas, In Paris Las Vegas, 3655 Las Vegas Blvd. S. (p 115)*

Best **Old-Fashioned Vegas Revue**
★★★ *Vegas! The Show, In Planet Hollywood, 3667 Las Vegas Blvd. S. (p 118)*

Best Chapel for **Kitsch**
Little White Wedding Chapel, *1301 Las Vegas Blvd. S. (p 120)*

Best Place to **be Married by an Elvis Impersonator**
★ *Graceland Wedding Chapel, 619 Las Vegas Blvd. S. (p 120)*

Best for a **Traditional Wedding**
★★ *Little Church of the West, 4617 Las Vegas Blvd. S. (p 120)*

When you just can't wait to get down the aisle, head for the 24-hour drive-up window at the Little White Wedding Chapel. Previous page: Cirque du Soleil has become a Vegas entertainment juggernaut, and its very first show in town, Mystère, is still going strong.

Las Vegas Arts & Entertainment A to Z

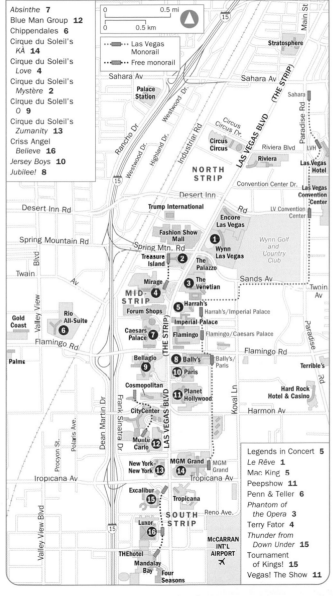

Absinthe **7**
Blue Man Group **12**
Chippendales **6**
Cirque du Soleil's *KÀ* **14**
Cirque du Soleil's *Love* **4**
Cirque du Soleil's *Mystère* **2**
Cirque du Soleil's *O* **9**
Cirque du Soleil's *Zumanity* **13**
Criss Angel *Believe* **16**
Jersey Boys **10**
Jubilee! **8**

Legends in Concert **5**
Le Rêve **1**
Mac King **5**
Peepshow **11**
Penn & Teller **6**
Phantom of the Opera **3**
Terry Fator **4**
Thunder from Down Under **15**
Tournament of Kings! **15**
Vegas! The Show **11**

A&E on the Strip

Live Shows

★★★ *Absinthe* MID-STRIP Cirque-style acrobatics mix with outrageous, often X-rated humor in this dizzyingly entertaining production. Performed in a small tent, the acts are literally feet from (and above) the audience, which contributes to the "anything can happen" atmosphere created by the hilariously inappropriate hosts. *In Caesars Palace, 3570 Las Vegas Blvd. S.* ☎ *800/745-3000. www.absinthevegas.com. Tickets $69–$99. Map p 113.*

★★★ kids Blue Man Group SOUTH STRIP Three men coated in blue paint play with more paint, marshmallows, and musical instruments made out of PVC pipe while the audience howls. It's middlebrow performance art, and no less enjoyable for all that. *In Monte Carlo, 3770 Las Vegas Blvd. S.* ☎ *877/386-8224. www.blueman.com. Tickets $74–$158. Map p 113.*

The Blue Man Group didn't start out in Vegas, but their performance art antics have found a welcome home here.

★ Chippendales WEST OF THE STRIP The famous beefcake gentlemen of Chippendales show off their impossibly buff bods in a series of fantasy fulfillment sketches (Cowboys! Construction workers!) that can send even the most proper lady into fits of unrestrained abandon. *In Rio Las Vegas, 3700 W. Flamingo Rd.* ☎ *888/746-7784. www.chippendales. com. Tickets $40–$50. Map p 113.*

★★★ kids Cirque du Soleil's *KÀ* SOUTH STRIP Factor in the actual story line (separated royal siblings battle various forces in their efforts to reunite), the special effects, the incredible moving stage, and the overall artistry of Cirque, and this is probably the best show in the city. *In MGM Grand, 3799 Las Vegas Blvd. S.* ☎ *866/740-7711 or 702/531-3826. www.cirquedusoleil.com. Tickets $69–$150 (plus tax). Map p 113.*

★ Cirque du Soleil's *Love* MID-STRIP Largely just a bunch of interpretive dances set to remixed Beatles tunes, with the usual Cirque arty and weird set design floating through. It's pretty, but even Beatles fans might be disappointed at the lack of substance. *In The Mirage, 3400 Las Vegas Blvd. S.* ☎ *800/963-9634 or 702/792-7777. www.cirque dusoleil.com. Tickets $79–$156 (plus tax). Map p 113.*

★★★ kids Cirque du Soleil's *Mystère* MID-STRIP The first big Cirque production in Vegas and still one of the best. Don't come looking for a story line; just settle back and let the imagery and acrobatics of this world-class show wash over you. *In TI Las Vegas, 3300 Las Vegas Blvd. S.* ☎ *800/392-1999 or 702/894-7722. www.cirquedusoleil.com. Tickets $60–$109 (plus tax & service fee). Map p 113.*

It's not the best of the Cirque du Soleil gang, but Love *might tickle the fancy of Fab Four fans.*

★★★ **Cirque du Soleil's** *O* MID-STRIP   The action in this dreamy and moving piece takes place in, around, and above a 1.5-million-gallon (5.7-million-ltr) pool. It's as if Dali and Magritte collaborated on an Esther Williams show. So beautiful, it might make you cry. *In Bellagio, 3600 Las Vegas Blvd. S.* ☎ *888/488-7111 or 702/693-7722. www.cirquedusoleil.com. Tickets $99–$155 (plus tax). Map p 113.*

Cirque du Soleil's *Zumanity* SOUTH STRIP   This ode to sexuality is a rare near-total miss by the otherwise reliable Cirque brand. Not so much erotic as it is trying too hard. *In New York–New York, 3790 Las Vegas Blvd. S.* ☎ *866/606-7111 or 702/740-6815. www.zumanity.com. Ages 18 & over only. Tickets $69–$125 (plus tax & service fee). Map p 113.*

★★ **Criss Angel** *Believe* SOUTH STRIP   Critically savaged when it first debuted, this show from magic's bad boy has been drastically improved by stripping out most of the dreamy Cirque elements and allowing Angel to do what he does best: eye-popping illusions that leave even jaded audiences gasping. *In the Luxor, 3900 Las Vegas Blvd. S.* ☎ *800/557-7428. Tickets $59–$160. Map p 113.*

★★ *Jersey Boys* MID-STRIP   The time-tested songs of the Four Seasons are the central draw of this enthusiastic and compelling Tony Award winner, which should satisfy both the theater veteran and the vacationing family. *In Paris Las Vegas, 3655 Las Vegas Blvd.* ☎ *800/237-7469. Tickets $64–$235. Map p 113.*

★ *Jubilee!* MID-STRIP   The last of the dying Vegas topless showgirl revues. Big set pieces, which include the story of Samson and Delilah and the sinking of the *Titanic* (no, I'm not making this up), not to mention enormous Bob Mackie wigs, make this more of a campy throwback than a good show, but put your tongue firmly in your cheek and you can have some cheesy fun. *In Bally's Las Vegas, 3645 Las Vegas*

These rubber-jointed contortionists are only one of the many delights found in Cirque du Soleil's sublime O.

High-End Headliners

The days when top-notch commercial talent regarded Vegas as a cheesy step in the wrong career direction are over. Céline Dion is back on the Strip, continuing to blaze a trail that other headliners are traveling. The good news: Garth Brooks, Elton John, Rod Stewart, and Donny and Marie Osmond all have high-profile gigs. The bad news: They're playing on limited contracts (and only go onstage a limited number of days each year)—and when they do perform, it'll cost you an arm, a leg, and who knows how many other body parts to see them. But if you have the cash to burn, here's how to spend it:

- ★★ **Céline Dion:** In Caesars Palace, 3570 Las Vegas Blvd. S. (☎ **877/423-5463**); tickets $55–$250.

- ★★ **Donny and Marie Osmond:** In The Flamingo, 3355 Las Vegas Blvd. S. (☎ **702/733-3333**); tickets $85–$250.

- ★★ **Elton John:** In Caesars Palace, 3570 Las Vegas Blvd. S. (☎ **888/435-8665**); tickets $55–$255.

- ★★★ **Garth Brooks:** In Encore Las Vegas, 3121 Las Vegas Blvd. S. (☎ **877/65-GARTH** [654-2784]); tickets $253.

- ★★ **Rod Stewart:** In Caesars Palace, 3570 Las Vegas Blvd. S. (☎ **800/745-3000**); tickets $55–$250.

Folksy Mac King does a first-rate magic/comedy act for a reasonable price—a Vegas miracle.

Blvd. S. ☎ 800/237-7469. www.bally slv.com. Ages 18 & over only. Tickets $57–$117 (plus tax). Map p 113.

★ **Legends in Concert** MID-STRIP The performers at this veteran celebrity impersonator show (over 25 years on the Strip!) do their best to make you believe they are the real thing with varying results. Most are passable, but some will have you wondering if they are the real thing (at one memorable 2008 show, that really was Ellen DeGeneres up there!). *In Harrah's, 3475 Las Vegas Blvd.* ☎ 702/396-5111. www.legendsinconcert.com. Tickets $50–$60. Map p 113.

★★ **Le Rêve** NORTH STRIP Originally a Cirque rip-off, right down to the utilization of a tank of water as a

Las Vegas Blvd. S. ☎ 800/427-7247. www.harrahs.com. Tickets $33 (plus tax & service fees). Discount coupons are almost always available in local magazines & handouts. Map p 113.

Buying Tickets

Many Vegas shows sell discounted tickets through local brokers. For information on getting these discounts, see p. 175.

★ **Peepshow** MID-STRIP Classic fairy tales collide with a topless Vegas review, producing surprisingly successful and sexy results. You'll never look at Little Bo Peep or Peter the Pumpkin Eater the same way again. In Planet Hollywood, 3667 Las Vegas Blvd. S. ☎ 877/333-9474. www.lasvegaspeepshow.com. Tickets $65–$125 (plus tax). Map p 113.

★★★ **Penn & Teller** MID-STRIP The smartest show in town, as the famous duo gleefully skewers the very magician tradition they happen to excel at. In the Rio, 3700 W. Flamingo Rd. ☎ 888/746-7784. www.riolasvegas.com. Ages 5 & over only. Tickets $75–$95 (plus tax). Map p 113.

★ **kids** **Terry Fator** MID-STRIP Fator won NBC's America's Got Talent with his comedic blend of ventriloquism and celebrity impersonation (the puppets sing like the stars). The shtick gets a little old after a while, but it's solid middle-of-the-road entertainment. In The Mirage, 3400 Las Vegas Blvd. S. ☎ 800/963-9634. www.mirage.com. Tickets $60–$150 (plus tax & service fee). Map p 113.

★★ *Thunder from Down Under* SOUTH STRIP Australian

The topless Vegas revue may be dying, but Jubilee! *with its signature showgirls, lives on.*

set, this show has evolved into a spectacular piece of art in its own right. The acrobatics and dance are first-rate, and the eerily dark visuals will stay with you long after you leave the theater. In Wynn Las Vegas, 3131 Las Vegas Blvd. S. ☎ 888/320-7110. www.wynnlasvegas.com. Tickets $99–$195. Map p 113.

★★★ **kids** **Mac King** MID-STRIP Given Vegas's sky-high ticket prices, this is possibly the best value in town. The affable King adroitly mixes comedy and magic (of the mind-blowing, close-up variety) and is an excellent choice for an afternoon break. In Harrah's, 3475

Top-notch acrobatic mix with adult humor at Absinthe.

The famous magical duo of Penn & Teller show off their skills and sense of humor at the Rio.

hunks strut their stuff in this ab-tastic revue that has a bit more "anything goes" atmosphere than rival Chippendales. Seriously, what women in the audience will do for a calendar is pretty amazing. Maybe it's the accents. *In Excalibur, 3850 Las Vegas Blvd. S.* ☎ *702/794-8200. www. thunderfromdownunder.com. Tickets $41–$51 (plus tax). Map p 113.*

★ **kids Tournament of Kings** SOUTH STRIP   This interactive dinner theater features heroic knights on horseback, fair maidens, and a few court jesters who encourage audience participation. One of the few family-friendly shows left in town. *In Excalibur, 3850 Las Vegas Blvd. S.* ☎ *702/597-7600. www. excalibur.com. Tickets $58 (plus tax). Map p 113.*

★★★ **Vegas! The Show** MID-STRIP   A rollicking look back at Vegas entertainment through the decades includes showgirls, tributes to Elvis and the Rat Pack, some amazing variety acts (Tap dancing! Magic!), and some of the best dancers in town. If "classic" Vegas shows were really this good, they'd all still be around. *In Planet Hollywood, 3667 Las Vegas Blvd. S.* ☎ *866/932-1818. www.vegastheshow.com. Tickets $80–$100 (plus tax). Map p 113.*

Making it Legal

Going to the chapel in Vegas isn't hard, but even spur-of-the-moment nuptials require Uncle Sam's approval. For details on getting a marriage license in Vegas, see p 28, ❻.

Vegas! The Show is a wonderful tribute to classic Sin City entertainment.

Best **Wedding Chapels**

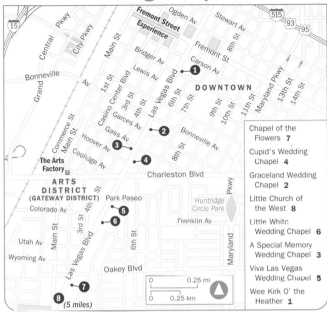

Wedding Chapels A to Z

★ **Chapel of the Flowers** This slick operation is your best bet for a traditional wedding (though no rice or confetti throwing—bummer!). Choose from among the friendly complex's five chapels (I like the Victorian best), use the drive-through, or opt for an outdoor ceremony. *1717 Las Vegas Blvd. S. (at E. Oakey Blvd.).* ☎ *800/843-2410 or 702/735-4331. www.littlechapel.com. Map p 119.*

★ kids **Cupid's Wedding Chapel** The self-described "little chapel with the big heart" lives up to its rep, and not only because it doesn't churn out ceremonies quite as fast as the other places in town (weddings are by appointment only). It also rolls out the red carpet to couples blending preexisting families,

If you want to take a more traditional route down the aisle, try A Special Memory Wedding Chapel.

making it a great option for those with kids. *827 Las Vegas Blvd. S. (btw. Gass & Hoover aves.).* ☎ *800/543-2933 or 702/598-4444. www. cupidswedding.com. Map p 119.*

★ Graceland Wedding Chapel

Elvis never slept here, and he didn't get married here, but this mom-and-pop joint has catered to a number of rock stars over the years (and you can get an Elvis impersonator if you want the King to officiate). It's not the nicest in town, but the tiny chapel (only 33 seats) is a pretty friendly place to get hitched. *619 Las Vegas Blvd. S. (at E. Bonneville Ave.).* ☎ *800/824-5732 or 702/382-0091. www.gracelandchapel.com. Map p 119.*

★★ Little Church of the West

Originally built in 1942, this historic, woodsy chapel has been relocated several times, but it hasn't lost any of the charm that has seen celebrity nuptials by everyone from Judy Garland to Angelina Jolie. *4617 Las Vegas Blvd. S.* ☎ *800/821-2452 or 702/739-7971. www.littlechurchlv. com. Map p 119.*

Little White Wedding Chapel

Are there better and friendlier

An Elvis-themed wedding at Viva Las Vegas.

places in town to tie the knot? Yes. But for pure Vegas kitsch, you can't beat this 24-hour wedding factory, which is little, is white, and has a really famous drive-through window, where many a celeb has embarked on a path to 48 hours of wedded bliss. Just avoid the noisy gazebo. *1301 Las Vegas Blvd. S. (btw. E. Oakey & Charleston blvd).* ☎ *800/545-8111 or 702/382-5943. www.alittlewhitechapel.com. Map p 119.*

★ A Special Memory Wedding Chapel

Want a traditional, non-tacky, big-production wedding? Here's the place. The pretty interior of the main New England–style chapel actually looks like a church, it holds up to 115, and there's even a cool staircase from which a bride can make a grand entrance. Of course, if you want that drive-through option, it's still there (this is Vegas). *800 S. Fourth St. (at Gass Ave.).* ☎ *800/962-7798 or 702/384-2211. www.aspecialmemory.com. Map p 119.*

★★★ Viva Las Vegas Wedding Chapel

Want to star in your own theatrical wedding production? This fun spot specializes in theme weddings—in addition to the eponymous Elvis, they've done everything from *Star Wars* to Camelot to James Bond! The Southwestern-style chapel holds up to 100. *1205 Las Vegas Blvd. S.* ☎ *800/570-4450 or 702/384-0771. www.vivalasvegas.com. Map p 119.*

★ Wee Kirk O' the Heather

Though it's the oldest wedding chapel in Vegas (opened in 1940), the decor at this veteran is fresh, the service is warm, and the whole package strikes just the right balance between kitsch and classic. *231 Las Vegas Blvd. S. (btw. Bridger & Carson aves.).* ☎ *800/843-2566 or 702/382-9830. www.weekirk.com. Map p 119.* ●

Hotel Best Bets

Most **Luxurious**
★★★ Four Seasons Hotel Las Vegas $$$$ 3960 Las Vegas Blvd. S. (p 128)

Best **Business Hotel**
★★ LVH: Las Vegas Hotel & Casino $$ 3000 Paradise Rd. (p 130)

Best **Views**
★★ Palms Casino Resort $$$ 4321 W. Flamingo Rd. (p 134)

Best **Room on the Strip**
★★★ Cosmopolitan of Las Vegas $$$ 3708 Las Vegas Blvd. S. (p 126)

Best **Classic Vegas Hotel**
★★ Caesars Palace $$$ 3570 Las Vegas Blvd. S. (p 126)

Best **Use of Wacky Theme**
★★ New York–New York Hotel & Casino $$ 3790 Las Vegas Blvd. S. (p 132)

Best **Moderately Priced Strip Rooms**
★★ The Flamingo Las Vegas $$ 3555 Las Vegas Blvd. S. (p 127)

Most **Improved Rooms**
★★ Tropicana Las Vegas $$ 3801 Las Vegas Blvd. S. (p 136)

Best **for Families**
★ Circus Circus Hotel & Casino $ 2880 Las Vegas Blvd. S. (p 126)

Best **Bathrooms**
★★ The Venetian $$$ 3355 Las Vegas Blvd. S. (p 138)

Best **Downtown Bargain**
★★ Main Street Station $ 200 N. Main St. (p 130)

Best **Gym**
★★ The Venetian $$$ 3355 Las Vegas Blvd. S. (p 138)

Best **Swimming Pool**
★★ The Mirage $$ 3400 Las Vegas Blvd. S. (p 131)

Best **Resort**
★★★ Red Rock Resort $$$ 11011 W. Charleston Blvd. (p 134)

Best **Getaway**
★★ JW Marriott $$$ 221 N. Rampart Blvd. (p 130)

Best **Lobby**
★★★ Cosmopolitan of Las Vegas $$$ 3708 Las Vegas Blvd. S. (p 126)

Best **Beds**
★★★ Red Rock Resort $$$ 11011 W. Charleston Blvd. (p 134)

Best **Rock 'N' Roll Hotel**
★★ Hard Rock Hotel & Casino $$$ 4455 Paradise Rd. (p 129)

Best **Strip Bargain**
★ Stratosphere Casino Hotel & Tower $ 2000 Las Vegas Blvd. S. (p 135)

Best **Non-Casino Hotel**
★★★ Mandarin Oriental Las Vegas $$$ 3752 Las Vegas Blvd. S. (p 131)

Best **"Locals" Hotel**
★★ South Point Hotel & Casino $$ 9777 Las Vegas Blvd. S. (p 135)

The Venetian has the best bathrooms in Vegas.

Previous page: The lobby of the Red Rock Resort.

South Strip Hotels

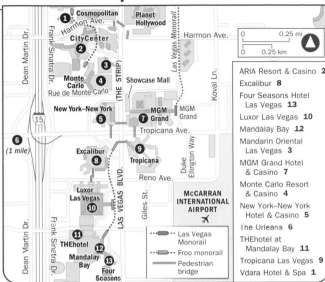

ARIA Resort & Casino **2**

Excalibur **8**

Four Seasons Hotel Las Vegas **13**

Luxor Las Vegas **10**

Mandalay Bay **12**

Mandarin Oriental Las Vegas **3**

MGM Grand Hotel & Casino **7**

Monte Carlo Resort & Casino **4**

New York–New York Hotel & Casino **5**

The Orleans **6**

THEhotel at Mandalay Bay **11**

Tropicana Las Vegas **9**

Vdara Hotel & Spa **1**

Mid-Strip Hotels

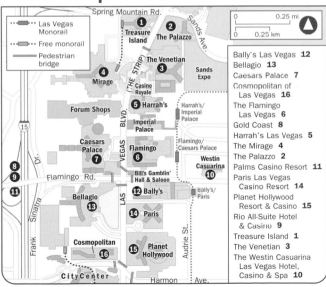

Bally's Las Vegas **12**

Bellagio **13**

Caesars Palace **7**

Cosmopolitan of Las Vegas **16**

The Flamingo Las Vegas **6**

Gold Coast **8**

Harrah's Las Vegas **5**

The Mirage **4**

The Palazzo **2**

Palms Casino Resort **11**

Paris Las Vegas Casino Resort **14**

Planet Hollywood Resort & Casino **15**

Rio All-Suite Hotel & Casino **9**

Treasure Island **1**

The Venetian **3**

The Westin Casuarina Las Vegas Hotel, Casino & Spa **10**

Las Vegas Hotels

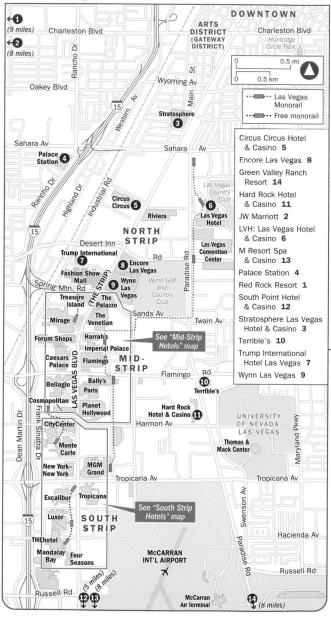

DOWNTOWN

ARTS DISTRICT (GATEWAY DISTRICT)

Charleston Blvd
Huntridge Circle Park

Charleston Blvd

Oakey Blvd

Wyoming Av

1 (9 miles)
2 (8 miles)

Rancho Dr

Western Av

Main St

0   0.5 mi
0   0.5 km

········ Las Vegas Monorail
····■··· Free monorail

Sahara Av

Sahara Av

Palace Station **4**

Stratosphere **3**

Circus Circus **5**

Riviera

Las Vegas Country Club

Las Vegas Hotel **6**

Las Vegas Convention Center

NORTH STRIP

Desert Inn

Trump International **7**

Fashion Show Mall

Spring Mtn. Rd

Encore Las Vegas **8**

Wynn Las Vegas **9**

Wynn Golf and Country Club

Treasure Island

The Palazzo

The Venetian

Mirage

Forum Shops

Harrah's

Imperial Palace

Flamingo

Caesars Palace

Bally's

Paris

Bellagio

Planet Hollywood

Cosmopolitan

CityCenter

Monte Carlo

New York–New York

MGM Grand

Excalibur

Tropicana

Luxor

THEhotel

Mandalay Bay

Four Seasons

MID-STRIP

Sands Av

Twain Av

Flamingo Rd

Terrible's **10**

Hard Rock Hotel & Casino **11**

Harmon Av

UNIVERSITY OF NEVADA, LAS VEGAS

Thomas & Mack Center

Tropicana Av

Hacienda Av

Russell Rd

Maryland Pkwy

Swenson Av

Paradise Rd

Industrial Rd

Highland Dr

Rancho Dr

Dean Martin Dr

Frank Sinatra Dr

Paradise Rd

See "Mid-Strip Hotels" map

See "South Strip Hotels" map

SOUTH STRIP

McCARRAN INT'L AIRPORT

McCarran Air Terminal

Russell Rd

12 (5 miles)
13 (8 miles)

14 (8 miles)

Circus Circus Hotel & Casino **5**

Encore Las Vegas **8**

Green Valley Ranch Resort **14**

Hard Rock Hotel & Casino **11**

JW Marriott **2**

LVH: Las Vegas Hotel & Casino **6**

M Resort Spa & Casino **13**

Palace Station **4**

Red Rock Resort **1**

South Point Hotel & Casino **12**

Stratosphere Las Vegas Hotel & Casino **3**

Terrible's **10**

Trump International Hotel Las Vegas **7**

Wynn Las Vegas **9**

Downtown Hotels

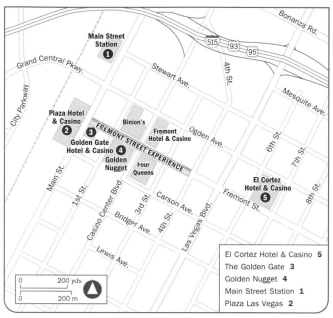

Main Street
Station ❶

Plaza Hotel
& Casino ❷

Binion's ❸

Golden Gate
Hotel & Casino ❹

FREMONT STREET EXPERIENCE

Fremont
Hotel & Casino

Golden
Nugget

Four
Queens

El Cortez
Hotel & Casino ❺

El Cortez Hotel & Casino	5
The Golden Gate	3
Golden Nugget	4
Main Street Station	1
Plaza Las Vegas	2

Las Vegas Hotels A to Z

★★ ARIA Resort & Casino

SOUTH STRIP   Cutting-edge decor mixes with high-tech wizardry in this luxe hotel's two curved glass towers. The plush guest rooms feature all manner of cool techno gizmos—and floor-to-ceiling windows. A soaring three-story lobby, vast pool area, fab spa, and more restaurants and bars than you could probably handle in a single visit round out the first-class offerings. *3730 Las Vegas Blvd. S. (at Harmon Ave.). ☎ 866/359-7757. www.arialasvegas.com. 4,004 units. Doubles $159 & up. AE, DC, MC, V. Map p 123.*

★ Bally's Las Vegas MID-STRIP

Bally's has one of the best locations on the Strip (dead center, and on the monorail line), but not much of a

wow factor in a city where that means a lot. Still, you can get a large, comfy room for a ridiculously low rate. It's a very pleasant place

The rooms at ARIA Resort & Casino offer marvelous views.

to stay for value seekers. *3645 Las Vegas Blvd. S. (at Flamingo Rd.).* ☎ *877/603-4390. www.ballyslv. com. 2,814 units. Doubles $99 & up. AE, DC, MC, V. Map p 123.*

★★ **Bellagio** MID-STRIP The first of the "luxury resort"–style Vegas casino hotels, which in this case means posh rooms, a classy Euro-style pool area, and access to some of the best restaurants in town. Accommodations feel a little small compared to some of the even newer resorts, but they are still handsome, especially after an over-haul that made them more modern. Though the size can be daunting (it's a nice trek to the pool and spa from most rooms), the grown-up atmosphere makes up for it. *3600 Las Vegas Blvd. S. (at the corner of Flamingo Rd.).* ☎ *888/987-6667 or 702/693-7111. www.bellagio.com. 3,933 units. Doubles $169 & up. AE, DC, DISC, MC, V. Map p 123.*

★★ **Caesars Palace** MID-STRIP Though they've toned down the cheese factor and upped this veteran to a ridiculous and often impossible-to-navigate size, no hotel is more Vegas spectacle than Caesars. Rooms vary from tower to tower in terms of size and no longer have that goofy romance that once characterized the place, but all are generically handsome and comfortable. The spa, Qua, is a sybaritic stunner, as is its heavenly Garden of the Gods pool complex. Toss in The Forum Shops (p 49), and a variety of bars and excellent restaurants, and leaving here isn't necessary—which is good, because it's so hard to find the door. *3570 Las Vegas Blvd. S. (just north of Flamingo Rd.).* ☎ *877/427-7243 or 702/731-7110. www.caesars palace.com. 4,084 units. Doubles $129 & up; suites $399 & up. AE, DC, DISC, MC, V. Map p 123.*

★ **kids** **Circus Circus Hotel & Casino** NORTH STRIP The circus acts still fly above the casino action and families still stay here, but its days as an attraction are long gone. Now it's the place to come for cheap rooms, though its Manor rooms are a bargain (or should be) for a reason. A dump-your-bags-and-head-to-more-interesting-climes location. *2880 Las Vegas Blvd. S. (btw. Circus Circus & Convention Center drives).* ☎ *800/634-3450 or 702/734-0410. www.circuscircus. com. 3,774 units. Doubles $39 & up. AE, DC, DISC, MC, V. Map p 124.*

★★★ **Cosmopolitan of Las Vegas** MID-STRIP The new defini-tion of eye candy, this visual won-derland of a hotel uses art as its theme, with a stunning contempo-rary design and lots of nonthreaten-ing hipster whimsy thrown in just for fun. Rooms are huge, well-appointed, and sleekly modern with unique touches like outdoor terraces and books that you will probably never

One of Bellagio's posh guest rooms; some rooms overlook the hotel's famous fountains.

A petite suite in the Augustus Tower at Caesars Palace.

read, but are fun anyway. A masterpiece. *3708 Las Vegas Blvd. S. ☎ 877/551-7778 or 702/698-7000. www.cosmopolitanoflasvegas.com. 2,995 units. Doubles $159 & up. AE, DC, DISC, MC, V. Map p 123.*

★★ El Cortez Hotel & Casino

DOWNTOWN   This Downtown veteran has been transformed into an unusually cool and contemporary place to stay, even while retaining its Old Vegas cred. And it's ultra-affordable, too. The traditionally furnished rooms (some quite large) have some useful modern features (minifridges, flatscreen TVs, and so on); the Cabana Suites are especially desirable. *600 Fremont St. (btw. Sixth & Seventh sts.). ☎ 800/634-6703 or 702/385-5200. www.elcortezhotelcasino.com. 428 units. Doubles $35 & up. AE, DISC, MC, V. Map p 125.*

★★ Encore Las Vegas

NORTH STRIP   This aptly named second act of Steve Wynn's scores on all the luxe fronts. The whimsically decorated public areas (Moroccan, red, and butterflies mix to good effect) are more fun than the guest rooms, which are nevertheless grand, modern, and richly appointed (especially those marble bathrooms!). Prices are stratospheric. *3121 Las Vegas Blvd. S. (near Spring Mountain Rd.). ☎ 888/320-7125 or 702/770-7171. www.encorelasvegas.com. 2,034 units. Doubles $159 & up. AE, DC, DISC, MC, V. Map p 124.*

★ kids Excalibur

SOUTH STRIP   No longer the sword-and-sorcery fantasy escape it once promised to be, this is the place to go if you simply must stay in an oversize cartoonish castle (whose theme has been sadly downsized of late) and/or you must stay on the Strip and need a bargain room—stick to the newer Widescreen rooms and avoid the Standard ones. The pool area might help make the stay feel a little more special. *3850 Las Vegas Blvd. S. (at Tropicana Ave.). ☎ 800/937-7777 or 702/597-7700. www.excalibur.com. 4,008 units. Doubles $49 & up. AE, DC, DISC, MC, V. Map p 123.*

★★ kids The Flamingo Las Vegas

MID-STRIP   This Strip veteran turned what were rather forgettable rooms into snazzy, modern digs. The GO rooms are retro wonders with hot pink accents, black-and-white photos of its heyday as Bugsy Siegel's hangout, and TVs embedded in the bathroom mirrors. The FAB rooms are simpler but still contemporary with flatscreens and rare hardwood floors. Bonus points for the pool area (complete with live birds), which is one of the city's best. Good for families who cover an age range. *3555 Las Vegas Blvd. S. (btw. Sands Ave. & Flamingo Rd.). ☎ 800/732-2111 or 702/733-3111. www.flamingolv.com. 3,999 units.*

The rooms at Circus Circus may not be much to write home about, but the resort is still a great place to stay if you're traveling with kids.

A room at The Flamingo Las Vegas, whose pool is still one of the best in the city.

Doubles $99 & up. AE, DC, DISC, MC, V. Map p 123.

★★★ kids Four Seasons Hotel Las Vegas SOUTH STRIP

Situated at the top of Mandalay Bay, and accessed through its own entrance, this is your home away from Vegas (though the Strip action is right at your door if you need a fix). This grown-up oasis (though kids are warmly welcomed) has posh yet quietly tasteful accommodations, plus the service the Four Seasons is renowned for. And unlike most of the other big-name hotels, there are no extra charges for such amenities as gym use. *3960 Las Vegas Blvd. S.* ☎ *877/632-5000 or 702/632-5000. www.fourseasons. com. 424 units. Doubles $199 & up. AE, DC, DISC, MC, V. Map p 123.*

★ Gold Coast MID-STRIP

Most locals' hotels offer high value at low costs but are often too far afield to

The first-rate pool area at the plush Green Valley Ranch Resort is great for lounging.

be genuinely good alternatives. This one has all the good stuff—low-cost casino, comfy but affordable rooms, lots of cheap eats—but has the bonus of being within walking distance of the Strip. Bargain hunters apply here. *4000 W. Flamingo Rd. (at Valley View Blvd.).* ☎ *800/331-5334 or 702/367-7111. www.goldengate casino.com. 106 units. Doubles $29 & up. AE, DC, DISC, MC, V. Map p 123.*

★ The Golden Gate DOWNTOWN

First opened in 1906 (the state's first hotel!), this classic bit of Vegas history has been upgraded and expanded to make it a modern boutique property with a decidedly retro charm. Rooms are microscopic but lovingly furnished—and often dirt-cheap. *1 E. Fremont St.* ☎ *800/ 426-1906 or 702/385-1906. www. goldcoastcasino.com. 711 units. Doubles $39 & up. AE, DC, DISC, MC, V. Map p 125.*

★★ Golden Nugget DOWNTOWN

One of the finest hotels in Downtown is currently on an upswing, with public areas sporting a fresh mix of the best of new and old Vegas. Rooms are attractive and comfortable (not quite at the level of similar Strip hotels, but comparatively bargain priced), and the snazzy pool is a major plus. *129 E. Fremont St. (at Casino Center Blvd.).* ☎ *800/846-5336 or 702/385-7111. www.goldennugget. com. 1,907 units. Doubles $69 & up. AE, DC, DISC, MC, V. Map p 125.*

★★★ Green Valley Ranch Resort
HENDERSON   Mash the Ritz-Carlton and W styles together and you have this greatly appealing resort. Its spacious rooms have supremely plush beds. The modern pool area, complete with sandy "beach" and mattresses for serious lounging, is terrific. The casino is small and a bit of a walk from the main hotel action but warmly decorated and full of low-limit wagering options. The resort's location about 20 minutes from the Strip can either be viewed as a roadblock or as a retreat from the Vegas madness. *2300 Paseo Verde Pkwy. (at I-215).* ☎ *866/782-9487 or 702/617-7777. www.greenvalleyranchresort.com. 490 units. Doubles $129 & up. AE, DC, DISC, MC, V. Map p 124.*

★★ Hard Rock Hotel & Casino
EAST OF THE STRIP   Still the place to stay if you sport tattoos or Pamela Anderson on your arm, but its hipster cred has been somewhat eclipsed by newer kids in town. The beach-party pool area remains a happening hangout, but the rooms try so hard for style that they sometimes forget comfort (some only have showers). Rock 'n' roll is always here to stay—but you shouldn't stay here if you need to ask, "Who was Kurt Cobain and why is there a glass case of his stuff over

The Hard Rock Hotel lures music lovers with a primo collection of rock memorabilia.

there?" *4455 Paradise Rd. (at Harmon Ave.).* ☎ *800/HRD-ROCK (473-7625) or 702/693-5000. www.hardrockhotel.com. 1,500 units. Doubles $129 & up. AE, DC, MC, V. Map p 124.*

★ Harrah's Las Vegas
MID-STRIP   A dated but adequate facility, best occupied if you can get a good rate, and ultimately acceptable because of its superconvenient mid-Strip location. The rooms are pedestrian but functional, and there are several good restaurants, a lively (and often rewarding) casino, and some fun shows like Mac King (p 117). *3475 Las Vegas Blvd. S. (btw. Flamingo & Spring Mountain roads).* ☎ *800/HARRAHS (427-7247)*

One of the handsome suites inside the huge MGM Grand, one of the largest hotels in the world.

The stylish rooms inside The Mirage are small, but the hotel itself impresses thanks to a vast array of amenities.

or 702/369-5000. www.harrahslv. com. 2,579 units. Doubles $79 & up. AE, DC, DISC, MC, V. Map p 123.

★★ **JW Marriott** WEST OF THE STRIP   One of the few true resorts in Las Vegas, this gorgeous and serene oasis on the northwest side of town has luxuriously comfortable rooms, lushly landscaped grounds, and a world-class spa on its amenities list. Of course if it's too quiet, the casino just down the hall out of earshot can provide you with all the excitement you need. *221 N. Rampart Blvd. (at Summerlin Pkwy.).* ☎ 877/869-8777 or 702/869-7777. www.jwlasvegasresort.com. 548 units. Doubles $129 & up. AE, DC, DISC, MC, V. Map p 124.

★★ **LVH: Las Vegas Hotel & Casino** EAST OF THE STRIP   Formerly known as the Las Vegas Hilton (it's a long, unimportant story), this is still a top choice for the businessperson, because, unlike most other hotels in town, this one is more about business than pleasure. Rooms are somewhat more geared to working customers than playing customers, though the smallish casino is a good retreat. There is plenty of on-site recreation, but the hotel's main draw is its proximity to the Convention Center. *3000 Paradise Rd. (at Riviera Blvd.).* ☎ 888/ 732-7117 or 702/732-5111. www. thelvh.com. 3,174 units. Doubles $49

& up. AE, DC, DISC, MC, V. Map p 124.

★★ **kids Luxor Las Vegas** SOUTH STRIP   The inexplicable decision to turn what was formerly a deliciously goofy, Egyptian-themed paradise into a generic cookie-cutter resort sent me into mourning. Rooms inside the pyramid (they couldn't get rid of that!) are small and shower only (and not great if you're tall, thanks to the slanted glass walls). Best of all are the corner rooms, where they plant a Jacuzzi tub right where those slanted windows meet. I prefer the Tower rooms, which are larger and have better bathrooms. *3900 Las Vegas Blvd. S. (btw. Reno & Hacienda aves.).* ☎ 888/777-0188 or 702/262-4000. www.luxor.com. 4,400 units. Doubles $69 & up. AE, DC, DISC, MC, V. Map p 123.

★★ **Main Street Station** DOWNTOWN   One of the best deals in town, this pretty hotel is clean, comfortable, and even kind of sweet, with a late-Victorian San Francisco style. Superior air circulation makes the public areas much less smoky than those at its counterparts. Rooms are unexpectedly stylish and cozy, though the location next to the freeway and train tracks means that noise can be an issue for some. It's only a couple of blocks from the action on Fremont Street. *200 N. Main St. (btw. Fremont St. & I-95).*

800/713-8993 or 702/387-1896. www.mainstreetcasino.com. 406 units. Doubles $59 & up. AE, DC, DISC, MC, V. Map p 125.

★★ kids **Mandalay Bay** SOUTH STRIP   It doesn't really live up to its South Asian theme, but this beauty is one of my personal favorites. It's oddly kid-friendly, thanks to the big rooms and bathrooms (dig those marble bathtubs), its famous pool area (including beach, wave pool, and lazy river), and the ability to access your room without traversing the casino. A great assortment of restaurants, clubs, and bars will please adults, thus rounding out the demographic appeal. *3950 Las Vegas Blvd. S. (at Hacienda Ave.).* 877/632-7800 or 702/632-7000. www.mandalaybay.com. *3,309 units. Doubles $99 & up. AE, DC, DISC, MC, V. Map p 123.*

★★★ **Mandarin Oriental Las Vegas** SOUTH STRIP   The Four Seasons has a worthy Strip competitor in this luxe boutique hotel. The public areas' sleek and subtle Asian theme carries over into the state-of-the-art and large guest rooms (the bathrooms notably have free-standing tubs). Toss in gourmet dining

The Monte Carlo's posh boutique Hotel 32 is worth the extra bucks.

and a bi-level spa, and you have a welcome respite smack in the middle of the Strip. And if you must gamble, there's a casino next door. *3752 Las Vegas Blvd. S. (at Harmon Ave.).* 888/881-9578 or 702/590-8888. www.mandarinoriental.com/lasvegas. *392 units. Doubles $375 & up. AE, DC, DISC, MC, V. Map p 123.*

★★ **MGM Grand Hotel & Casino** SOUTH STRIP   A 360-degree property overhaul turned what was handsome but bland into sparkly, modern, and hip from the accommodations to the massive casino and beyond. They couldn't make the rooms bigger, but they sure did make them sassier, with contemporary furnishings, plus high-tech gizmos galore. MGM also has a variety of restaurant options and the largest pool area apart from Mandalay Bay, complete with a lazy river. *3799 Las Vegas Blvd. S. (at Tropicana Ave.).* 800/880-0880 or 702/891-7777. www.mgmgrand.com. *5,034 units. Doubles $99 & up. AE, DC, DISC, MC, V. Map p 123.*

★★ **The Mirage** MID-STRIP   Its pretty rooms are now running with the Vegas generic upscale pack (though the bathrooms are small), but the rest of the hotel is chic and Asian sleek. The raintorest entrance is still one of the most impressive hotel welcomes in town, and the pool area is a tropical marvel complete with water slide. Good restaurants, terrific bars, and hot clubs complete the mix. *3400 Las Vegas Blvd. S. (btw. Flamingo & Spring Mountain roads).* 800/627-6667 or 702/791-7111. www.mirage.com. *3,044 units. Doubles $109 & up. AE, DC, DISC, MC, V. Map p 123.*

★ **Monte Carlo Resort & Casino** SOUTH STRIP   Though its name evokes classic and classy, beyond the crystal chandelier–filled lobby this is a fairly generic hotel.

A chic Red Room at Paris Las Vegas.

Rooms are merely average, though the Hotel 32 boutique level is worth the splurge. The touted pool area allows for frolicsome fun but is now overshadowed by other versions on the Strip. Affordable rates and a great location may make the general lack of sparkle unimportant. *3770 Las Vegas Blvd. S. (btw. Flamingo Rd. & Tropicana Ave.).* ☎ *800/311-8999 or 702/730-7777. www.montecarlo.com. 3,002 units. Doubles $99 & up. AE, DC, DISC, MC, V. Map p 123.*

★★★ M Resort Spa & Casino SOUTH OF THE STRIP Famous for hosting Bravo's *Top Chef: Las Vegas*, M Resort is a hike from the Strip, but if you don't mind the commute, this sophisticated "boutique" property (in Vegas that means 400 rooms) has everything you could ask for in a casino resort: large comfortable rooms, floor-to-ceiling views, giant tubs, two flatscreen TVs (one in the bathroom mirror!), and reasonable rates. *12300 Las Vegas Blvd. S., Henderson.* ☎ *877/673-7678 or 702/797-1000. www.themresort.com. 390 units. Doubles $99 & up. AE, DISC, MC, V. Map p 124.*

★★ kids New York–New York Hotel & Casino SOUTH STRIP This chaotic location was a bit more tolerable when the heavy Manhattan theme made it more of an attraction. Now that the spectacle has been toned down (on the inside at least) into more of the new Vegas blandness, the inconveniences are starting to outweigh the pleasures. The guest rooms are middlebrow sophisticated, but nothing startling, and can vary dramatically in size and shape; they're also overpriced when compared with what you get at other spots on the Strip. *3790 Las Vegas Blvd. S. (at Tropicana Ave.).* ☎ *800/693-6763 or 702/740-6969. www.newyorknewyork.com. 2,023*

The lobby of the sophisticated M Resort Spa & Casino; a stay here is worth the commute to the Strip.

units. *Doubles $79 & up. AE, DC, DISC, MC, V. Map p 123.*

★ kids **The Orleans** SOUTH STRIP   Easily overlooked because it's sort of in the middle of nowhere off the Strip, The Orleans has no fancy reputation to help draw attention. It's still worth considering because you can often find bargain rates on the surprisingly roomy accommodations, which sport the occasional sweet Victorian touch. Free shuttle services to the Strip help with the isolation, as do the 70-lane bowling alley (open really late) and 18-screen multiplex. *4500 W. Tropicana Ave. (west of the Strip & I-15).* ☎ *800/ORLEANS (675-3267) or 702/365-7111. www.orleans casino.com. 1,886 units. Doubles $49 & up. AE, DC, DISC, MC, V. Map p 123.*

★ kids **Palace Station** WEST OF THE STRIP   Although it is just a stone's throw from the Strip geographically, this pleasantly middle-of-the-road property is miles away in terms of price. Rooms in the main tower are modern but small while those in the pool-side motel units are best left to those who can't afford something better. Still, the costs here are bargain basement from the rooms to the restaurants to the casino, so it may just be worth it to skip a few niceties. *2411 W. Sahara Ave. (west of the Strip & I-15).* ☎ *800/678-2846 or 702/367-2411. www.palacestation.com. 1,029 units. Doubles $29 & up. AE, DC, DISC, MC, V. Map p 124.*

★ **The Palazzo** MID-STRIP   This expansion of The Venetian functions as its own hotel, with its own massive grand lobby, own restaurants, and own (pricey) rates. Its "suites" are virtually identical to its sister property, but the rest of the resort is nowhere near as interesting, verging on bland. If the rates are the same (which they usually are) go for The Venetian instead. *3325 Las Vegas Blvd. S.* ☎ *877/883 6423 or 702/607-7777. www.palazzo.com. 3,000 units. Doubles $179 & up. AE, DC, DISC, MC, V. Map p 123.*

The Vegas Hotel Experience

Vegas hotels are not your average hotel experience. Most hotels are content to be located near attractions. Vegas hotels *are* the attraction. Or they bring attractions into the hotel. Or both. Expect access to all kinds of unusual goodies, from happening nightclubs to roller coasters to, oh yes, casinos. But hotel size brings its own issues; 3,000-room (or more) resorts simply do not have the kind of service one expects at a true resort. Personal attention can be spotty, maintenance can be a bit slow (that stain on the carpet will likely stay there for some time), and it's highly likely you will hear plumbing and other noises emanating from nearby rooms. The final caveat is the hidden price. Most hotels charge extra for almost everything beyond bed and bath, including gym use, Wi-Fi use, pool cabana use—it all adds up. Many casino hotels now audaciously automatically add that charge to the room rate as a mandatory "resort fee." Only true resorts, such as the Four Seasons, have inclusive room prices. Factor that in when making your decision.

A palazzo bedroom at the Rio, whose accommodations are among the largest in Vegas.

★★ Palms Casino Resort

MID-STRIP   Still one of the hipper hotels, and a bit daunting because of that. But look past the zero-body-fat types lining up to get into one of the many happening clubs and bars, and you will find a good, cheap food court; a multiplex; and a fine child-care facility. It's not the first place I would suggest for a family, but those elements might sway you. Rooms have especially comfortable beds and lots of pizazz. Try to get a high-level unit for some of the best views of the city. *4321 W. Flamingo Rd. (just west of I-15).* ☎ *866/942-7777 or 702/942-7777. www.palms. com. 703 units. Doubles $99 & up. AE, DC, DISC, MC, V. Map p 123.*

★★ Paris Las Vegas Casino

Resort MID-STRIP   Now here's a hotel that remains dedicated to its theme—an element of Vegas that is vanishing, to my despair. *Merci!* It's also perfectly located on the Strip. Regular rooms are a little generically pretty (though the bathtubs are satisfyingly deep), but the Red Rooms are done up in sort of a masculine

French bordello and are worth the extra price. *3655 Las Vegas Blvd. S.* ☎ *888/BONJOUR (266-5687) or 702/946-7000. www.parislv.com. 2,916 units. Doubles $119 & up. AE, DC, DISC, MC, V. Map p 123.*

★★ Planet Hollywood Resort

& Casino MID-STRIP   Those hoping for kitsch will be disappointed in this hotel's classy and clubby design, which has obliterated all traces of its previous incarnation as the Aladdin. And the chain's memorabilia angle works well in the very comfy rooms, which all have a movie or entertainment theme (needless to say, the Judy Garland room has a very different vibe than the *Pulp Fiction* one). *3667 Las Vegas Blvd. S.* ☎ *866/919-7472 or 702/785-5555. www.planethollywoodresort.com. 2,567 units. Doubles $99 & up. AE, DC, DISC, MC, V. Map p 123.*

★★ Plaza Las Vegas DOWN-

TOWN   A multimillion-dollar make-over turned a dump into one of Downtown's most desirable gems. The rooms got brand-new furnishings from a bankrupt hotel project, which makes them the nicest in the area—much nicer than they should be at these bargain-basement prices. An updated casino, restaurants, and entertainment offerings complete a great new package. *1 Main St.* ☎ *800/634-6575 or 702/ 386-2110. www.plazahotelcasino. com. 1,000 units. Doubles $39 & up. AE, DC, DISC, MC, V. Map p 125.*

★★★ Red Rock Resort SUM-

MERLIN   A fantastic resort—right across from the eponymous red rocks themselves—that's not that many minutes from the Strip, giving you both privacy and ready access. It's one of the best settings in Vegas. Rooms are striking, the comfy beds will make you disinclined to get up (especially with the big flatscreen TV in front of you), and the bathrooms are positively sprawling. The pool attracts celebrities pretending they want to keep a low profile. The gym and spa are not worth the mandatory additional price. *11011 W. Charleston Blvd.* ☎ *866/767-7773 or 702/797-7625. www.redrockstation.com. 800 units. Rooms $139 & up (up to 4 people). AE, DC, DISC, MC, V. Map p 124.*

★ **Rio All-Suite Hotel & Casino** MID-STRIP   Still some of the largest rooms in Vegas, though no more "suites" than at The Venetian (you just get a living/sitting area along with your bedroom area) and outstripped in style by so many others. Because the place is also hectic—it feels like spring break all the time and bringing kids is not encouraged—and located off the Strip, it's not a first-choice venue. *3700 Las Vegas Blvd. S. (just west of I-15).* ☎ *888/752-9746 or 702/777-7777. www.riolv.com. 2,582 units. Doubles $99 & up. AE, DC, DISC, MC, V. Map p 123.*

★★ **kids South Point Hotel & Casino** SOUTH OF THE STRIP   This "locals" joint is lower profile and south of the Strip. But given the size of the rooms here, the frills (squishy beds, flatscreen TVs), and the access to plenty of on-site entertainment (movie theaters, bowling alley, a first-rate equestrian center, budget food choices)—all for a much lower price than its on-the-Strip competition—the (rather minor) distance from the main action hardly matters. *9777 Las Vegas Blvd. S.* ☎ *866/796-7111 or 702/796-7111. www.southpointcasino.com. 650 units. Doubles $79 & up. AE, DC, DISC, MC, V. Map p 124.*

★ **kids Stratosphere Las Vegas Hotel & Casino** NORTH STRIP

Think of this place as a motel, with prices to match, and the difference between its humble yet adequate rooms and the much more lavish numbers down the Strip won't bother you a bit. The very friendly service makes it that much more attractive. You will need a car if you stay here because it's much too far to walk to the main Strip action or to Downtown. *2000 Las Vegas Blvd. S. (btw. St. Louis & Baltimore aves.).* ☎ *800/99-TOWER (998-6937) or 702/ 380-7777. www.stratospherehotel. com. 2,444 units. Doubles $49 & up. AE, DC, DISC, MC, V. Map p 124.*

★ **Terrible's** EAST OF THE STRIP This unexpected bargain isn't terrible at all (its namesake is convenience store and gas station magnate Ed "Terrible" Herbst). And it's near the Strip! Rooms are as basic as can be, though accommodations in the tower have fresher furnishings and flatscreen TVs. The pool area is particularly nice for a budget operation. *4100 Paradise Rd. (at Flamingo Rd.).* ☎ *800/640-9777 or 702/733-7000. www.terriblescasinos.com. 325 units. Doubles $39 & up. AE, DC, DISC, MC, V. Map p 124.*

One of the sleek suites at THEhotel at Mandalay Bay, arguably the best place to stay in Las Vegas.

The Westin Casuarina's lack of pizazz makes it a somewhat bland option, but the Heavenly Beds do make for a good night's sleep.

★★★ THEhotel at Mandalay Bay

SOUTH STRIP   Without a doubt one of the best hotels on the Strip. It's sophisticated, with its Manhattan-style sleekly contemporary lobby; and it has large rooms, each a dark-wood and gleaming black one-bedroom suite, complete with two flatscreen TVs and a deep soaking tub. Its separate-from-but-attached-to Mandalay Bay location means you can have your getaway and gamble too. *3950 Las Vegas Blvd. S.* ☎ *877/632-7800 or 702/632-7777. www.mandalaybay.com. 1,120 units. Suites $149 & up. AE, DC, DISC, MC, V. Map p 123.*

★★ Treasure Island

MID-STRIP   Strip away the TI's original theme (pirates and treasure) and what you have left is a more bland experience, but one that now caters to a more middle-class market. Good-size rooms with some unexpected careful details (including decent art on the walls and large soaking tubs in the bathroom) are superior to those at the neighboring Mirage, even if that hotel is more interesting overall. The pool is a disappointment. *3300 Las Vegas Blvd. S. (at Spring Mountain Rd.).* ☎ *800/944-7444 or 702/894-7111. www.treasureisland.com. 2,885 units. Doubles $89 & up. AE, DC, DISC, MC, V. Map p 123.*

★★ Tropicana Las Vegas

SOUTH STRIP   In a stunning reversal of fortune, the dusty and dingy Tiffany of the Strip has gotten a new lease on life with a bright and sunny South Beach makeover. If you haven't been here in a while, you won't recognize the joint. Rooms are beachy pleasures with rattan furnishings and plantation shutters, while the all-new casino, restaurants, and pool area give the place a festive and fresh atmosphere. *3801 Las Vegas Blvd. S. (at Tropicana Ave.).* ☎ *888/826-8767 or 702/739-2222. www.troplv.com. 1,375 units. Doubles $59 & up. AE, DC, DISC, MC, V. Map p 123.*

Sign Up!

Most Vegas hotels offer discounted packages and room rates to those who friend them on Twitter or Facebook. It's a "friends with benefits" arrangement that you should definitely take advantage of.

The huge guest rooms inside The Venetian are among the best in the city.

★ **Trump International Hotel Las Vegas** NORTH STRIP This huge, nongaming tower parlays the opulence that The Donald is known for, with gilded windows, lots of marble, and ubiquitous crystal chandeliers. Plush and sizable studio "suites" boast Jacuzzi-style tubs, two flatscreen TVs, and small kitchens, complete with coffeemakers—a Sin City rarity. And if you find yourself missing a casino, there are plenty within walking distance. *2000 N. Fashion Show Dr. (at Las Vegas Blvd.).* ☎ *702/982-0000. www. trumplasvegashotel.com. 1,282 units. Studio suites $99 & up. AE, DISC, MC, V. Map p 124.*

★★ **Vdara Hotel & Spa** SOUTH STRIP A luxury, nonsmoking, non-gaming all-suite hotel right in the middle of the Strip? And it's seriously committed to sustainability? It's a winner in my book. The earth-toned suites come in various sizes, all with minikitchens (stove tops and

The lobby at CityCenter's Vdara Hotel & Spa.

dishwashers!), deep soaking tubs, and the high-tech wizardry one expects in the latest crop of Vegas hotels. It just might be the most restful of the CityCenter properties, though it's right on Bellagio's back

Playing the Hotel Rate Game

Hotel rates in Las Vegas fluctuate more wildly than the stock market and can be just as hard to predict. Rates in this chapter are the listed minimum rack rates (without the 9%–10% hotel tax included), but the same room at the same hotel can range from $50 to $300 to a lot more (or a lot less), depending on when you book. You will, for example, always pay top dollar around New Year's, on weekends, and when a major convention is in town. Take the prices I list with a grain of salt and always do your homework. Check out the going rates on the major hotel booking sites (Expedia.com, Travelocity.com, and Travelaxe.com) and always check the websites of the hotels themselves for available discount packages and rates.

Also note that rates listed here are for double occupancy only; most Vegas hotels usually charge extra (sometimes as much as $35 per person, per night) for another person in the room, even if the extra guest happens to be your child. If you're bringing kids along, always ask about the hotel's policy when booking.

The nifty rooms inside the Wynn Las Vegas come with all sorts of bells and whistles, but they're also very pricey for what you get.

doorstep if you need a Vegas fix. *2600 W. Harmon Ave. (at Las Vegas Blvd. S.). ☎ 866/745-7767 or 702/590-2767. www.vdara.com. 1,495 units. Suites $159 & up. AE, DISC, MC, V. Map p 123.*

★★ **The Venetian** MID-STRIP Some of the largest and best rooms on the Strip, though not precisely the "suites" they advertise. Instead, it's one big space encompassing both bedroom and sunken living room, with plenty of stately touches and marble bathrooms with double sinks. The Venezia tower (worth the extra cash) has its own entrance and more of a Ritz-Carlton vibe. The immense property can be hard to navigate. *3355 Las Vegas Blvd. S. ☎ 877/883-6423 or 702/414-1000. www.venetian.com. 4,029 units. Doubles $149 & up. AE, DC, DISC, MC, V. Map p 123.*

★ **The Westin Casuarina Las Vegas Hotel, Casino & Spa** MID-STRIP   Brand-name reliability means those Westin Heavenly Beds—though, oddly, not the best beds in town—and various features

that make this more business traveler–friendly than pleasure seeker appropriate. The gym is free, the casino small and forgettable. It has more pizazz than other chain hotels in town, but so much less than the powerhouse hotels that the prices seem a bit of a cheat. *160 E. Flamingo Rd. ☎ 866/837-4215 or 702/836-9775. www.starwoodhotels. com. 825 units. Doubles $139 & up. AE, DC, DISC, MC, V. Map p 123.*

★★ **Wynn Las Vegas** NORTH STRIP   An adult luxury resort on steroids. The enormous rooms are full of nifty touches—high-thread-count linens, Warhol silk-screens, curtains that operate with a push button, long tubs in the bathroom, fancy amenities—and the rest of the property is equally upscale. The prices are sky-high, but if you're looking for a Vegas-style luxury experience, this is one of your best options. *3131 Las Vegas Blvd. S. (at the corner of Sands Ave.). ☎ 888/ 320-9966 or 702/770-7100. www. wynnlasvegas.com. 3,933 units. Doubles $159 & up. AE, DC, DISC, MC, V. Map p 124.* ●

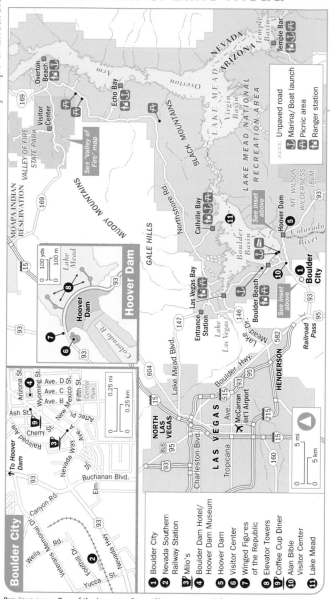

Hoover Dam & Lake Mead

Hoover Dam

Boulder City

- ① Boulder City
- ② Nevada Southern Railway Station
- ③ Milo's
- ④ Boulder Dam Hotel/ Hoover Dam Museum
- ⑤ Hoover Dam
- ⑥ Visitor Center
- ⑦ Winged Figures of the Republic
- ⑧ Elevator Towers
- ⑨ Coffee Cup Diner
- ⑩ Alan Bible Visitor Center
- ⑪ Lake Mead

Unpaved road · · · · · ·
Marina/Boat launch
Picnic area
Ranger station

Previous page: One of the immense Seven Sisters, giant rock formations set inside the Valley of Fire.

The architectural and engineering marvel that is Hoover Dam is probably the major reason there is a Vegas today (those lights on the Strip need lots of power). It's one of the world's major electrical-generating plants, but it's also a wonder of Art Deco design and a remarkable combination of beauty and function. It's also responsible for the creation of the 110-mile-wide (177km) Lake Mead, an unexpected recreational oasis smack in the middle of the desert. START: **From Las Vegas, take U.S. 93 S. U.S. 93 becomes U.S. 93/95 S, which then becomes the Nevada Highway.**

1 ★★ **Boulder City.** This charming small town (originally built by the Bureau of Reclamation to house the workers building Hoover Dam, originally called Boulder Dam) is all the more unexpected because it's only 20 miles (32km) from Vegas. It doesn't hurt that this is the only place in Nevada where it's not legal to gamble. Wander through the adorable downtown area (construction and growth are strictly regulated to maintain its character) as a Mayberry antidote to the "bright lights, big city" atmosphere, which despite its proximity seems another lifetime away. ⏱ *30 min. Off Nevada Hwy. www.bouldercity.com.*

2 ★ 🧒 **Nevada Southern Railway Station.** This seasonal train ride offers visitors the chance to take a 3-mile (4.8km) journey along a historic train route (built in 1931 as a supply route for the Hoover Dam) aboard refurbished 1911 Pullman cars. A can't-miss for train buffs and a sweet outing for everyone else. ⏱ *45 min. Allow 15 min. before departure time to buy tickets & choose a seat. Reservations are unnecessary. 600 Yucca St., Boulder City.* ☎ *702/486-5933. www.nevadasouthern.com. Admission $10 adults, $9 seniors 65 & over, $5 kids 12 & under. Trains depart Feb–Dec Sat–Sun 10am, 11:30am, 1pm & 2:30pm from Boulder City.*

Recharge your own dam power with a healthy salad, cheese plate, or glass of wine at **3** **Milo's Cellar.** Dine indoors or alfresco and soak in Boulder City's small-town charm. *538 Nevada Hwy., Boulder City.* ☎ *702/293-9540. $.*

Lake Mead is known for both its scenery and its outdoor recreational opportunities.

❹ Boulder Dam Hotel/Hoover Dam Museum. This still-active hotel is set in a Dutch-colonial-style building built to house VIPs visiting the dam construction. The structure also holds a museum that neatly explains why the dam and related construction projects represented virtually the only economic possibility for the area during the Depression. The great emphasis on the human-interest element of construction makes this a good counterpart to the more engineering-oriented exhibit at the dam itself. ⏱ *30 min. 1305 Arizona St., Boulder City. Hotel* ☎ *702/293-3510. www. boulderdamhotel.com. Museum* ☎ *702/294-1988. www.bcmha.org. Admission $2 adults, $1 seniors & kids. Open Mon–Sat 10am–5pm. Closed New Year's Day, Thanksgiving & Christmas.*

Take U.S. 93 S to the Nevada-Arizona border. Pass the turnoff for Lake Mead, and as you near the dam, you'll see the parking structure on your left. Parking is $7, cash only. *Note:* This drive can get very backed up on Sunday and at the end of holiday weekends, so if you must visit on those days, go early in the morning or late in the day.

❺ ★★★ Hoover Dam. The star of the show and a wonder of the modern engineering world. You may not realize how beautiful a monolithic structure can be until you behold the dam. Note how the design reflects the Art Deco period so influenced by the post–King Tut tomb–discovery Egyptian revival. Construction on this National Historic Landmark lasted from 1931 to 1936 and, once completed, the face of the Southwest was changed forever. Anytime someone turns on a light switch in California or Nevada,

The huge Winged Figures of the Republic *guard the entrance to Hoover Dam on the Nevada side.*

they can thank the Hoover Dam engineers and the workers who gave so much (more than 100 people died during construction) to make it come true. *See* ❻.

❻ Visitor Center. All the information you could possibly want about Hoover Dam is contained in this three-level exhibition and information center. Videos, interactive displays, photos, and more help illustrate what a massive feat this was. Two tours are available. The **Powerplant Tour** is a partly docent-guided, partly self-guided tour of the dam, including a 500-foot (152m) elevator ride down to one of the generators, a journey through a tunnel drilled through rock, and a trip to the observation deck overlooking Lake Mead. The **Hoover Dam Tour** (worth the extra time and expense) travels deeper into the dam's rocky hallways to view its inner workings. ⏲ *2 hr. Off U.S. 93 S.* ☎ *866/730-9097 or 702/494-2517. www.usbr.gov/lc/ hooverdam. Powerplant tour $11 adults, $9 seniors & military, $9 children 4–16, free for kids 2 & under & military in uniform. Dam tour $30 per person. Open 9am–6pm daily except Thanksgiving and Christmas. Last admission 5:15pm.*

❼ ★★ Winged Figures of the Republic. Should you opt to walk the dam on your own, stop on the Nevada side to pay homage to these 30-foot-high (9.1m) winged mythological figures representing the higher nature of all humankind (they were designed by sculptor Oskar J. W. Hansen). The bronze-shelled statues were originally erected, along with an astrological star chart, as a memorial to higher intelligence, but after World War II, they were rededicated to the men who built the dam, plus their little mascot dog. *Off U.S. 93 S. Free admission.*

❽ ★ Elevator Towers. Exhibits on local flora and fauna are found on the exterior of the dam's elevator towers, thus combining nature and industry. Note how the clock on the tower on the Nevada side gives one time, and the one on the Arizona side gives another; the latter is on Mountain Standard Time, 1 hour ahead of the former—except during daylight saving time, because Arizona does not observe it. *Viewing the exterior is free. See ❺.*

Get a cup of joe or a burger at the classic greasy spoon **❾ Coffee Cup Diner.** *512 Nevada Hwy., Boulder City. www.worldfamouscoffee cup.com.* ☎ *702/294-0517. $.*

Take U.S. 93 N to Lakeshore Drive/NV 166.

❿ Alan Bible Visitor Center. Staffed by eager, knowledgeable locals, Lake Mead's main visitor center is a great place to pick up information on area recreational activities. Do explore its small but interesting exhibits on local nature and history. It's also here that you pay your fee for the Lake Mead scenic drive (see ⓫). ⏲ *20 min. on U.S. 93 at NV 166 (4 miles/6.4km northeast of Boulder City).* ☎ *702/293-8990. Free admission. Open daily 8:30am–4:30pm. Closed New Year's Day, Thanksgiving & Christmas.*

Follow the scenic Lakeshore Drive/NV 166 into Lake Mead National Recreational Area.

⓫ ★★★ Lake Mead. Created in 1935 by the building of Hoover Dam (and named for the commissioner of the Bureau of Reclamation at the time), Lake Mead is the largest manmade lake in the United States. The best way to view the lake (whose beauty isn't lessened by its artificial origins) is to take its 30-mile (48km) scenic drive. Expect colorful desert landscape, panoramic views, and mountain vistas. There are several beaches and campgrounds along the way, with plenty of opportunities for various recreational activities. The water is a bit chilly and the beaches are rocky; so the lake is used more for fishing and sailing purposes than swimming. ⏲ *1½ hr., longer if you indulge in the recreational facilities. www.nps.gov/lame. Admission $10 per vehicle, $5 per person on foot or bike. Open daily 24 hrs. (some spots in the park have shorter hours so inquire at the visitor center, see ❿).*

The scenic route becomes Northshore Road, and from here you can head to the Valley of Fire or take U.S. 93/95 N back to Las Vegas.

Valley of Fire State Park

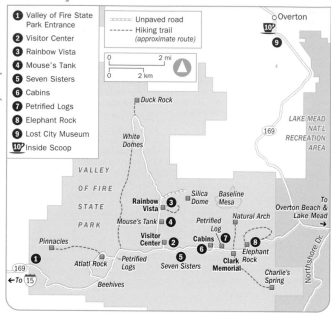

1. Valley of Fire State Park Entrance
2. Visitor Center
3. Rainbow Vista
4. Mouse's Tank
5. Seven Sisters
6. Cabins
7. Petrified Logs
8. Elephant Rock
9. Lost City Museum
10. Inside Scoop

===== Unpaved road
----- Hiking trail
(approximate route)

0 — 2 mi
0 — 2 km

F or those who think a desert is brown, flat, and feature-less, the Valley of Fire comes as a shock. This almost other-worldly tundra of brilliant red sandstone formations was created 150 million years ago as wind twisted and shaped the landscape into what could be called a Jurassic zoo of creaturelike configurations. The man-made structures that make Las Vegas a marvel have noth-ing on what nature can do, given enough time. **START: From Las Vegas, take I-15 N to exit 75 (Valley of Fire turnoff); trip time is 1 hour. For a more scenic route, take I-15 N, then take Lake Mead Boulevard East to Northshore Road/NV 167 and proceed to the Valley of Fire exit; trip time is 1½ hours. Be sure to bring plenty of water.**

1 Valley of Fire State Park Entrance. As you enter the 25,000-acre (10,117-hectare) park (Nevada's oldest state park) on a windy little road, the first major sight will be on your left. The Atlatl Rock was a basic training camp for Native American tribes in the area (an *atlatl* was a stick used to throw spears) and is full of old petro-glyphs. Men came here for coming-of-age ceremonies and to learn hunting and survival skills. ⏱ *5 min. 60 miles (97km) northeast of Las Vegas, Overton. http://parks.nv.gov/ vf.htm. Admission $6 per car. Open daily sunrise–sunset.*

2 Visitor Center. Accessed from the Old Arrowhead road (the first car road running from Los Angeles to Salt Lake City), this is where you can purchase various materials concerning information on the park, talk to park rangers, and check out some small displays on the local landscape. Be sure to pick up a map before you head into the park. 🕐 *15 min. On NV 169 (6 miles/9.7km west of Northshore Rd.).* ☎ *702/397-2088. Open daily 8:30am–4:30pm. Closed Christmas.*

3 Rainbow Vista. From the visitor center, drive through this palette of multicolored sandstone, all the colors of the spectrum splashed down to the earth. The drive dead-ends at the pure white silica domes. At this point, you can take a hiking trail to the site where the bawdy western *The Professionals* (1966) with Burt Lancaster and Lee Marvin was filmed. A bit of the set is still there. 🕐 *1 hr. round-trip for gardens; 1 hr. for hike.*

4 Mouse's Tank. Take a hike down a deep sandy wash (no sandals, shoes only) with many well-executed petroglyphs lining the way. The glyphs are the most ancient and historic in the Southwest, thousands of years old—even the local Paiute people don't know who did them. The titular Mouse's Tank (named for a fugitive who hid out here in the 1890s) lies at the end of the hike and is a natural sandstone bowl *tanaha,* which is a hole in the desert that fills up when it rains (don't come here after a storm), but it's something of a let-down postpetroglyphs. 🕐 *30 min.*

5 Seven Sisters. Named after an Indian legend that describes how the seven stars of the Big Dipper were created, these girls are seven huge red-rock formations of Mesozoic sandstone. It was originally an ancient sand dune that hardened and cracked over the years, and erosion has separated it into seven distinct shapes with one little brother in the middle.

From Valley of Fire, follow NV 169 southeast toward Scenic Loop Road. Make a left to stay on NV 169 into Overton. NV 169 becomes South Moapa Valley Boulevard. Trip time is 30 minutes.

Valley of Fire State Park is filled with beautiful and eerie rock formations, including the famed Elephant Rock.

An ancient pueblo village is one of the top attractions at the Lost City Museum.

Heat Alert

Daytime temperatures in the Valley of Fire can reach 120°F (49°C) in the height of summer. This tour is best done in late fall, early spring, or early winter, when the climate is more tolerable. Even during those times, carry at least a gallon of water per person.

6 Cabins. These native stone structures are now used for picnicking (bring fixings along with you to the park), but were originally constructed in the 1930s by the Civilian Conservation Corps to provide nighttime shelter for weary travelers. It's a good location for taking a breather before hitting the road again.

7 Petrified Logs. These prime examples of fossilized wood have been fenced off to prevent treasure hunters from walking off with them. It's believed that the colorful trunks are the remnants of a forest, whose trees were washed into this area about 225 million years ago.

8 Elephant Rock. This red stone formation is easily accessed via a short trail from the main park road. And it really does look like the head of a giant pachyderm. Can we say prime photo op?

9 Lost City Museum. A sweet little museum focusing on an ancient Anasazi village (named Pueblo Grande de Nevada because the Pueblo Indians occupied it after the Anasazi disappeared) discovered in the area in 1924. Along with exhibits whose contents date back some 12,000 years, there are some displays on the area's 19th-century Mormon settlers. ⏱ *30 min. 721 S. Moapa Valley Blvd./NV 169, Overton.* ☎ *702/397-2193. http://museums. nevadaculture.org. Admission $5 adults, free for kids 18 & under. Open Thurs–Sun 8:30am–4:30pm. Closed New Year's Day, Thanksgiving & Christmas.*

A sweet old-fashioned ice-cream parlor, **10 Inside Scoop** also offers soups, sandwiches, and box lunches for picnics inside the park. *395 S. Moapa Valley Blvd.* ☎ *702/ 397-2055. $.*

To get back to Vegas, head northeast on South Moapa Valley Boulevard/NV 169 toward South Pioneer Road. Merge onto I-15 S to Las Vegas. ●

The
Savvy Gambler

Playing the **Games**

As you walk through the labyrinthine twists and turns of a casino floor, your attention will likely be dragged to the various games and, your interest piqued, your fingers may begin to twitch in anticipation of hitting it big. Before you put your money on the line, it's imperative to know the rules of the game you want to play.

Some casinos offer free gambling lessons at scheduled times on weekdays. This provides a risk-free environment for you to learn the games that tickle your fancy. Casinos may follow their lessons with low-stakes game play, enabling you to put your newfound knowledge to the test at small risk. During those instructional sessions, and even when playing on your own, dealers in most casinos will be more than happy to answer any questions you might have. Remember, the casino doesn't need to trick you into losing your money . . . the odds are already in their favor across the board; that's why it's called gambling.

Another rule of thumb: Take a few minutes to watch a game being played in order to familiarize yourself with the motions and lingo. Then go back and reread this chapter—things will make a lot more sense at that point. Good luck!

Players' Clubs

If you gamble, it definitely pays to join a players' club. These so-called clubs are designed to attract and keep customers in a given casino by providing incentives: meals, shows, discounts on rooms, gifts, tournament invitations, discounts at hotel shops, VIP treatment, and (more and more) cash rebates. Join a players' club (it doesn't cost a cent to sign up), do some gambling, and you will start getting offers—discounted or free rooms; show tickets; and even free slot or table game play. (This is one way to beat high hotel rates in Vegas.) Of course, your rewards are often greater if you play in just one casino, but your mobility is limited.

When you join a players' club (inquire at the casino desk), you're given something that looks like a credit card, which you must insert into an ATM-like device whenever you play. Yes, many casinos even have them for the tables as well as the machines. (Don't forget to retrieve your card when you leave the machine, as I sometimes do.) The device tracks your play and computes bonus points.

Which players' club should you join? Actually, you should join one at any casino where you play because even the act of joining usually entitles you to some benefits. It's convenient to concentrate play where you're staying; if you play a great deal, a casino hotel's players' club benefits may be a factor in your accommodations choice. Consider, though, particularly if you aren't a high roller, the players' clubs Downtown. You get more bang for your buck because you don't have to spend as much to start raking in the goodies.

Previous page: There are a myriad number of card games that you can play in Las Vegas.

Another advantage is to join a players' club that covers many hotels under the same corporate umbrella. For example, MGM Resorts International runs The Mirage, Bellagio, MGM Grand, and more, and their players' club offers discounts and point awards at all of their properties.

One way to judge a players' club is by the quality of service you receive when you enroll. Personnel should politely answer all your

questions (for instance, is nickel play included, and is there a time limit for earning required points?) and be able to tell you exactly how many points you need for various bonuses.

Maximizing your players' club profits and choosing the club that's best for you is a complex business. To get into it in depth, see **www. lasvegasadvisor.com**. Also visit the sites for the individual casinos, many of which allow you to join their clubs online.

Baccarat

The ancient game of baccarat, or chemin de fer, is played with eight decks of cards. Firm rules apply, and there is no skill involved other than deciding whether to bet on the bank or the player. No, really—that's all you have to do. The dealer does all the other work. You can essentially stop reading here. Oh, all right, carry on.

Any beginner can play, but check the betting minimum before you sit down, as this tends to be a high-stakes game. The cards are shuffled by the croupier and then placed in a box called the "shoe." Players may wager on "bank" or "player" at any time. Two cards are dealt from the shoe and given to the player who has the largest wager against the bank, and two cards are dealt to the croupier, acting as the bank. If the rules call for a third card, the player or the bank, or both, must take the third card. In the event of a tie, the hand is dealt over. **Note:** The

guidelines that determine if a third card must be drawn (by the player or the bank) are provided at the baccarat table upon request.

The object of the game is to come as close as possible to the number 9. To score the hands, the cards of each hand are totaled and the *last digit* is used. All cards have face value. For example: 10 plus 5 equals 15 (score is 5), 10 plus 4 plus 9 equals 23 (score is 3); 4 plus 3 plus 3 equals 10 (score is 0); and 4 plus 3 plus 2 equals 9 (score is 9). The closest hand to 9 wins.

Each player has a chance to deal the cards. The shoe passes to the player on the right each time the bank loses. If the player wishes, he or she may pass the shoe at any time.

Note: When you bet on the bank and the bank wins, you are charged a 5% commission. This must be paid at the start of a new game or when you leave the table.

Blackjack

The dealer starts the game by dealing each player two cards. In some casinos, they're dealt to the player faceup, in others facedown, but the

dealer always gets one card up and one card down. Everybody plays against the dealer. The object is to get a total that is higher than that of the dealer without exceeding 21. All face cards count as 10; all other number cards, except aces, are counted at their face value. An ace may be counted as 1 or 11, whichever you choose it to be.

Starting at his or her left, the dealer gives additional cards to the players who wish to draw (be "hit") or none to players who wish to "stand" or "hold." If your total is nearer to 21 than the dealer's, you win. If it's less than the dealer's, you lose. Ties are a push and nobody wins. After all the players are satisfied with their cards, the dealer exposes his or her facedown card. If his or her two cards total 16 or less, the dealer must "hit" (draw an additional card) until reaching 17 or more. If the dealer's total exceeds 21, he or she must pay all the players whose hands have not gone "bust." It is important to note here that the blackjack dealer has no choice as to whether he or she should stay or draw. A dealer's decisions are predetermined and known to all the players at the table.

If you're a novice or just rusty, do yourself a favor and buy one of the small laminated cards available in shops all over town that illustrate proper play for every possible hand in blackjack. Even longtime players have been known to pull them out every now and then, and they can save you from making costly errors.

How to Play

Here are eight "rules" for blackjack:

1. Place the number of chips that you want to bet on the betting space on your table.

2. Look at the first two cards the dealer gives to you. If you wish to stand, then wave your hand over your cards, palm down (watch your fellow players), indicating that you don't want any additional cards. If you elect to draw an additional card, you communicate with the dealer by tapping the table with a finger (watch your fellow players).

3. If your total goes over 21, you are bust and lose, even if the dealer also goes bust afterward.

4. If you have 21 in your first two cards (any picture card or 10 with an ace), you've got blackjack. Blackjack should ideally pay off at 3 to 2 (you make $3 for every $2 bet), but many casinos now pay out at the less stellar 6 to 5, especially if you're playing a single deck. **Note:** You won't be paid at all if the dealer also has blackjack, in which case it's a push and nobody wins.

5. If you find a pair in your first two cards (say, two 8s or two aces), you may "split" the pair into two hands and treat each card as the first card dealt in two separate hands. You will need to place an additional bet, equal to your original bet, on the table. The dealer will then deal you a new *second* card to each hand and play commences as described above. **Note:** When you split aces you will receive only one additional card per ace and must stand.

6. After seeing your two starting cards, you have the option to "double down." You place an amount equal to your original bet on the table and you receive only one more card. Doubling down is a strategy to capitalize on a potentially strong hand against the dealer's weaker hand. **Tip:** Some casinos allow you to double down for less than your original bet but this is rare.

7. Anytime the dealer deals himself or herself an ace for the up card, you may insure your hand against the possibility that the down card is a 10 or face card, which would give him or her an automatic blackjack. To insure, you place an

amount up to one-half of your bet on the "insurance" line. If the dealer does have a blackjack, you get paid 2 to 1 on the insurance money while losing your original bet: You break even. If the dealer does not have a blackjack, he or she takes your insurance money and play continues in the normal fashion.

8. **Remember:** The dealer must stand on 17 or more and must hit a hand of 16 or less.

Professional Tips

Advice of the experts in playing blackjack is as follows:

1. *Do not* ask for a card if you have a total of 17 or higher, *ever*.

2. *Do not* ask for a card when you have a total of 12 or more if the dealer has a 2 through 6 showing in his or her up card.

3. *Ask* for a card or more when you have a count of 12 through 16 in your hand if the dealer's up card is a 7, 8, 9, 10, or ace.

There's a lot more to blackjack strategy than the above, of course. So consider this merely as the bare bones of the game. Blackjack is played with a single deck or with multiple decks; if you're looking for a single-deck game, your best bet is to head to a Downtown casino.

A final tip: Avoid insurance bets; they're sucker bait!

Craps

The most exciting casino action is usually found at the craps tables. Betting is frenetic, play is fast-paced, and groups quickly bond while yelling and screaming in response to the action.

The Possible Bets

The craps table is divided into marked areas (Pass, Come, Field, Big 6, Big 8, and so on), where you place your chips to bet. The following are a few simple directions.

PASS LINE A "Pass Line" bet pays even money. If the first roll of the dice adds up to 7 or 11, you win your bet; if the first roll adds up to 2, 3, or 12, you lose your bet. If any other number comes up, it's your

Look, but Don't Touch!

1. **Never touch your cards (or anyone else's),** unless it's specifically stated at the table that you may. While you'll only receive a verbal slap on the wrist if you violate this rule, you *really* don't want to get one.

2. **Players must use hand signals to indicate their wishes to the dealer.** All verbal directions by players will be politely ignored by the dealer, who will remind players to use hand signals. The reason for this is the "Eye in the Sky," the casino's security system, which focuses an "eye" on every table, and must record players' decisions to avoid accusations of misconduct or collusion.

"point." If you roll your point again, you win, but if a 7 comes up again before your point is rolled, you lose.

DON'T PASS LINE Betting on the "Don't Pass Line" is the opposite of betting on the Pass Line. Here, you lose if a 7 or an 11 is thrown on the first roll, and you win if a 2 or a 3 is thrown on the first roll.

If the first roll is 12, however, it's a push (standoff), and nobody wins. If none of these numbers is thrown and you have a point instead, in order for you to win, a 7 will have to be thrown before the point comes up again. A Don't Pass Line bet also pays even money.

COME Betting on "Come" is the same as betting on the Pass Line, but you must bet after the first roll or on any following roll. Again, you'll win on 7 or 11 and lose on 2, 3, or 12. Any other number is your point, and you win if your point comes up again before a 7.

DON'T COME This is the opposite of a Come bet. Again, you wait until after the first roll to bet. A 7 or an 11 means you lose; a 2 or a 3 means you win; 12 is a push, and nobody wins. You win if 7 comes up before the point. (The point, you'll recall, was the first number rolled if it was none of the above.)

FIELD This is a bet for one roll only. The "Field" consists of seven numbers: 2, 3, 4, 9, 10, 11, and 12. If any of these numbers is thrown on the next roll, you win even money, except on 2 and 12, which pay 2 to 1 (at some casinos 3 to 1).

BIG 6 AND 8 A "Big 6 and 8" bet pays even money. You win if either a 6 or an 8 is rolled before a 7. Mathematically, this is a sucker's bet.

ANY 7 An "Any 7" bet pays the winner 5 for 1. If a 7 is thrown on the first roll after you bet, you win.

"HARD WAY" BETS In the middle of a craps table are pictures of several possible dice combinations together with the odds the casino will pay you if you bet and win on any of those combinations being thrown. For example, if double 3s or 4s are rolled and you had bet on them, you will be paid 7 to 1. If double 2s or 5s are rolled and you had bet on them, you will be paid 9 to 1. If either a 7 is rolled or the number you bet on was rolled any way other than the "Hard Way," then the bet is lost. In-the-know gamblers tend to avoid Hard Way bets as they are an easy way to lose money.

ANY CRAPS Here you're lucky if the dice "crap out"—if they show 2, 3, or 12 on the first roll after you bet. If this happens, the bank pays 7 to 1. Any other number is a loser.

PLACE BETS You can make a "Place Bet" on any of the following numbers: 4, 5, 6, 8, 9, and 10. You're betting that the number you choose will be thrown before a 7 is thrown. If you win, the payoff is as follows: 4 or 10 pays at the rate of 9 to 5; 5 or 9 pays at the rate of 7 to 5; 6 or 8 pays at the rate of 7 to 6. Place Bets can be removed at any time before a roll.

Some Probabilities

The probability of a certain number being rolled at the craps table is not a mystery. As there are only 36 possible outcomes when the dice are rolled, the probability for each number being rolled is easily ascertained. See the "Dice Probabilities" chart, below, to help you in case you decided it was more fun to pass notes or sleep during your math classes.

So 7 has an advantage over all other combinations, which, over the long run, is in favor of the casino. You can't beat the law of averages, but if you can't beat 'em, join 'em. (Play the Don't Pass bet.)

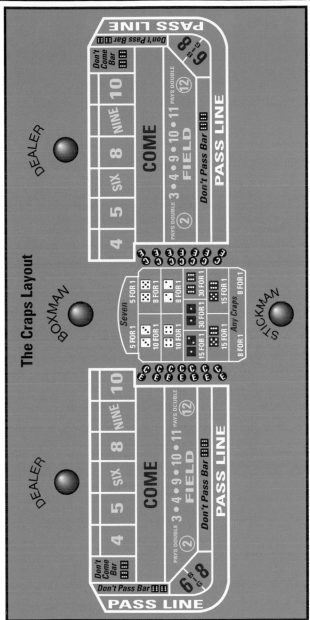

A typical craps table.

DICE PROBABILITIES

NUMBER	POSSIBLE COMBINATIONS	ACTUAL ODDS	PERCENTAGE PROBABILITY
2	1	35:1	2.8%
3	2	17:1	5.6%
4	3	11:1	8.3%
5	4	8:1	11.1%
6	5	6.2:1	13.9%
7	6	5:1	16.7%
8	5	6.2:1	13.9%
9	4	8:1	11.1%
10	3	11:1	8.3%
11	2	17:1	5.6%
12	1	35:1	2.8%

Poker

Poker is the game of the Old West. There's at least one scene in every Western in which the hero faces off against the villain over a poker hand. In Las Vegas, poker is a tradition, although it isn't played at every casino.

Traditional Poker

There are lots of variations on the basic game, but one of the most popular is **Hold 'Em.** Two cards are dealt facedown to the players. After a betting round, five community cards (everyone can use them) are dealt faceup on the table, with betting rounds in between each card. The player makes the best five-card hand, using his own cards and the "board" (the community cards), and the best hand wins. The house dealer takes care of the shuffling and the dealing and moves a marker around the table to alternate the start of the deal. The house usually rakes in around 10% (it depends on the casino) from each pot. Most casinos also provide tables for playing Seven-Card Stud, Omaha High, and Omaha Hi-Lo. A few will even have Seven-Card Stud Hi-Lo split. To learn

how these variations are played, either read a book or take lessons.

Warning: If you don't know how to play poker, don't attempt to learn at a table. Card sharks are not a rare species in Vegas; they will gladly feast on fresh meat (you!). Find a casino that provides free gaming lessons and learn, to paraphrase Kenny Rogers, when to hold 'em, and when to fold 'em.

Table Games

Beyond the traditional poker games, Vegas is also home to a number of table games that capitalize on the popularity of poker, everything from a variation on Texas Hold 'Em to three-card poker. The biggest difference between these games and the real thing? You play against the house, not other players (some people find this less intimidating). And the house usually holds a serious advantage in these games, though many of them feature bonus or progressive payouts should you manage to hit a given hand (a flush, for example).

It's actually more difficult to explain many of these games than it

Poker Hands

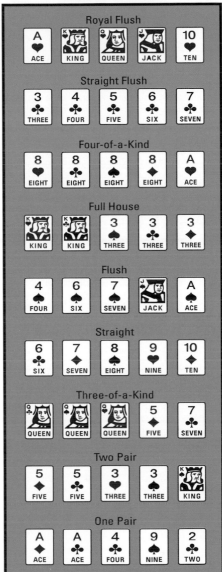

All the major poker hands.

is to play them (though I do cover Let It Ride, below). For this reason, I recommend watching a table for a while or taking a lesson (when offered). **Note:** Many of the poker-related table games often have explanation cards in a small dispenser on the side of the table—if you're interested in a game, take one and read it. If you have questions, feel free to ask the dealer.

Warning: The table games can be lots of fun, but do not assume that you will learn strategy that you can use later on at a real poker table. The poker hands might be the same, but the approach is very different. Hands that you routinely play at a table game because you aren't playing against a slew of opponents will often leave you dead in the water in an actual game.

Let It Ride

Let It Ride is another popular game that involves poker hands. You place three bets at the outset and are dealt three cards. The dealer is dealt two cards that act as community cards (you're not playing against the dealer). Once you've seen your cards, you can choose to pull the first of your three bets back, or "Let It Ride." The object of this game is to get a pair of 10s or better by combining your cards with the dealer's. If you're holding a pair of 10s or better in your first three cards, you want to let your bets ride the whole way through. Once you've decided whether or not to let your first bet ride, the dealer exposes one of his or her two cards.

Once again you must make a decision to take back your second bet or keep on going. Then the dealer exposes the last of his or her cards; your third bet must stay. The dealer then turns over the hands of the players and determines whether you've won. Winning bets are paid on a scale, ranging from even money for a single pair up to 1,000 to 1 for a royal flush. These payouts are for each bet you have in play. Like Caribbean Stud, Let It Ride has a progressive jackpot that you can win for high hands if you cough up an additional dollar per hand, but be advised that the house advantage on that $1 is obscene. But hey, that's why it's called gambling.

Roulette

Roulette is an extremely easy game to play, and it's really quite colorful and exciting to watch. The wheel spins and the little ball bounces around, finally dropping into one of the slots, numbered 1 to 36, plus 0 and 00 (on American wheels, which is what you'll find mostly in Vegas; European wheels eschew the 00 so they lower the house advantage—not a beloved prospect for the casinos in Vegas). You can place bets

"Inside" the table and "Outside" the table. Inside bets are bets placed on a particular number or a set of numbers. Outside bets are those placed in the boxes surrounding the number table (see illustration, below). If you bet on a specific number and the ball lands on that number in the wheel, you'll be paid 35 to 1 on your bet. Bear in mind, however, that the odds of a particular number coming up are actually 38 to 1 (don't forget 0 and

00!), so the house has a 5.26% advantage the moment you place an Inside bet. For payoffs on Outside bets, such as Red/Black, Odd/Even, and so forth, see the illustration below. The methods of placing single-number bets, column bets, and others are fairly obvious. The dealer will be happy to show you how make many interesting betting combinations, such as betting on six numbers at once. Each player is given different-colored chips so that it's easy to follow the numbers you've bet on.

Some typical bets are indicated by means of letters on the roulette layout depicted in the illustration. The winning odds for each of these sample bets are listed. These bets can be made on any corresponding combinations of numbers.

Tip: The latest trend in Vegas is "electronic" roulette, where you bet electronically (no need to manually distribute all of those chips) on the spin of an actual wheel. The biggest difference in games that use this technology is that they go a lot faster, which (given the large house advantage on this game) means you can lose your money even more quickly.

Slots

You put the coin in the slot and pull the handle. What, you thought there was a trick to this?

Actually, there is a bit more to it. But first, some background. Old-timers will tell you slots were invented to give wives something to do while their husbands gambled. Slots used to be stuck at the edges of the casino and could be counted on one hand, maybe two. But now they *are* the casino. The casinos make more from slots than from craps, blackjack, and roulette combined. There are some 150,000 slot machines (not including video poker) in the county. Some of these are at the airport, steps from you as you deplane. It's just a matter of time before the planes flying into Vegas feature slots that pop up as soon as you cross the state line.

But in order to keep up with the increasing competition, the plain old machine, where reels just spin, has become nearly obsolete. Now, they are all computerized and have added buttons to push, so you can avoid getting carpal tunnel syndrome from yanking the handle all night. (The handles are still there on many of them.) Many don't even have reels any more, but are entirely video screens, which offer a number of little bonus extras that have nothing to do with actual play. The idea is still simple: Get three (sometimes four or five) cherries (clowns, sevens, dinosaurs, whatever) in a row and you win something. Each machine has its own combination. Some will pay you something with just one symbol showing; on most, the more combinations there are, the more opportunities for loot. Some will even pay if you get three blanks. Study each machine carefully to learn what it does. *Note:* The **payback** goes up considerably if you bet the limit (from 2 to as many as 90 coins).

Progressive slots are groups of linked machines (sometimes spread over several casinos) where the jackpot gets bigger every few moments (just as lottery jackpots build up). Bigger and better games keep showing up; for example, the popular **Wheel of Fortune** machines, which offer you a chance to spin a wheel (electronically of course) and win bonuses; slots that have a gorilla attempt to

A typical roulette table.

climb the Empire State Building, heading up as you win; and machines with themes like *Star Trek* or the *Wizard of Oz*.

Penny slots, which for a long time were overlooked, relegated to a lonely spot somewhere by a back wall because they were not as profitable for the casinos as quarter and dollar slots, are now everywhere. Machines now offer upwards of a 300-penny maximum (meaning a larger bet on those machines than on the five-quarter-maximum slots), and gamblers have been flocking to them. As a result, more cash is pocketed by the casino (which keeps a higher percentage of cash off of penny slots than it does off of quarter slots), which is happy to accommodate this trend by offering up more and more penny slots. (See how this all works? Are you paying attention?)

Of course when we're talking about pennies or quarters, I don't mean actual coins. Most slot machines in Las Vegas do not take or dispense coins anymore, instead accepting paper currency and paying you out with a paper ticket that can be cashed in (at an ATM-like machine or with the casino cashier) or stuck into another slot machine. Purists miss the sound of coins raining down in the bins after a big win, but the vast majority of people appreciate the convenience, remembering what it was like to lug around buckets of quarters and wait while they refilled the hoppers when they ran dry.

Are there surefire ways to win on a slot machine? No. But you can lose more slowly. The slot machines use minicomputers known as random number generators (RNGs) to determine the winning combinations on a machine, but though each spin may indeed be random, individual machines are programmed to pay back different percentages over the long haul. As a result, a machine programmed to return a higher percentage might be "looser" than others. A bank of empty slots probably (but not certainly) means the machines are tight. Go find a line where lots of people are sitting around with a lot of credits on the meter. (Of course, yours will be the one that doesn't hit.) A good rule of thumb is that if your slot doesn't hit something in four or five pulls, leave it and go find another. It's not as though you won't have some choice in the matter. Also, each casino has a bank of slots that they advertise as more loose or with a bigger payback. Try these. It's what they want you to do, but what the heck.

Tip: For a pretty good explanation of slot odds, check out **http://wizardofodds.com/slots**. The site also has a wealth of information on gambling in general.

Sports Books

Most of the larger hotels in Las Vegas have sports-book operations, which look a lot like commodities-futures trading boards. In some, almost as large as theaters, you can sit comfortably, occasionally in recliners and sometimes with your own video screen, and watch ballgames, fights, and, at some casinos, horse races on huge TV screens. To add to your enjoyment, there's usually a deli/bar nearby that serves sandwiches, hot dogs, soft drinks, and beer. As a matter of fact, some of the best sandwiches in Las Vegas are served next to the sports books.

Sports books take bets on virtually every sport (and not just on who'll win, but also what the final score will be, who'll be first to hit a home run, who'll be MVP, who'll wear red shoes, you name it). They are best during important playoff games or big horse races, when everyone in the place is watching the same event—shrieking, shouting, and moaning, sometimes in unison. Joining in with a cheap bet (so you feel like you too have a personal stake in the matter) makes for bargain entertainment.

Video Poker

Video poker works the same way as regular poker, except you play against the machine. You are dealt a hand, you pick which cards to keep and which to discard, and then you get your new hand. And, it is hoped, you collect your winnings. This is somewhat more of a challenge and more active than slots because you have some control (or at least the illusion of control) over your fate, and it's easier than playing actual poker with a table full of folks who probably take it very seriously.

There are a number of varieties of this machine, with **Jacks or Better, Deuces Wild,** and so forth. Be sure to study your machine before you bet. (The best returns are offered on the 10/7 **Double Bonus Poker** machine, where, theoretically, if you play perfectly, you can, in fact, beat the house.) The Holy Grail of general video-poker machines is the 9/6 (it pays nine coins for a full house, six coins for a flush), but you'll need to pray a lot before you find one in town. Some machines offer **double down:** After you have won, you get a chance to draw cards against the machine,

with the higher card the winner. If you win, your money is doubled, and you are offered a chance to go again. Your money can increase nicely during this time, and you can also lose it all very quickly, which is most annoying.

Technology is catching up with video poker, too. Now they even have touch screens, which offer a variety of different poker games, blackjack, and video slots—just touch your screen and choose your poison.

Tip: The key to winning at video poker (where the strategy is very different than playing actual poker) is playing your cards perfectly at each individual machine. To do that, a little study time is in order. I suggest perusing the video poker books in the "LVA Store" section of the website of the very reputable *Las Vegas Advisor* (www.lasvegas advisor.com). If, like me, you prefer a more hands-on tutorial, Bob Dancer's Video Poker for Winners software is a real champ when it comes to teaching proper strategy for video poker; it's also for sale on the *Las Vegas Advisor* website. ●

Before You Go

Government Tourist Offices

For advance information, call or write the **Las Vegas Convention and Visitors Authority**, 3150 Paradise Rd., Las Vegas, NV 89109 (☎ 877/VISIT-LV [847-4858] or 702/892-0711; www.visitlasvegas.com).

For information on all of Nevada, including Las Vegas, contact the **Nevada Commission on Tourism** (☎ 800/638-2328; www.travelnevada.com).

The Best Times to Go

Most of a Las Vegas vacation is usually spent indoors, so you can have a good time here year-round. That said, the most pleasant seasons in this area are spring and fall (when crowds are everywhere and prices are high), especially if you want to experience the great outdoors. Summers here mean ultrahigh temps, but also fewer crowds and lower prices. Winters can get downright cold, so you can forget about using the hotel pool (almost all are outdoors and many close from Labor Day to Memorial Day); but prices in mid-December and mid-January usually descend into good-value territory.

Holidays (especially New Year's) in Vegas are a mob scene—and for Vegas, "holiday" includes Super Bowl Sunday, anytime during the NCAA Basketball Championships (especially the Final Four), boxing matches, and all other important pro and college sporting events. Hotel prices skyrocket not only during the holidays, but also when big conventions and special events take place. If a major convention is to be held during your trip, you might want to change your date. You can check convention dates by contacting the **Las Vegas Convention and Visitors Authority** (☎ 877/VISIT-LV [847-4858] or 702/892-0711; www.visitlasvegas.com).

Festivals & Special Events

Before you arrive, contact the **Las Vegas Convention and Visitors Authority** (☎ 877/VISIT-LV [847-4858] or 702/892-0711; www.visitlasvegas.com), or the **Chamber of Commerce** (☎ 702/735-1616; www.lvchamber.com), to find out what other events are scheduled during your visit. Once you're in town, check *Las Vegas Weekly* (www.lasvegasweekly.com), a free magazine you'll find in your hotel room, or **www.lasvegasevents. com**.

FEB The **Super Bowl** may not be held in Las Vegas, but that doesn't stop people from flocking to the city for the big game. Sports books, bars, and pretty much anywhere with a TV are usually packed with football fans, which drives up room rates.

MAR The start of spring sees the running of two of the most important **NASCAR Sprint Cup** races in the country. Held at the **Las Vegas Motor Speedway,** 7000 Las Vegas Blvd. N. (☎ 800/644-4444; www.lvms.com), the Sam's Town 300 and the Kobalt Tools 400 attract thousands of rabid racing fans each year.

Speaking of rabid fans, the **NCAA** basketball tournament (March Madness) is also a big draw at the sports books and bars, especially during the final few games of the championship.

JUNE The **World Series of Poker,** held at the **Rio All-Suite Hotel &**

Casino, 3700 W. Flamingo Rd. (☎ 866/746-7671; www.riolv.com), in June, July, and August, is *the* gambling event in Vegas, featuring high-stakes gamblers and showbiz personalities. There are daily events in June and July, with entry stakes ranging from $125 to $5,000. For a chance at the main event's multimillion-dollar Final Table held in November, players must ante up $10,000. You can crowd around the tables and watch for free, or if you want to avoid the throngs, you can catch a lot of it on TV. For more information, visit **www.wsop.com**.

OCT Pro golf's best players hit the greens at the televised 4-day **Justin Timberlake Shriners Hospitals for Children Open** (☎ 702/873-1010; www.jtshrinersopen.com), which is played at TPC Summerlin and TPC at the Canyons in October.

DEC The **National Finals Rodeo** (☎ 866/388-3267 for tickets; www. nfrexperience.com) is the Super Bowl of rodeos, attended by about 200,000 people each year, suddenly turning Vegas into Cowboy Country. Order tickets as far in advance as possible.

In mid-December, the winners of college football's Pac-10 Conference and the Mountain West Conference square off against each other in the **Maaco Bowl Las Vegas.** The action takes place at the 32,000-seat Sam Boyd Stadium. Call ☎ 702/732-3912 or visit www.lvbowl.com for ticket information.

New Year's Eve is the biggest day of the year on the Vegas calendar; reserve your hotel room early (and be prepared to pay top dollar). Downtown, at the Fremont Street Experience, there is a big block party with two dramatic countdowns to midnight at 9pm (midnight on the East Coast) and midnight. The Strip is usually closed to street traffic and hundreds of thousands of people pack the area for the festivities.

Weather

Vegas isn't always hot, but when it is hot, it's melting. Still, the humidity averages a low 22% and even on hot days there's apt to be a breeze. Also, except on the hottest of summer days, there is relief at night, when temperatures drop by as much as 20°. Keep in mind, however, that this is the desert and it's not hot year-round; it can get quite cold, especially in the winter. That summer breeze can become a cold, biting, strong wind of up to 40 mph (64kmph) and more in winter. And there are entire portions of the year when you won't be using your hotel pool at all (even if you want to, because many of the hotels close huge chunks of their fabulous pool areas for "the season," which can be as long as from Labor Day to Memorial Day). If you aren't traveling at the height of summer, bring a jacket. Also remember sunscreen (apply it often!) and a hat—even if it's not all that hot, you can burn easily and very quickly.

Useful Websites

- **www.vegas4visitors.com**: A sweeping and comprehensive site on Las Vegas, with lots of practical advice and strong opinions.

- **www.lvchamber.com**: The Chamber of Commerce's official website has a calendar of events, lots of practical tips, info on getting married in Vegas, and more.

- **www.vegas.com**: Using resources from the city's free weeklies, this site features plenty of locally written reviews and opinions.

- **www.lasvegasadvisor.com**: Veteran Vegas bargain hunter Anthony DeCurtis gives out all sorts of valuable tips, plus trivia, gambling advice, and lots of cool info.

LAS VEGAS'S AVERAGE TEMPERATURES (°F/°C) & PRECIPITATION

	JAN	FEB	MAR	APR	MAY	JUNE
High °F	56	63	69	78	88	99
High °C	13	17	21	26	31	37
Low °F	34	38	44	51	60	69
Low °C	1	3	7	11	16	21
Avg. Precip. (in.)	.59	.50	.53	.15	.24	.08
(cm)	1.5	1.8	1.5	.4	.6	.2

	JULY	AUG	SEPT	OCT	NOV	DEC
High °F	104	102	94	81	66	57
High °C	40	39	34	27	19	14
Low °F	75	74	66	54	42	34
Low °C	24	23	19	12	6	1
Avg. Precip. (in.)	.44	.45	.31	.24	.31	.40
(cm)	1.1	1.1	.8	.6	.8	1.0

- **www.visitlasvegas.com**: The Convention and Visitor Bureau's official site is well organized by subject matter and offers lots of information and practical tips on hotels, dining, entertainment, and more. There's also information on discount vacation packages.

Cellphones

It's a good bet your phone will work in Las Vegas, but take a look at your wireless company's coverage map on its website before heading out. I've had problems with reception every now and then (using two different providers), especially inside some of the casino hotels.

Car Rentals

If you stick to one section of the Strip, or concentrate solely on Downtown, then you technically don't need a car. I used to strongly recommend getting one anyway because a car does make it easier to get around, parking doesn't cost you anything beyond the valet tip, and if you want to do some serious touring off the Strip, it's almost a must. But that was before rental car taxes and fees in Vegas rose to 27.5%, plus a $3-per-day fee if you rent out of McCarran International Airport. On my last trip I figured out it would have been cheaper if a little less efficient to use public transport and some cabs than to rent a car. So now I say that if you're not planning on venturing off the Strip and you have no mobility issues, a car is more of a maybe than a must.

National companies with outlets in Las Vegas include **Alamo** (☎ 877/227-8367; www.alamo.com), **Avis** (☎ 800/230-4898; www.avis.com), **Budget** (☎ 800/527-0700; www.budget.com), **Dollar** (☎ 800/800-3665; www.dollar.com), **Enterprise** (☎ 800/261-7331; www.enterprise.com), **Hertz** (☎ 800/654-3131; www.hertz.com), **National** (☎ 800/227-7368; www.nationalcar.com), **Payless** (☎ 800/729-5377; www.paylesscarrental.com), and **Thrifty** (☎ 800/847-4389; www.thrifty.com).

If you're visiting from abroad and plan to rent a car in the United States, keep in mind that foreign driver's licenses are usually recognized in the U.S., but you should get an international one if your home license is not in English.

For decent car-rental rates, consult the major travel websites (Travelocity.com, Expedia.com) to comparison shop. You should also check out **Breezenet.com** (www. bnm.com), which offers domestic car-rental discounts with some of the most competitive rates around.

Getting **There**

By Plane

For a list of airlines that have regularly scheduled flights into Vegas see "Toll-Free Numbers & Websites," later in this chapter.

Las Vegas is served by **McCarran International Airport** (☎ 702/261-5211; www.mccarran.com), just a few minutes' drive from the southern end of the Strip, where the bulk of casinos and hotels are concentrated. This big, modern airport is rather unique in that it includes several casino areas with more than 1,000 slot machines.

Getting to your hotel from the airport is a cinch. **Bell Trans** (☎ 800/274-7433 or 702/739-7990; www. bell-trans.com) runs 20-passenger minibuses daily between the airport (minibuses depart just west of the baggage-claim area) and all major Las Vegas hotels and motels (7:45am–midnight). Several other companies offer similar ventures—just stand outside on the curb, and one will be flagged for you. The cost is $6.50 per person each way to hotels on the Strip or around the Convention Center, $8 to Downtown or other off-Strip properties (north of Sahara Ave. and west of I-15). Other similarly priced shuttles run 24 hours and can be found in the same place. Minibuses from the airport leave about every 10 minutes. When you want to check out of your hotel and head back to the airport, call at least 2 hours in advance to be safe (though often you can just flag down one of the minibuses outside any major hotel).

Even less expensive are **Citizens Area Transit (CAT)** buses

(☎ 702/CAT-RIDE [847-4858]; www. rtcsnv.com/transit). The no. 108 bus departs from the airport and takes you to the Stratosphere, where you can transfer to the Deuce or SDX bus lines, which stop close to most Strip- and Convention Center–area hotels. The no. 109 goes from the airport to the South Strip Transfer Terminal (Gillespie St. and Sunset Rd.) where you can also catch one of the Strip buses. Bus fares (depending on the route you take) are $2 to $5 for adults, $1 to $5 for seniors and children 6 to 17, and free for children 5 and under. It's cheaper than a minibus, but it might not be enough to put up with the added hassle (buses do not stop in front of hotel main entrances, while minibuses do—you could be in for a long walk if you opt for the bus), especially if you have luggage.

You can also take a taxi from the airport to the Strip (around $15–$25) or Downtown ($20–$30); the maximum number of passengers allowed in a cab is five (infants and kids included).

By Car

The main highway connecting Las Vegas with the rest of the country is **I-15;** it links Montana, Idaho, and Utah with Southern California. From the east, take **I-70** or **I-80** west to Kingman, Arizona, and then **U.S. 93** north to Downtown Las Vegas (Fremont St.). From the south, take **I-10** west to Phoenix and then U.S. 93 north to Las Vegas. From San Francisco, take **I-80** east to Reno and then **U.S. 95** south to Las Vegas.

Getting **Around**

By Public Transportation

The **Deuce** and **SDX** lines, operated by the Regional Transportation Commission (RTC) of Southern Nevada (☎ 702/CAT-RIDE [847-4858]; www.rtcsouthernnevada.com) are the primary ways to get up and down the Strip. The Deuce is a fleet of modern double-decker buses that run the length of the Strip into Downtown and near the airport while SDX (Strip & Downtown Express) features sleek double-carriage buses that make fewer stops. A 2-hour pass is $5, while a $7 all-day pass lets you get on and off as many times as you like and also lets you ride other RTC buses all day. Exact change is required. **Note:** Discounted fares are available to seniors, students, and children, but you have to apply for a reduced fare ID card at the Bonneville Transit Center in Downtown Las Vegas, which may not be worth the hassle. Visit the RTC website for more information.

By Taxi

Cabs line up in front of all major hotels and are an easy way to get around town, although certainly not the cheapest. Cabs charge $3.30 at the meter drop and 20¢ for each additional 1/13 mile ($2.60 per mile), plus an additional $1.80 fee for being picked up at the airport; time-based penalties are assessed when you get stuck in a traffic jam. You can often save money by sharing a cab—up to five people can ride for the same fare. Do not attempt to hail a taxi from anywhere but an approved stand when you're on the Strip; it's illegal for cabs to pick up fares off the street.

Cab companies in the area include **Desert Cab Company** (☎ 702/386-9102), **Whittlesea Blue Cab** (☎ 702/394-6111), and

Yellow/Checker Cab/Star Company (☎ 702/873-2000).

By Monorail

The Las Vegas Monorail (www.lvmonorail.com) is a rider's best shot at getting from one end of the Strip to the other with a minimum of frustration (though the expense can add up). The 4-mile (6.4km) monorail route runs from the MGM Grand at the southern end of the Strip to Sahara Avenue at the northern end, with stops at Paris/Bally's, The Flamingo, Harrah's, the Las Vegas Convention Center, and the Las Vegas Hotel & Casino along the way. Keep in mind that it can be a long walk from the monorail stops to the action; wear comfy shoes.

Trains can accommodate more than 200 passengers (standing and sitting) and make the end-to-end run in about 15 minutes. Operating hours are Monday through Thursday from 7am to 2am and Friday through Sunday from 7am to 3am. Fares are an exceedingly steep $5 for a one-way ride, no matter what distance you travel; discount multiride/multiday passes are sold and can bring the price of a ride down to about $3.50. Kids ages 5 and under ride free.

It's worth noting that the system, while convenient, has not been very popular and has sunk into bankruptcy. Its future is in doubt as of this writing, so be sure to check the Las Vegas Monorail website for updates.

By Car

If you plan on venturing beyond the Strip (or far from the general area surrounding your hotel), a car is your best bet. The Strip is too spread out for walking (and often Las Vegas is too hot or too cold to make those strolls pleasant), Downtown is too far away for a cheap cab ride, and public transportation is often ineffective in getting you where you want to go in a timely manner. You should note that places with addresses some 60 blocks east or west of the Strip are actually less than a 10-minute drive—provided there is no traffic.

Having advocated traveling by car, I should warn you that traffic is reaching horrifying proportions, and it's harder and harder to get around town with any certain swiftness. A general rule of thumb is to avoid driving on the Strip whenever you can and avoid driving at all during peak rush hours (8–9:30am and 4:30–6pm). Notable back roads that can help you access the major hotels while avoiding the Strip include Harmon Avenue, Koval Lane, and Frank Sinatra Drive. Get yourself a good map (most Vegas car-rental agencies hand out excellent ones) and familiarize yourself with chosen routes before you set out.

Parking in Vegas is usually a pleasure because all the casino hotels offer free valet service. That means for a mere $2 to $3 tip you can park right at the door, though valet parking usually fills up on busy nights (or is offered to guests only on busy evenings). In those cases, you can use the gigantic self-parking lots that all hotels have.

On Foot

The best way to navigate Downtown is on your own two feet, especially in the Glitter Gulch area on Fremont Street, which is now pedestrian only.

Walking also makes sense on the Strip, if you're going short distances and want to avoid traffic tie-ups. I know people who walk up and down the Strip as a matter of course, but despite the flat terrain, it can get very tiring (especially when it might very well be a mile from your room to a hotel's entrance). Keep in mind the following:

1. **Distances in Las Vegas can be very deceiving.** That hotel that looks really close to where you're standing may be more than a mile away. And if it's broiling hot outside or freezing cold (and it can get very chilly in winter), that may be the longest mile you've ever walked.

2. **Don't even think of jaywalking.** Pushing your luck in this area will likely result in you getting hurt. Badly. Use the provided escalators and pedestrian walkways to cross the Strip and its major side streets.

3. **Make use of indoor walkways and free shuttles.** A free monorail connects Mandalay Bay with Luxor and Excalibur (and indoor walkways connect all three hotels as well), and a free tram shuttles between The Mirage and TI at The Mirage. Monte Carlo and Bellagio are connected to CityCenter via a monorail. And you can walk from Paris Las Vegas to Bally's without ever stepping outside. A free shuttle also runs from Paris Las Vegas and Harrah's to the Rio.

Fast **Facts**

APARTMENT RENTALS Note that most home and apartment rentals in Las Vegas are located off the Strip and that a car becomes a necessity if you go this route. **Las**

Vegas Retreats (☎ 888/887-0951 or 702/966-2761; www.lasvegas retreats.com) is a reputable firm that offers upscale accommodations at decent prices. A pricier (and more upscale) option is **Las Vegas Luxury Home Rentals** (☎ 702/871-9727; www.lasvegasluxury homerentals.com).

AREA CODES The area code for Las Vegas is 702.

ATMs/CASHPOINTS An ATM (automated teller machine) is pretty much right at your elbow no matter where you are in Vegas. Particularly in casinos.

The **Cirrus** (☎ 800/424-7787; www.mastercard.com) and **PLUS** (☎ 800/843-7587; www.visa.com) networks span the globe; look at the back of your bank card to see which network you're on, then call or check online for ATM locations in Vegas.

Be sure you know your personal identification number (PIN) and daily withdrawal limit before you depart. *Note:* Remember that ATMs in Vegas charge transaction fees of between $3 and $5 in addition to whatever your bank will charge you for not using one of their ATMs.

BABYSITTERS Contact Around the Clock Child Care (☎ 800/798-6768 or 702/365-1040). In business since 1987, this reputable company clears its sitters with the health department, the sheriff, and the FBI, and carefully screens references. Rates are $75 for 4 hours for one or two children, $15 for each additional hour, with surcharges for additional children and on holidays. Call at least 3 hours in advance.

BANKS Banks are generally open from 9 or 10am to 5 and sometimes 6pm, and most have Saturday hours.

BUSINESS HOURS Casinos and most bars are open 24 hours a day. Stores generally open between 9 and 10am and close between 7 and 8pm Monday through Saturday; on Sunday they usually open around 11am and close by 6pm. Stores in the casino hotels sometimes keep longer hours.

CONSULATES & EMBASSIES All embassies are located in the nation's capital, Washington, D.C. Some consulates are located in major U.S. cities, and most nations have missions to the United Nations in New York City. For addresses and phone numbers of embassies in Washington, D.C., call ☎ 202/555-1212, or log on to www.embassy.org/embassies.

CUSTOMS U.S. airports have considerably beefed up security clearances in the years since the September 11, 2001, terrorist attacks, and clearing Customs and Immigration can take as long as 2 hours, especially on summer weekends.

DENTISTS Hotels usually keep lists of dentists, should you need one. For dental referrals, you can also call the **Southern Nevada Dental Society** (☎ 702/733-8700; www.sndsonline.org) weekdays from 9am to noon and 1 to 5pm; when the office is closed, a recording will tell you who to call for emergency service.

DINING Vegas is used to all kinds, so unless a restaurant specifies a dress code (and if you're headed to a "name" restaurant, be sure to check in advance), business-casual attire should get you in anywhere. Always make reservations way in advance for higher-end locations (a month early isn't unheard of).

In the budget department, you'll almost always save money by splurging at lunch instead of dinner; prices can be 20% to 50% less at lunchtime in some fancy restaurants. Most restaurants start serving lunch between 11:30am and noon; dinner usually starts at around 5:30pm.

DOCTORS Hotels usually keep lists of doctors, should you need one. For physician referrals, call the **Desert Springs Hospital** (☎ 702/388-4888;

www.desertspringshospital.com).
Hours are Monday to Friday from
8am to 8pm and Saturday from 9am
to 3pm, except holidays.

DRUGSTORES There's a 24-hour
Walgreens (which also has a 1-hr.
photo) at 3765 Las Vegas Blvd. S.
(☎ 702/739-9645; www.walgreens.
com), and a **CVS** at 3758 Las Vegas
Blvd. S. (☎ 702/262-9284; www.
cvs.com)—both are just across from
the Monte Carlo. **White Cross
Drugs,** 1700 Las Vegas Blvd. S.
(☎ 702/382-1733), is another
24-hour option.

ELECTRICITY Like Canada, the
United States uses 110–120 volts
AC (60 cycles), compared to 220–
240 volts AC (50 cycles) in most of
Europe, Australia, and New Zealand.
If your small appliances use 220–
240 volts, you'll need a 110-volt
transformer and a plug adapter with
two flat parallel pins to operate
them here. Downward converters
that change 220–240 volts to 110–
120 volts are difficult to find in the
United States, so bring one with you.

EMERGENCIES Dial ☎ **911** to contact the police or fire department or
to call an ambulance.

EVENT LISTINGS In order to make
sure the show you want isn't dark
during your visit, or to see what
headliner has hit town, you can
check events through the following:
The **Las Vegas Review-Journal**
(www.lvrj.com) is the city's daily
paper, and its Friday edition carries
a special "Weekend" section with a
guide to shows and other entertainment options. **Las Vegas CityLife**
(www.lasvegascitylife.com) and **Las
Vegas Weekly** (www.lasvegas
weekly.com) are free weekly alternative papers with plenty of club
and bar listings. **What's On** (www.
whats-on.com) is the free magazine
you will usually find in your hotel
room. It's mostly a rehash of press
releases, but often has discount

coupons for some shows, buffets,
and more.

FAMILY TRAVEL Think twice (and
then again) before you bring kids to
Vegas these days. The "Vegas is for
families" concept died ages ago, so
not only is there considerably less
to do with children, but you also
have to do it while constantly distracting them from casinos, booze,
four-story-tall billboards featuring
nearly bare bottoms, and other
adult material. On top of that, some
casino hotels ban children if they
aren't guests of that property—and
they will check your room keys for
proof. If you must bring your children to town, I suggest you look at
my "Las Vegas with Kids" tour on
p 30. Another good source of information is *Frommer's Las Vegas with
Kids.*

GAMBLING LAWS You must be 21
years of age to enter, much less
gamble in, any casino. If you look
young, carry your identification with
you as you may be asked to prove
your age. Most casinos are open 24
hours a day.

HOLIDAYS Banks, government
offices, post offices, and many
stores, restaurants, and museums
are closed (but not the casinos!) on
the following legal national holidays:
January 1 (New Year's Day), the third
Monday in January (Martin Luther
King Day), the third Monday in Feb-
ruary (Presidents' Day), the last Monday in May (Memorial Day), July 4
(Independence Day), the first Monday
in September (Labor Day), the second Monday in October (Columbus
Day), November 11 (Veterans Day/
Armistice Day), the fourth Thursday
in November (Thanksgiving Day),
and December 25 (Christmas Day).
The Tuesday after the first Monday
in November is Election Day, a fed-
eral government holiday in presi-
dential-election years (held every
4 years, and next in 2012).

For more information on holidays see "Festivals & Special Events," earlier in this chapter.

HOSPITALS Emergency services are available 24 hours a day at **University Medical Center,** 1800 W. Charleston Blvd., at Shadow Lane (☎ 702/383-2000; www.umcsn.com); the emergency-room entrance is on the corner of Hastings and Rose streets. **Sunrise Hospital and Medical Center,** 3186 Maryland Pkwy., between Desert Inn Road and Sahara Avenue (☎ 702/731-8080; www.sunrisehospital.com), also has a 24-hour emergency room.

For minor problems, try the **Harmon Medical Center**—the closest to the Strip—at 150 E. Harmon at Koval Lane, near the MGM Grand (☎ 702/796-1116; www.harmonmedicalcenter.com). It's open Monday to Friday from 8am to 5pm; it has X-ray machines, and there is a pharmacy on-site.

INSURANCE The cost of travel insurance varies widely, depending on the destination, the cost and length of your trip, your age and health, and the type of trip you're taking, but expect to pay between 5% and 8% of the vacation itself. You can get estimates from various providers through **www.insuremytrip.com**. Enter your trip cost and dates, your age, and other information, for prices from more than a dozen companies.

U.K. citizens and their families who make more than one trip abroad per year may find an annual travel insurance policy works out cheaper. Check **www.moneysupermarket.com**, which compares prices across a wide range of providers for single- and multi-trip policies.

Most big travel agents offer their own insurance and will probably try to sell you their package when you book a holiday. Think before you sign.

Britain's **Consumers' Association** recommends that you insist on seeing the policy and reading the fine print before buying travel insurance. The **Association of British Insurers** (☎ 020/7600-3333; www.abi.org.uk) gives advice by phone and publishes *Holiday Insurance,* a free guide to policy provisions and prices. You might also shop around for better deals: Try **Columbus Direct** (☎ 0870/033-9988; www.columbusdirect.net).

Trip Cancellation: Trip-cancellation insurance will help retrieve your money if you have to back out of a trip or depart early, or if your travel supplier goes bankrupt. Trip cancellation traditionally covers such events as sickness, natural disasters, and U.S. State Department advisories. The latest news in trip-cancellation insurance is the availability of **"any-reason"** cancellation coverage—which costs more but covers cancellations made for any reason. You won't get back 100% of your prepaid trip cost, but you'll be refunded a substantial portion. **TravelSafe** (☎ 888/885-7233; www.travelsafe.com) offers this coverage, and Expedia.com offers any-reason cancellation coverage for its air-hotel packages.

For details, contact one of the following recommended insurers: **Access America** (☎ 800/284-8300; www.accessamerica.com); **Travel Guard International** (☎ 800/826-4919; www.travelguard.com); **Travel Insured International** (☎ 800/243-3174; www.travelinsured.com); or **Travelex Insurance Services** (☎ 800/228-9792; www.travelex-insurance.com).

Medical Insurance: Although it's not required of travelers, health insurance is highly recommended. Most health-insurance policies cover you if you get sick away from home—but check your coverage before you leave.

International visitors should note that unlike many European countries, the United States does not usually offer free or low-cost medical care to its citizens or visitors. Doctors and hospitals are expensive, and in most cases will require advance payment or proof of coverage before they render their services. Packages such as **Europ Assistance's Worldwide Healthcare Plan** are sold by European automobile clubs and travel agencies at attractive rates. **Worldwide Assistance Services, Inc.** (☎ 240/330-1000; www.worldwide assistance.com), is the agent for Europ Assistance in the United States. Though lack of health insurance may prevent you from being admitted to a hospital in nonemergencies, don't worry about being left on a street corner to die: The American way is to fix you now and bill the living daylights out of you later.

Insurance for British Travelers: Travelers from the U.K. should carry their European Health Insurance Card (EHIC), which replaced the E111 form as proof of entitlement to free/reduced cost medical treatment abroad (☎ 0845/606-2030; www.ehic.ie). *Note:* The EHIC only covers "necessary medical treatment," and for repatriation costs, lost money, baggage, or cancellation, travel insurance from a reputable company should always be sought. For other options visit **www.travelinsuranceweb.com**.

Insurance for Canadian Travelers: Canadians should check with their provincial health-plan offices or call **Health Canada** (☎ 866/225 0709; www.hc-sc.gc.ca) to find out the extent of their coverage and what documentation and receipts they must take home in case they are treated in the United States.

INTERNET ACCESS Most resort hotels in Vegas offer wireless access, but for a hefty daily fee (usually around $15). Some chain hotels offer free Wi-Fi in public areas, while others still offer high-speed access. In Las Vegas, you can find free Wi-Fi at most stand-alone McDonald's, Starbucks, and in the Fashion Show Mall. To find additional public Wi-Fi hot spots, go to **www.jiwire.com**; its Wi-Fi Finder holds the world's largest directory of public wireless hot spots.

There are usually no easily accessible cybercafes in Vegas, and even those that open tend to close without warning. To check for possibilities, try **www.cybercaptive. com** and **www.cybercafe.com**.

LIMOUSINES Hotels will often provide airport limos for high rollers or VIP guests—in the latter case, that often means someone merely staying in a higher-level room. Ask and see. Otherwise, try **Las Vegas Limo** (☎ 888/696-4400 or 702/736-1419; http://lasvegaslimo.com) or **Presidential Limo** (☎ 800/423-1420 or 702/731-5577; www.presidential limolv.com).

LIQUOR LAWS The legal age for purchase and consumption of alcoholic beverages is 21; proof of age is required and often requested at bars, nightclubs, and restaurants, so it's always a good idea to carry ID when you go out.

Beer, wine, and liquor are all sold in all kinds of stores pretty much around the clock, plus cocktail waitresses are ready to ply you moments after you sit down at a slot machine or gaming table. You won't have a hard time finding a drink in this town.

Do not carry open containers of alcohol in a car or any public area that isn't zoned for alcohol consumption. It is also forbidden to have an open container of alcohol in a vehicle, even if you're the passenger.

The Strip and Fremont Street in Downtown Las Vegas are the only areas in town where you can have open containers on public sidewalks; otherwise, the police can fine you on the spot. And nothing will ruin your trip faster than getting a citation for DUI (driving under the influence), so don't even think about driving while intoxicated.

LOST PROPERTY Be sure to tell all of your credit card companies the minute you discover your wallet has been lost or stolen, and file a report at the nearest police precinct. Your credit card company or insurer may require a police report number or record of the loss. Most credit card companies have an emergency toll-free number to call if your card is lost or stolen; they may be able to wire you a cash advance immediately or deliver an emergency credit card in a day or two. Visa's U.S. emergency number is ☎ 800/847-2911 or 410/581-9994. American Express cardholders and traveler's check holders should call ☎ 800/221-7282. MasterCard holders should call ☎ 800/307-7309 or 636/722-7111. For other credit cards, call the toll-free number directory at ☎ 800/555-1212.

MAIL & POSTAGE At press time, domestic postage rates were 32¢ for a postcard and 45¢ for a letter. For international mail, a first-class letter of up to 1 ounce costs $1.05 (85¢ to Canada and Mexico); a first-class postcard costs the same as a letter. For more information go to **www.usps.com** and click on "Calculate Postage."

MONEY Vegas runs on money, in all its forms. Most places, except the smallest stores and restaurants, take credit cards. The gaming tables and slot machines run on cold hard cash. If you prefer using traveler's checks, they are accepted in many places in Las Vegas.

American Express (☎ 800/807-6233; 800/221-7282 for cardholders); **Visa** (☎ 800/732-1322); and **MasterCard** (☎ 800/223-9920) all issue traveler's checks.

Be sure to keep a copy of the traveler's checks serial numbers separate from your checks in the event that they are stolen or lost. You'll get a refund faster if you know the numbers.

PARKING Free valet parking is one of the great pleasures of Las Vegas and well worth the $2 or $3 tip (given when the car is returned) to save walking a city block from the far reaches of a hotel parking lot, especially in the summer heat. Valet service can fill up late on weekend nights, but the self-parking lots are vast (*always* write down where you parked if you go this route).

PASSPORTS International visitors should always keep a photocopy of their passport with them when traveling. If your passport is lost or stolen, having a copy significantly facilitates the reissuing process at a local consulate or embassy. Keep your passport and other valuables in your room's safe or in the hotel safe.

POLICE For nonemergencies call ☎ 702/795-3111. For emergencies, call 911.

SAFETY While otherwise quite safe for a big city, Las Vegas always has vast amounts of money on display, and criminals find many easy marks. At gaming tables and slot machines, men should keep wallets well concealed and out of reach of pickpockets, and women should keep handbags in plain sight (on your lap). If you're playing slots, do not forget to take your winnings ticket with you. If you win a big jackpot, ask the pit boss or slot attendant to cut you a check rather than give you cash; it's also perfectly reasonable to ask security to escort you to your car. Outside casinos, popular spots for pickpockets and thieves are restaurants and outdoor shows. Stay alert. Unless your hotel room has an in-room safe, check your valuables in a safe-deposit box at the front desk.

SMOKING Smoking has been banned in most public indoor spaces including restaurants, malls, and hotel lobbies. The exceptions are bars and nightclubs and the casinos, of course, although most poker rooms in Las Vegas do not permit smoking.

SPECTATOR SPORTS Las Vegas isn't known for its sports teams. Except for minor-league baseball and hockey, the only consistent spectator sports are those at UNLV. For the pros, it watching Triple A ball (in this case, a Los Angeles Dodgers farm team) in potentially triple-degree heat sounds like fun, the charmingly named and even-better merchandised **Las Vegas 51s** (as in Area 51, as in alien-themed gear!) is a great bet. This ball team's schedule and ticket info are available by calling ☎ 702/386-7200 or online at **www.lv51.com**. Ice hockey might be a better climate choice; get info for the **Las Vegas Wranglers** at **www.lasvegaswranglers.com** or by calling ☎ 702/471-7825.

The **Las Vegas Motor Speedway** (p 35) is a major venue for car racing that draws major NASCAR events to Las Vegas.

Because the city has several top-notch sporting arenas, important annual events take place in Las Vegas. The **PGA Tour** (www.pgatour.com) regularly makes a stop in Las Vegas each October. The **National Finals Rodeo** is held in UNLV's Thomas and Mack Center each December. From time to time, you'll also find NBA exhibition games, professional ice-skating competitions, or gymnastics exhibitions.

Finally, Las Vegas is well known as a major location for boxing matches. These are held in several Strip hotels, most often at Caesars or the MGM Grand, but sometimes at The Mirage. Tickets are hard to come by and quite expensive.

Tickets to sporting events at hotels are available either through **Ticketmaster** (☎ 702/893-3000; www.ticketmaster.com) or through the hotels.

TAXES Sales tax is 8.1%. (**Note:** It's also levied on show tickets.) The Clark County hotel room tax is 12%, and in Downtown it's 13%. The United States has no value-added tax (VAT) or other indirect tax at the national level. Every state, county, and city may levy its own local tax on all purchases, including hotel and restaurant checks and airline tickets. These taxes will not appear on price tags.

TAXIS See "By Taxi" in "Getting Around," earlier in this chapter.

TELEPHONES For **directory assistance** ("information"), dial **411**; for long-distance information, dial **1,** then the appropriate area code and **555-1212.** Generally, hotel surcharges on long-distance and local calls are astronomical. You are often charged even for making a toll-free or phone card call. You're better off using your **cellphone** or a **public pay telephone.** Some hotels are now adding on an additional "resort fee" to the cost of the room, which is supposed to cover local calls (as well as using the pool and other elements that ought to be givens). The fee can range from $1 (Motel Six) to $15 per day. Many convenience grocery stores and packaging services sell **prepaid calling cards** in denominations up to $50; for international visitors, these can be the least expensive way to call home. Local calls made from public pay phones in Las Vegas cost from 25¢

to 50¢. Pay phones do not accept pennies, and few will take anything larger than a quarter.

Most long-distance and international calls can be dialed directly from any phone. **For calls within the United States and to Canada,** dial **1** followed by the area code and the seven-digit number. **For other international calls,** dial 011 followed by the country code, the city code, and the number you are calling.

TICKETS To avoid surcharges and obtain better seating options, it's usually best to go through the box office for the show in question (some box offices can be accessed online). Top-draw shows can sell out months in advance, so try to order tickets as early as possible. Ticket agencies generally charge obscene markups and should be consulted only if you're desperate. For more information on buying discount tickets, check out "Getting Discount Tickets," below.

TIPPING You can get tip fatigue in Vegas, but try to remember that this city runs on the service sector and tipping is often an important part of certain workers' income. In hotels, tip bellhops at least $1 per bag ($2–$3 if you have a lot of luggage) and tip the chamber staff $1 to $2 per day (more if you've left a disaster area). Tip the doorman or concierge only if he or she has provided you with some specific service (for example, calling a cab for you or obtaining difficult-to-get theater tickets). Tip the valet-parking attendant $2 to $3 every time you get your car.

In restaurants, bars, and nightclubs, tip service staff 15% to 20% of the check, tip bartenders 10% to 15%, tip checkroom attendants $1 per garment, and tip valet-parking attendants $1 per vehicle.

As for other service personnel, tip cabdrivers 15% of the fare; tip

skycaps at airports at least $1 per bag ($2–$3 if you have a lot of luggage); and tip hairdressers and barbers 15% to 20%.

TOILETS There are large, clean, and often rather glamorous toilets scattered throughout every hotel casino. Just look for the signs. Some city restaurants and bars may reserve their restrooms for patrons. You can avoid arguments by paying for a cup of coffee or a soft drink, which will qualify you as a patron.

TOURIST OFFICES The main tourist office is the **Las Vegas Convention and Visitors Authority,** 3150 Paradise Rd., Las Vegas, NV 89109 (☎ 877/847-4858 or 702/892-0711; www.visitlasvegas.com). They're open daily from 9am to 5pm.

Another excellent source of information is the **Las Vegas Chamber of Commerce,** 3720 Howard Hughes Pkwy., #100, Las Vegas, NV 89109 (☎ 702/735-1616; www.lvchamber.com). They can answer all your Vegas questions. They are open Monday to Friday from 8am to 5pm.

TOURS Just about every hotel in town has a tour desk offering a seemingly infinite number of sightseeing opportunities in and around Las Vegas.

Gray Line (☎ 800/634-6579; www.grayline.com) is a reputable company with a rather comprehensive roster, including 5- to 6-hour city tours (both day and evening), half-day excursions to Hoover Dam and Red Rock Canyon, and full-day trips to the Grand Canyon in Arizona. Call for details or inquire at your hotel's tour desk, where you'll also find free magazines with coupons for discounts on select tours.

TRAVELERS WITH DISABILITIES On the one hand, Las Vegas is fairly well equipped for travelers with disabilities, with virtually every hotel having accessible rooms, ramps, and other

Getting Discount Tickets

Las Vegas ticket prices keep on climbing every year. The good news is that Vegas has discounters to shop from (though you must purchase tickets in person).

Tix 4 Tonight (www.tix4tonight.com) offers day-of-show discounts (as well as dining discounts at major buffets and restaurants) from 10am to 9pm. It has seven locations scattered throughout the city, including a Downtown branch in the Four Queens Hotel & Casino, and a Strip location in the Showcase Mall (next to MGM Grand). It also will sometimes offer a sneak peek of tickets available on its website.

Discounts can range from 10% to as high as 50% on between 35 and 50 performances daily (shows that I've seen sold include *Phantom of the Opera, Blue Man Group*, and *Zumanity*). **Note:** Tickets are released for sale throughout the day, so getting there early won't necessarily net you a better selection.

requirements. On the other hand, the distance between hotels (particularly on the Strip) makes a vehicle of some sort virtually mandatory for most people with disabilities, and it may be extremely strenuous and time-consuming to get from place to place (even within a single hotel, because of the crowds).

Even if you don't intend to gamble, you still may have to go through the casino, and casinos can be quite difficult to maneuver in, particularly for a guest in a wheelchair. Casinos are usually crowded, and the machines and tables are often laid out close together, with chairs, people, and other items blocking easy access. You should also consider that it is often a long trek through larger hotels between the entrance and the room elevators (or, for that matter, anywhere in the hotel), and then add a crowded casino to the equation.

For more on organizations that offer resources to travelers with limited mobility, go to **Frommers.com**.

WEATHER For current weather conditions, the radio station 970 FM does regular weather reports. You can also consult **www.weather.com**.

A Brief **History**

1831–48 Artesian spring waters of Las Vegas serve as a watering place on the Old Spanish Trail.

1855 A Mormon colony of 30 missionaries establishes a settlement just north of today's Downtown.

Unsuccessful in its aims, the colony disbands in 1858.

1864 President Lincoln proclaims Nevada the 36th state of the Union. Las Vegas, however, is still part of the territory of Arizona.

1865 Gold prospector Octavius D. Gass builds Las Vegas Ranch, the first permanent settlement in Las Vegas, on the site of the old Mormon colony.

1880s Due to the past 2 decades' of mining fever and the fervor for westward migration, the population of Nevada soars to more than 60,000 in 1880. The Paiutes are forced onto reservations.

1895 San Francisco inventor Charles Fey creates a three-reel gambling device—the first slot machine.

1907 Fremont Street, the future "Glitter Gulch," gets electric lights.

1909 Gambling is made illegal in Nevada, but Las Vegas pays little heed.

1928 Congress authorizes construction of Boulder Dam 30 miles (48km) from Vegas, bringing thousands of workers to the area. Later, Las Vegas capitalizes on the hundreds of thousands who come to see the engineering marvel.

1931 Gambling is legalized once again.

1932 The 100-room Apache Hotel opens in Downtown.

1933 Prohibition is repealed. Las Vegas's numerous speak-easies become legit.

1934 The city's first neon sign lights up the Boulder Club Downtown.

1941 The luxurious El Rancho Vegas becomes the first hotel on the Strip. Downtown, the El Cortez opens.

1942 The Last Frontier opens 2 miles (3.2km) south of El Rancho Vegas.

1946 Benjamin "Bugsy" Siegel's Flamingo extends the boundaries of the Strip. Sammy Davis, Jr., debuts at the El Rancho Vegas. Downtown (now dubbed "Glitter Gulch") gets two new hotels: the Golden Nugget and the Eldorado.

1947 United Airlines inaugurates service to Las Vegas.

1948 The Thunderbird becomes the fourth hotel on the Strip.

1950 The Desert Inn adds country-club panache to the Strip.

1951 The first of many atom bombs is tested in the desert just 65 miles (105km) from Las Vegas. Frank Sinatra debuts at the Desert Inn.

1952 The Club Bingo (opened in 1947) becomes the desert-themed Sahara. The Sands' Copa Room enhances the city's image as an entertainment center.

1954 The Showboat pioneers buffet meals and bowling alleys in a new area of Downtown.

1955 The Strip gets its first high-rise hotel, the nine-story Riviera, which pays Liberace the unprecedented sum of $50,000 to open its showroom.

1957 The Dunes introduces bare-breasted showgirls in its *Minsky Goes to Paris* revue. The most luxurious hotel to date, the Tropicana, opens on the Strip.

1958 The 1,065-room Stardust opens as the world's largest resort complex with a spectacular show from France, the *Lido de Paris*.

1959 The Las Vegas Convention Center goes up, presaging the city's future as a major convention city.

1960 A championship boxing match, the first of many, takes place at the convention center. El Rancho Vegas, the Strip's first property, burns to the ground.

1963 McCarran International Airport opens.

1966 The Aladdin, the first new hotel on the Strip in 9 years, is soon eclipsed by the unparalleled grandeur of Caesars Palace. The Four Queens opens in Downtown. Pioneer aviator Howard Hughes takes up residence at the Desert Inn; he buys up big chunks of Las Vegas and helps erase the city's gangland stigma.

1967 Elvis Presley marries Priscilla Beaulieu at the Aladdin.

1968 Circus Circus gives kids a reason to come to Las Vegas.

1973 The ultraglamorous 2,100-room MGM Grand assumes the mantle of "world's largest resort." Siegfried & Roy debut at the Tropicana.

1976 Howard Hughes dies aboard a plane en route to a Houston hospital. Dean Martin and Jerry Lewis make up after a 20-year feud.

1979 A new international arrivals building opens at McCarran International Airport.

1980 McCarran International Airport embarks on a 20-year, $785-million expansion program. A devastating fire destroys the MGM Grand, leaving 84 dead and 700 injured.

1981 Siegfried & Roy begin a record-breaking run in their own show, *Beyond Belief,* at the Frontier.

1982 A Las Vegas street is named Wayne Newton Boulevard.

1989 Steve Wynn makes headlines with his spectacular Mirage, fronted by an erupting volcano.

1990S The family-friendly medieval Arthurian realm of Excalibur opens as the new "world's largest resort" titleholder with 4,032 rooms, a claim it relinquishes when the MGM Grand's new 5,005-room megaresort/theme park opens in 1993, with a *Wizard of Oz* theme. Other properties geared toward families open in the 1990s, most notably Luxor, with its pyramid and Egyptian motifs, and the pirate-themed Treasure Island. The rock-'n'-roll Hard Rock, Mandalay Bay, Bellagio, New York–New York, The Venetian, and Paris Las Vegas carry concept gaming resorts to new heights. Celebrity chefs come to town.

2004 The Strip Monorail debuts.

2005 Wynn Las Vegas, the first major new casino resort to open in 5 years, debuts on the Strip.

2006 The Red Rock Resort opens off the Strip.

2007 The Stardust is demolished to make way for the new Echelon (which was put on hold). The Aladdin is renamed Planet Hollywood.

2008 The tanking U.S. economy and plunging real estate values send Las Vegas into a tailspin, causing hotels to discount massively in order to attract visitors.

2009 CityCenter opens on the Strip.

2010 The Cosmopolitan of Las Vegas opens on the Strip. Due to the recession, it is most likely the last major resort to open in Las Vegas for years to come.

Toll-free Numbers and Websites

Airlines

AIR CANADA
☎ 888/247-2262
www.aircanada.ca

AIRTRAN AIRLINES
☎ 800/247-8726
www.airtran.com

ALASKA AIRLINES/HORIZON AIR
☎ 800/252-7522
www.alaskaair.com

AMERICAN AIRLINES
☎ 800/433-7300
www.aa.com

ATA AIRLINES
☎ 800/1-FLY-ATA (135-9282)
www.ata.com

DELTA AIR LINES
☎ 800/221-1212
www.delta.com

FRONTIER AIRLINES
☎ 800/432-1359
www.frontierairlines.com

HAWAIIAN AIRLINES
☎ 800/367-5320
www.hawaiianair.com

NORTHWEST AIRLINES
☎ 800/225-2525
www.nwa.com

SOUTHWEST AIRLINES
☎ 800/435-9792
www.southwest.com

UNITED AIRLINES
☎ 800/241-6522
www.united.com

US AIRWAYS
☎ 800/428-4322
www.usairways.com

VIRGIN ATLANTIC AIRWAYS
☎ 800/862-8621 in the continental U.S.
☎ 0870/380-2007 in Britain
www.virgin-atlantic.com

Major Hotel & Motel Chains

BEST WESTERN INTERNATIONAL
☎ 800/528-1234
www.bestwestern.com

COMFORT INN
☎ 800/228-5150
www.hotelchoice.com

DAYS INN
☎ 800/325-2525
www.daysinn.com

HILTON HOTELS & RESORTS
☎ 800/HILTONS (445-8667)
www.hilton.com

HOWARD JOHNSON
☎ 800/654-2000
www.hojo.com

INTERCONTINENTAL HOTELS & RESORTS
☎ 877/424-2449
www.ichotelsgroup.com

LA QUINTA INNS & SUITES
☎ 800/531-5900 or 866/725-1661
www.lq.com

MARRIOTT
☎ 800/228-9290
www.marriott.com

MOTEL 6
☎ 800/4-MOTEL6 (466-8356)
www.motel6.com

SHERATON HOTELS & RESORTS
☎ 800/325-3535
www.sheraton.com

SUPER 8
☎ 800/800-8000
www.super8.com

Index

Photo **Credits**

Photo **Credits**

p. 1 © Ken Ross / Viestiphoto.com; p. 3 © Naomi P. Kraus; p. 4, top © James Glover II Photography; p. 4, bottom © James Glover II Photography; p. 5 © Courtesy Atomic Testing Museum; p. 6, top © Courtesy Bally's Las Vegas; p.6, bottom © Eric Parsons; p. 7 © James Glover II Photography, p. 9 © James Glover II Photography; p. 10, top © Paul Cichocki/ FremontStock.com; p. 10, bottom © James Glover II Photography; p. 11, top © Naomi P. Kraus; p. 11, bottom © Eric Parsons; p. 12, top © James Glover II Photography; p. 12, bottom © James Glover II Photography; p. 13 © Naomi P. Kraus; p. 15, middle © James Glover II Photography; p. 15, bottom © Paul Cichocki/FremontStock.com; p. 16 © Courtesy The Mirage; p. 17, bottom © Courtesy Wynn Las Vegas; p. 17, top © Courtesy Cirque du Soleil; p. 19 © Paul Cichocki/FremontStock.com; p. 20 © Paul Cichocki/FremontStock.com; p. 21 © Martin S. Fuentes; p. 23 © James Glover II Photography; p.24, bottom © Paul Cichocki/FremontStock.com; p. 24, top © Eric Parsons; p. 25 © Sean DuFrene; p. 27, middle © Brian Janis/Thunder from Down Under; p. 27, bottom © James Glover II Photography; p. 28, top © Paul Cichocki/FremontStock.com; p. 28, bottom © Paul Cichocki/FremontStock. com; p. 29, bottom © James Glover II Photography; p. 29, middle © Courtesy Alize Restaurant; p. 31, bottom © Paul Cichocki/FremontStock.com; p. 31, middle © Paul Cichocki/FremontStock.com; p. 32 © Paul Cichocki/FremontStock.com; p. 33 © James Glover II Photography; p. 35 middle © Sean DuFrene; p. 35 bottom © James Glover II Photography; p. 36 bottom © James Glover II Photography; p. 36 top; © Ken Ross / Viestiphoto.com ; p. 37 top; © James Glover II Photography; p. 37 bottom © James Glover II Photography; p. 39 © Courtesy Clark County Heritage Museums ; p. 40 bottom © James Glover II Photography; p. 40 top; © James Glover II Photography; p. 41 © Eric Parsons; p. 43 top © Paul Cichocki/FremontStock.com; p. 43 bottom © Courtesy Mandalay Bay; p. 44 top © Ken Ross / Viestiphoto.com ; p. 44 bottom © Eric Parsons; p. 45 © James Glover II Photography; p. 47 © Ken Ross / Viestiphoto.com ; p. 49 top © Paul Cichocki/ FremontStock.com; p. 49 bottom © ©Cosmopolitan™ of Las Vegas; p. 50 top © Paul Cichocki/FremontStock.com; p. 50 bottom © Eric Parsons; p. 51 top © Naomi P. Kraus; p. 51 bottom © Eric Parsons; p. 53 © Paul Cichocki/FremontStock.com; p. 55 top © James Glover II Photography; p. 55 bottom © Martin S. Fuentes; p. 56, top © Paul Cichocki/ FremontStock.com; p. 56, bottom © James Glover II Photography; p.57; © James Glover II Photography; p. 58, top © Martin S. Fuentes; p. 58, bottom © Eric Parsons; p. 59; © Paul Cichocki/FremontStock.com; p. 60; © Paul Cichocki/FremontStock.com; p. 63; © James Glover II Photography; p. 64; © Paul Cichocki/FremontStock.com; p. 65, top © James Glover II Photography; p. 65, bottom © Paul Cichocki/FremontStock.com; p. 66, top © ;